To Theresa

my very best to you on continued winning in the game of your life!!

Tom Petty

11-30-98

Praise for
Winning in the Game of Life

"Tom Gegax writes from deep personal experience about the secrets he's learned for a vibrantly healthy, creative, and fulfilling life. This book is a gift. Tom Gegax knows what he's talking about.

—John Robbins, author of
Diet for a New America and *Reclaiming Our Health*

"*Winning in the Game of Life* is one of those books that will be passed from friend to friend. Tom Gegax is an inspirational coach for living a full and purpose-filled life."

—Walter F. Mondale, former vice president of United States

"Listen up Michael Jordan: the real coach for the new millennium is Tom Gegax. Phil Jackson and Pat Riley are okay. If you play by Tom's rules, there's no telling what you can achieve in the game of life. Your best plays are yet to come."

—Eric Utne, founder, *Utne Reader*

"*Winning in the Game of Life* is a playbook for becoming the best person you can be. I heartily recommend it."

—Curt Carlson, founder/chairman, Carlson Companies
(Radisson Hotels, TGI Friday's, and Carlson Travel)

"I've watched Tom Gegax grow and prosper in life and business for years; now you can benefit from his experience and down-to-earth "game plan" for a life that works."

—Richard M. Schulze, founder/chairman and CEO, Best Buy

Winning
in the
Game
of
Life

Self-Coaching Secrets for Success

TOM GEGAX

Harmony Books ✦ New York

Publishing by Harmony Books, 201 East 50th Street, New York, New York 10022. Member of the Crown Publishing Group.

Random House, Inc. New York, Toronto, London, Sydney, Auckland

www.randomhouse.com

Harmony Books is a registered trademark and Harmony Books colophon is a trademark of Random House, Inc.

Editors Jana Branch and T. Trent Gegax

Printed in The United States of America

Design by Cynthia Dunne

Cover photograph by Christopher Gegax

Gegax, Tom.
    Winning in the game of life: self-coaching secrets for success / Tom Gegax.
    Includes bibliographical references and index.
    1. Success—Psychological aspects. 2. Self-actualization (Psychology). I. Title.

BF637.S8G38   1999   99-13919
158.1—dc21

ISBN: 0-609-60392-2

First Edition

Definitions are used by permission. From *Merriam-Webster's Collegiate® Dictionary, Tenth Edition* © 1998 by Merriam-Webster, Incorporated.

For Mom and Dad, who helped bring me to this life.
Mom, thanks for your unconditional love and constant encouragement, for reading to me, for focusing more on what I did right than on what I did wrong. Dad, thanks for teaching me the importance of empathy, openness to learning, and the wisdom to "ask, and ye shall receive." I hope that this winter of your lives continues to fulfill you and that when it's time to transcend, you'll be met with pure joy and peace.

For my children, Trent and Chris, who carry life on.
Thanks for the love, coaching, and humor. Watching you both grow in wisdom and happiness—so much earlier than I—is a pleasure beyond measure.

Contents

Foreword
...or, More Appropriately, FORWARD!

The journey of a thousand miles begins with one step.
—LAO TZU (570–490 B.C.E.)

A GOOD BOOK can be a step on a journey. You may not know where it will take you, but it sparks discussion, new thinking, sometimes even controversy, and certainly growth.

A book can also be an eye-opening new play in a game—the game of your life. The ideas in this book are strategies waiting to be played. Left on the page, they're just words. Manifested in your thoughts and actions, they begin to beat with life. *Winning in the Game of Life* lays out a personal, self-coaching game plan for success, gleaned from the laboratory of my life and those I've observed—fifty-two years of lessons simple and complex, uplifting and heart-wrenching. It's designed to meet you where you live and then show you what's beyond. Use these ideas in the way that makes the most sense to you, synthesizing them with the person you *are* to help you become the person you *want to be.* This book can be read cover to cover or dipped into at the point that speaks to you most. Each chapter offers strategies you can use independently of the rest of the plan, yet, taken as a whole, each chapter builds a piece of a harmonious whole.

You'll see my personal philosophy and business practices expressed in terminology you won't find in a standard lexicon. I use the words *Universal Source, Higher Power, Divine Source, Spirit,* and *God* interchangeably to refer to the inner and outer spirituality that I believe is an inseparable part of being human. I use the word *psyche* to encompass aspects of emotion, psychology, and behavior. I use the word *coach* instead of *manager.* Likewise, *teammate* takes the place of *employee,* and *guest* replaces *customer.* These words reflect a paradigm shift from *working* together to *teaming* together.

That said, it's time to get busy.

Hungry for success, inner and outer? Want a win in the game that really counts? The game's not over yet, and it's not too late to step in. Your team's waiting for you—body, intellect, psyche, spirit. They need a playing coach who's willing to get in the game, use the right plays, and take life to the next level.

But where to begin?

What about errors? Wrong moves?

Let go of doubt. Let go of fear. Get off the sidelines. Take a step. Turn the page and get in the game...of life...*your* life.

Preface

by Deepak Chopra

WHILE CHANGE IS a defining character of the universe, I firmly believe in the unchanging idea that consciousness creates reality. Expectation decisively influences outcome—whether applied to improving health or relationships, learning new skills, or building a business.

When I first met Tom, he was in the throes of transformation, recovering from near disaster in his personal and business life. At a time when it would be easy to be guided by negatives, he instead saw opportunity and realized the power of his own consciousness to change his outcome. Tom's evolution in the ensuing years has been remarkable. I've watched him gather insights from a number of sources and weave from them a life philosophy that connects principles and actions, body and mind, spirit and soul. He has a particular talent for making real what others may only imagine. With passion and practicality, dreams and daring, he has rebuilt his life with clear intention grounded in real-world skills.

He effectively integrates leading edge concepts of time management, organization, and workplace communication with personal wellness and spiritual connection. Growth on a personal level goes hand in hand with growth in relationships, work, and an evolving sense of self in connection with the divine. This book is an answer for the growing numbers who sense that business and personal life need not divide the self but can unite to flow toward greater health and energy.

I believe a particular value of Tom's message is his view of business not in purely materialist terms but rather in human terms. Coming from the tire industry, he demonstrates that a holistic perspective benefits in fields of endeavor that may seem surprising hosts for such ideas. He sees money, for example, as a form of energy exchange and human relationships as the real "gold" of business life. That heartening viewpoint has the potential to improve the time we spend in and beyond business dealings.

When Tom told me that he planned to write a book, it seemed a natural step. I was also pleased to learn that the idea was born in India during the week of festivities held for my daughter's wedding. Perhaps the atmosphere reflected Tom's own awareness that the pain that motivated his evolution in

1989 had fully given way to a hopeful, joyous face. And joy is always best shared with others.

Just as I've devoted my life to exploring the interconnectedness of our universe, so Tom retraces his steps of exploration to share the skills and insights that personal and business life hold in common. As an extension of his own life, I know this book to be a sincere and valuable reflection of an ongoing journey of growing consciousness.

Acknowledgments

THANKS TO MY mate, Mary Wescott, for constant encouragement, understanding, flexibility, love—and patience while this book came into being.

Thanks to the team for going into fifth gear often to get this book where it needed to go. Your persistence, belief in our team approach, and special talents converged to co-create a book that couldn't have happened any other way. Thanks to Shawn Hollembeak for deciphering my handwriting and typing long hours; to Kirk Olson and Amy Goldberger for their tireless research; to Vickie Abrahamson for thought-provoking counsel and creative genius beyond measure; to Dorie Thrall, Tires Plus Advertising Coach and my assistant of twelve years, for never-ending support, coordination, and a knack for picking up dropped balls.

Words seem wholly inadequate to express my deepest gratitude to Jana Branch and T. Trent Gegax for helping me find excellent words to convey my message. Thanks to Jana, project coach and phase-one editor, for asking the right questions, for her ideas, improvements, patience, and organization. When I read her first edits, I knew immediately we were meant to team together. My thanks to T. Trent Gegax, phase-two editor, for making sentences soar and concepts come alive. Like his life, I find his words vibrant, exciting, and uplifting. He gives words life and makes reading fun. I'm grateful for the chance to learn from him and team across the generations with the writing pro of the Gegax family.

Numerous friends and colleagues willingly offered substantial comments and refinements to the manuscript in progress. Their expertise and insight helped put clearer information on the page. My thanks to Dr. Jim Calli; Allen Fahden; Ron L. Fronk, Ph.D.; Rev. Mark Holman; Rev. Kurt P. Kalland; Earnie Larsen, MRE; John R. Leach; Prof. Carl V. Phillips, Ph.D.; John Robbins; Gayle S. Rose; Brenda M. Schaeffer, M.A., C.A.S.; Pete Selleck; Dr. Robert Simmermon; and Rev. Duke Tufty. See additional acknowledgments on page 303.

Thanks to my agent, Kim Witherspoon, my editor, Patricia Gift, and the publishing team at Harmony Books. Your encouragement and belief in this book early in its development brought a part of my own personal mission one step closer.

Finally, boundless gratitude goes to my Source, Higher Power, and constant companion who has gifted me with ideas as well as the inner kick to keep them flowing even when the process could have bogged down. I put pen to paper, and You sent me the message. My only hope is that I heard it with clarity.

Winning in the Game of Life

1

Determine Your Mission

Success. Arguably the most sought after and least understood prize in America. Many hunger for it, and some never realize when they've got it. Most of us want to be successful human beings, mates, parents, workers, managers, homemakers, salespeople. To achieve it, many work their nails bloody logging long hours and packing more activity into already bloated schedules.

Yet it's startling to consider that while this effort may yield some of the usual trappings, many still don't *feel* successful. Underneath the satisfaction of good performance reviews, a bigger house, and committee memberships, many still feel that success is somewhere out there yet to be snared.

No wonder. Our eyes are bleary from reading business-success tomes and taking notes at "achievement" seminars. Still, we're left asking the same questions: What makes us tick? What makes us sick? What drives us? While the average American works more hours than ever, little of the effort actually helps us understand anything about *ourselves*. Crowded out by the often manic push for success, simple, reflective inquiry rarely hits anyone's radar screen.

Many of us are encouraged to train our attention outward, toward such linear concepts as the latest managerial trend, and toward consuming and producing on time, on trend, and in step. We're often so concerned with learning how to manage others—employees, children, mates, even friends—that we're left with little energy to manage ourselves. Obsessed with mastering the world around us, we often fail to notice the unexplored world within. As French author Édouard Schuré writes, "Modern man seeks pleasure without happiness, happiness without knowledge, and knowledge without wisdom." Meanwhile, the search goes on for the secret to success, as if there were a single pill that would make all the difference.

In my experience, there is no magic bullet. Success, however, is forever within reach, personal and professional growth evolving hand in hand through a winning life game plan. This "whole person" approach focuses on every aspect of our being to support a well-lived personal and professional life. Every aspect is a player and every player is necessary. No one need be left on the bench. Recognizing that a win-lose dichotomy only fragments your mission, this winning life game plan redefines "winning" into a venture of cooperation and integration. Win-lose evolves into win-win. Everyone and everything benefits.

This integrated approach is a path to success, but what kind of "success" are we talking about? This life game plan isn't just about making more money, ascending the corporate ladder, or cramming in one more goal in the name of efficiency. That narrow view of what constitutes success stands between us and deeper satisfaction. With our eyes locked only on the prize, we forget that a winning life is a product of how we play the game.

Success, like a jewel, has many facets, and it can be easy to focus on two of the most eye-catching: money and career. Important? Sure, polishing those are part of the plan. Turn the jewel in your hand, though, and take a look at all the other glints of well-rounded success: loving relationships, community consciousness, physical and psychological health, intellectual balance, spiritual connection—to name just a few. An effective life plan polishes them all. While no single facet defines success, the sum reflects a life well-lived.

Creating a Winning Life Game Plan

This winning life game plan starts by showing you how to tap your inherent wisdom, desires, and values to discover your life's compass: your personal mission. Compass in hand, the plan then combines theory and practical skills to show you the key plays and the support systems you can develop to coach yourself toward your mission—the bedrock of your success.

Creating a Winning Life Game Plan

After determining your mission in chapter 1, chapter 2 shows you how to transform it into practical action plans and how to support it with time-competency, a crucial skill in our ever-changing, round-the-clock world. Chapter 3 zooms in on six distinctive traits I call "COPPSS"—caring, optimism, persistence, passion, systems-discipline, and spirit-filled behavior—that put our action plans into play.

Chapters 4, 5, and 6 explore key plays to support and nurture body, intellect, psyche, spirit—what I call the "Inner Team." In harmony, they produce unmatched energy, clarity of mind, and tranquillity. In the process, you'll learn how to get out of ruts (old habits that no longer contribute to what you want) and into grooves (habits that promote what you want). Standing on the shoulders of wellness, you begin to see beyond what may be blocking your path—fears, unfulfilling relationships and careers, narrow ideas, or egotism.

Chapter 7 provides strategies for remaining a step ahead of change and overcoming the all-too-human tendency to forget what we learn. These lifetime learning lessons are crucial to cultivating an open mind that gathers wisdom no matter where it's found. Chapter 8 zeroes in on communication skills that help you sail smoothly through the occasionally choppy seas of work and family life. Chapter 9 turns the spotlight on specific tips for improving and balancing a variety of relationships, the field where the endeavors of chapters 1 through 8 bear fruit. Relationships are where the rubber meets the road.

This game plan teaches you how to synchronize your personal and professional lives by unearthing common values and skills. Ultimately, this moves you closer to your unique life goals and translates into new ways of being in a company and a family. It also grants permission to break the taboos against seeking personal growth inside the workplace and applying workplace wisdom inside the home.

What is Self Coaching?

I carry out this life game plan through a process I call "Self Coaching." If you consider a winning life game plan the *what,* Self Coaching is the *how.* More than simple goal-setting and performance measurement, Self Coaching's whole-person, or holistic, approach can revive slumbering potential and dismantle longstanding barriers to a fuller life. You experience a quantum leap in your career as well as your connection with loved ones, friends, coworkers, community, Earth, and God—the true yardstick for success.

At first blush, the concept of coaching yourself may sound odd, perhaps a little like talking to yourself. Sure enough, that *is* part of it—giving yourself coaching the way tennis or Lamaze coaches work with students. It also means bending an ear to what you want out of life so you can follow your own path to success rather than some route predetermined by others. To be sure, nobody else has the answer to how you should live your life. However, as you'll discover, *you do*. Self Coaching can help you access, listen to, and live by your own answers.

Everyone has a Self Coach who can determine a game plan, send in key plays, and assess it on the move. The Self Coach inside each of us can then analyze the results and make adjustments to produce a winning strategy. In the process, surprising results crop up. Solutions appear. Stress becomes more manageable. Self-confidence grows. Fears fade. Looking in the mirror, you see the person you've always wanted to be.

I say that coaching yourself is job one for leading a fulfilling life. Moreover, it's the best way to navigate the treacherous crosscurrents that swirl at the intersection of your professional and personal lives. Most approaches to self-improvement focus largely on theory or, alternatively, on skills. Self Coaching, however, combines both to reveal the "why" behind the "how-to." In my own life, the bounty of a winning life game plan put into action through Self Coaching represents a qualitative, fundamental change in the way I approach daily life—the way I see my past, the way I view the future, and my attention to the present.

The Drive to Thrive

There's an old saying: If you do what you've always done, you'll get what you've always gotten. But given today's out-of-control change "inflation," if you keep doing what you've always done, you'll get *less* than you have now.

Until I reached my early forties, I armored up with my business suit every Monday through Friday. An artificial upbeat attitude pulled me through each week. Many of my relationships were somewhat superficial; when I wasn't glad-handing, I could be master of the subtle browbeating. I was also pretty selfish. I saw events mostly through my own prism and gave scant notice to how they affected others. Getting my way was often the most important thing. In short, I knew how to play the game. If you'd met me then, you would have encountered a person who appeared every inch a portrait of awareness and control: healthy intellect, body, marriage, and company. But in reality, I was fast asleep.

I was a post, nailed with all the signs of what most call success—a nice home, an expensive car, a beautiful family, a prominent position in the community. No one could see through the smile. No one could see me sweat. My secret, that my life was seriously out of balance, was kept safely hidden from others—and myself.

Then my house of cards collapsed. I'd recently received a wake-up call that took three rings to answer: divorce, cancer, and a troubled business.

The first ring sounded at the collapse of my twenty-five-year marriage. Wed at nineteen, I'd lived my entire adult life as a married man. That traumatic end affected my relationships with nearly everyone—my kids, friends, church, and colleagues.

The second ring came one morning some months later. While shaving, I discovered a lump on the side of my neck. I saw several doctors, all of whom said it was nothing to worry about—until the lump was removed and a biopsy revealed a malignancy. "We need you to come in to talk about options from here," the internist told me.

As if divorce and cancer weren't enough, the third ring of my wake-up call came in the form of a sudden cash crisis in the retail chain I'd started fifteen years earlier. Despite years of hard work, my tire company was strapped for cash; the company's slack earnings and unchecked growth were gobbling up capital. My chief financial officer had come into my office with a desperate look on his face. "We're short a million dollars, and our credit line is exhausted," he said. "What are we going to do?"

Those three blows left me on the mat. For six months I spent mornings pinned to my bed in the sterile suburban condominium to which I moved after the end of my marriage. Its blank walls projected a blank future.

Daily showers of radiation for the cancer temporarily killed my sense of taste and coated the walls of my mouth with burns. Eating, once a pleasure, became excruciating. I gargled a potion to coat the burns and make chewing tolerable, but it quickly wore off. Most meals were exhausting rounds of what seemed like gargling chalk and chewing cardboard. Muscle tension often locked my jaw shut. My weight dropped from 200 to 165 pounds. It's a weight-loss plan I don't recommend.

On the days when I managed to drag myself into the office, I pressed DND (do not disturb) on the phone, tacked up the same sign on the door, closed the drapes, and collapsed on the couch where I'd lay for hours, a monochromatic kaleidoscope of grays and blacks playing across my mind's screen.

It got worse. My personal finances were in a shambles. Two mortgages and attorneys' fees for the divorce burned a hole through my savings and credit. Pushed to live off credit cards, I wondered if I'd ever get back in the black.

Thousands of thoughts rained down. *You really screwed up. You hurt your family. You ruined your business. There's no way out of this one.* My smile was gone, nothing was right, and it seemed as if nothing would ever be right again. The traits that had bailed me out before were now utterly failing me. My positive mental attitude couldn't will me out of this mess, nor could exercise send enough endorphins to the rescue. For the first time ever, I couldn't manage to push my life into a successful mold. My strategies were bankrupt.

Desperate, I sought a psychologist who could help me escape this nightmare. I was still convinced that if I could just get back to being my old self, everything would be all right. I'd be back at the helm of my business and standing in good stead with the people around me. *Heck,* I thought, *maybe a therapist can tell me what's wrong with other people. After all, this mess can't really be my fault.*

It's always easier to believe that problems rest elsewhere. What I couldn't see was that my own life was a house of cards. All my energy was focused outward—studying intellectual concepts, working out, managing others. I was gliding on life's surface. I could talk the talk, but I didn't really understand what people meant when they spoke of emotional insights or their belief in a Higher Power. I was listening; I just couldn't tune in.

A wicked storm was brewing inside me, unlike anything I'd ever experienced. But why did I have to feel this way? What was the message? I was under the mistaken impression that my intellectual powers could take care of everything. My willpower and brain power had always come to the rescue. Who needs this psychological and spiritual stuff? "Show me where it says it's healthy to feel my feelings!" I remember snapping at my girlfriend one night not long after my divorce. Yet I was quickly finding that I could only outthink my emotions and spirit for so long. The cards were tumbling.

Reeling in My Mission

Out of these fumbles and stumbles emerged my first step toward the concept of Self Coaching. On a mild June afternoon in 1989, I slouched on a couch in the office of a psychologist, Brenda Schaeffer. Unaware, I was about to embark, in that little office, on a journey that would forever change my life.

I was skeptical when Brenda began by asking me to close my eyes. As she guided me through ten minutes of rhythmic deep breathing, I wondered where she was going with this exercise. Suddenly my anxiety began to quiet, and my mind grew calmer than it had been for months. She asked me to see my life as if it were a movie and to roll the reel backward. I did, going back farther and farther, until I found myself in Connersville, Indiana, on October 4, 1946, the place and day of my birth.

To my surprise, Brenda asked me to continue turning the reel backward to a time before my birth. *Before* my birth? I was puzzled, but, astonishingly, the movie screen lit up, and I saw a time prior to my conception. Brenda said, "Imagine being in spirit form somewhere in the cosmos. A most perfect spiritual being, sometimes known as God, approaches you. In whatever way the being communicates with you, the being asks if you're willing to be born so that you can fulfill a mission to help the Earth. What's your answer?" Brenda said.

"I said yes," I told her.

"Tell me what God is asking you to do on Earth."

By the time that amazing hour was up, I knew. Messages came to me about what I understood I was to do in my lifetime. I repeated them to Brenda, who took notes. I couldn't tell whether these messages—they came in images, words, and half-thoughts—were from God or from my imagination. I did feel an unmistakable power in them, stronger than anything I had ever experienced. Perhaps they came from my Higher Power or my own higher wisdom—or both at once. Who's to say they're not simultaneously different and the same?

The words and images on that movie screen disclosed that I was willing to come to Earth to live out a multipart mission. Then Brenda asked, "Is that something you're willing to do?"

"I'm willing to do it," I said, "but I'm so obsessed with finding the perfect mate. I put too much energy into it and into my business."

That day I resolved to get into balance. It was the moment I began to awaken, and from that day forward I've done my best to wake up a little more each day.

Mining My Mission: Wellness

Through my discoveries that afternoon, and by way of further explorations, I arrived at the seven-part mission that now guides my actions. The first piece of my mission was clear. While my intellect was overused, my body, psyche, and spirit all felt empty. My new priority: to learn how to strike a balance among all aspects of myself. For the first time, intellectual growth would have to take a backseat to other development.

I spent the next five years coursing an uncharted world—myself. I found time that I didn't think existed for weekly therapy sessions and retreats, which slowly revealed the hows and whys behind my out-of-balance life. Every step was painful. No matter how unhealthy a habit I uncovered, I wanted desperately to cling to it. It was, and still is, a gradual process to discard more and more layers of harmful habits and philosophies.

And then a funny thing happened. The healthier I became emotionally, the more I wanted a deeper spiritual life. I had attended church regularly for years with my family, yet the sermons (while eloquent) never struck a genuine chord. But how could they have? I was in spiritual hibernation. I began reading the Big Books of major religions as well as *A Course in Miracles,* then began attending Course study groups and a nondenominational church.

I began practicing t'ai chi, an ancient Chinese form of meditative movement, which made me gently aware of my body and my relationships with the people and world around me. Years of superficially relating to people gave way to the first inklings of concrete connections that reached deeper than the usual small talk about work, school, sports, hobbies. I was beginning to wake up.

My mind, still noisy, craved quiet. Meditation, I was told, was the prescription. It sounded Greek to me, but I was open to trying anything that wasn't loaded with nasty side-effects. I learned to meditate at a t'ai chi retreat and then in workshops taught by Deepak Chopra, who was little known at the time. It wasn't long before meditation became my primary way to clear my spiritual airwaves, calm my day, and establish better connections with people.

No stranger to regular workouts and eating well, I nevertheless realized that my routine was only one-dimensional: food was energy in, exercise and exertion were energy out—the kind of linear equation that cancels out to zero. To begin rounding out my approach, I improved the quality of foods I was eating, eliminating meat and most dairy and concentrating instead on whole foods—grains, beans, fruits, vegetables, and some fish. I stopped drinking alcohol except on rare occasions. The nature of the food I ate reflected the qualities I wanted to nurture in myself: whole, essential, rooted in authenticity rather than highly processed and manufactured. In addition, I began "feeding" my body from the outside with weekly massage and energy work (a practice similar to massage, designed to balance the physical body, intellect, emotions, and spirit).

I can't complain about the results. My cancer left and has not returned. Despite being knocked for the cancer, an extensive 1996 physical exam for a life-insurance policy rated me in the best of six risk categories. My agent was floored. He told me he'd never seen anything like it in the thirty years he'd been selling insurance.

I also discovered that I didn't need to abandon intellectual growth. I merely had to balance it. I still attended seminars and read books on leadership and current business concepts. While valuable, they became just one part of the great lessons I was learning.

Like spring retiring winter, I was waking up to a healthy future. I still had the usual challenges at work and in my personal life, but the negative stuff occurred less frequently and no longer penetrated quite so deeply. I was discovering that what happens internally manifests externally. It's an inside job. The result: more energy; more insight; clearer decisions. The success of synergy.

Mining My Mission: The Rest of the Story

It was a major life change, but tuning up my wellness was only the first part of my mission. The second part was to create a personal space to share this information when others asked.

My mission's third part is to create a business environment that nurtures the whole-person wellness I do my best to live. This strikes some people as odd, because I have a chain of 150 retail tire stores. My reason— or rather, the Universal reason—I foster a holistic business environment is that it's a chance to provide a healthy setting through which my teammates (co-workers, in standard business parlance) can live healthier, happier lives. It also improves the relationships between my teammates and the 1.7 million guests they serve each year.

With the help of our "team wellness coach," Tires Plus adds a healthful approach to life to the usual mix of memos. When she isn't bringing in psychologists and behaviorists to speak to teammates, our wellness coach promotes exercise, healthy diet, and smoking cessation. It pays off. People throughout the company, as well as their families, regale me with their stories of personal growth. The side effects aren't bad, either. The more we promote holistic living within the walls of my company, the higher our guests' enthusiasm rises (shown in our customer satisfaction rate). This by-product created a company that reaps material abundance I'd never dared to imagine—$160 million in total sales in 1998, a figure that dwarfs the sales as well as earnings before my 1989 wake-up call. A healthy company is built partially on healthy earnings. Moreover, our earnings affirm that doing the right thing, by both the guest and the teammate, is right universally and makes sound economic sense.

To be sure, this doesn't exempt my team and me from the usual challenges every company faces. Competition and changing economic conditions require us to stay on top of prevailing conditions. In our region and business, even the weather can plow our profits up or down. My team and I are far from perfect, yet we're headed in the right direction, thanks to a way of business life that enhances our well-being. Our headquarters hums with meditation and nutritional cooking classes, shiatsu massages, and a workout facility. Team concepts are the staple of our culture, which our job titles have long reflected. We don't have "managers" or "executives," only "coaches."

The fourth part of my mission is to share leadership skills with people and organizations that do right by the world. I set my sights on two important thinkers, Dr. Deepak Chopra and John Robbins, who champion whole-body wellness. Within five years of discovering this part of my mission, I was sitting on their boards of advisers, trading my mentorship in organizational matters for their mentorship in matters of spirit and health.

The fifth and sixth parts of my mission are to nurture relationships with those close to me and recognize the connectedness of all living beings. Only by doing what I can to be a beneficial presence on the planet can I feel part of the circles of relationships that bind us all together.

The final part of my mission, the one that prompted this book, is to share my Self Coaching concepts. My hope is that you discover options in these pages that help you become more satisfied and effective at work and at home and help you forge a tighter bond with yourself and your friends, family, mate, co-workers, and community. Those, best as I can tell, are the ingredients for a fulfilled life.

Elements of a Winning Life Game Plan

The Personal Mission

At the core of a winning life game plan is identification of your personal mission. It's a matter of discovering who we are, why we're here, and what we want. Stuck on the treadmill of mortgages, lease payments, and carpools, many of us are so busy with the demands of everyday life that we lose sight of the most basic guiding principles: namely, our deepest desires for what we hope to give and get in life.

Your personal mission is the product of your higher wisdom and conscious will. It's a process of discovery and decision. The discovery begins when we open ourselves to information, or wisdom, whose source is anywhere but our analytical minds. The decision comes into play when you filter that information into a clear message. This combination creates a mission grounded in purpose and launched by inspiration.

DETERMINATION PART 1: DISCOVERY ✦ How to identify our deepest guiding principles? It's tempting to rely on intellect, to simply look around and think about all the things we want. But for many of us these are things that either make us more comfortable or raise our public profile. Intellect often can't see past our limited current reality. To reach beyond, we need a different kind of wisdom.

Imagination is one source of the wisdom of discovery. It taps not only into what is but also into what could be. Some people discount imagination, equating it with make-believe. Imagination, however, often yields a better map to our inner desires than does our intellect. In the process of discovery, I counsel setting aside for a moment Descartes' notion, "I think, therefore I am." Instead, think about this wise nugget popularized on a button: "I dream, therefore I become."

The other crucial source of wisdom for my personal mission was God. When I'm tuned in at this level, I feel both energized and strangely calm, a feeling unlike any other. I don't get hung up on whether this is a message from God or from my imagination. Those considerations only lead people to dismiss the message or to give it excessive power.

Every message, whether arising from wisdom within or from wisdom beyond, first must be heard—unedited and unquestioned. After discovery, we can determine whether those messages are useful and beneficial. The origin of wisdom ultimately is less important than what we choose to do with the message.

Connecting with higher wisdom is crucial for creating missions that aren't simply as large (or small) as our egos. We stand no chance of becoming more than we are today if our personal mission is founded on ego and doesn't give consideration to what others, including our Higher Power, may want. Listen to the noises outside your rational mind, and you'll hear a beat that will help you grow into the person you are destined to become.

DETERMINATION PART 2: DECISION ✦ Now that you've opened yourself to your imagination and higher wisdom, can you trust everything you hear? I'm guided by the following rules when I evaluate whether my discoveries are messages I can feel good about (morally and ethically) or messages to set aside:

"GOOD TO GO" MESSAGES

1. challenge me to move beyond my usual routine and expectations

2. forge stronger bonds between myself and others

3. directly or indirectly benefit others or the world at large

4. energize and motivate me with positive feelings

JETTISON ANY MESSAGE THAT

1. discounts myself or others

2. promotes harm to myself or others

3. encourages me to judge or control others

The crucial point is that if a thought contains negative feelings toward myself or other people, I know that it cannot be issuing from my higher wisdom.

The Success of Synergy

When your personal mission is your guiding light, decisions about any aspect of life are weighed in its glow and become much clearer. That allows you to put your values to work. As philosopher Friedrich Nietzsche wrote, "He who has a *why* to live for can bear almost any *how*."

Self Coaching zeroes in on the areas illustrated on p. 14.

Action plans geared for various time periods—a year, a few months, a week, a day—put grease in the gears of the traits, skills, and wellness strategies that make up a balanced life.

These elements may be familiar (no-brainers, perhaps), but notice that all of them are part of one continuum: you. The hub of a winning game plan is the integration of all the players.

Most of us are out of balance in one or more of these areas. No wonder; our early education and cultural values tend to ignore an integrated approach to life. In school we learn plenty of math and science but precious little about how to care for our own bodies. At the office we're prodded every day to ante up our "intellectual capital," with not a mention of spiritual or psychological wealth. We live in an age of specialization which preaches that one strong suit can compensate for a wardrobe of other weaknesses. That may be true for some people, but not in this winning game plan, which shows that imbalance never works over the long haul.

Here's an idea of how it works: Think about the last time you had the flu. Technically, only your physical body was sick. Yet could you think

Your Personal Mission and Its Supporting Players

CHAPTER 8
Communication
Skills

CHAPTER 2
Seven
Take-Action
Steps

CHAPTER 7
Lifetime
Learning

CHAPTER 1
You &
Your
Mission

CHAPTER 3
Six Traits
for the Trip

CHAPTER 6
Spiritual
Wellness

CHAPTER 4
Physical
Wellness

CHAPTER 5
Psychological
Wellness

CHAPTER 5
Intellectual
Wellness

clearly? Did you feel spiritually centered? Did you feel emotionally strong? How did you interact with the people around you? Obviously, poor physical health knocks the feet out from under many other parts of our being. Likewise, an underdeveloped or sick psyche can pull the rug out from under us and drag down our physical, spiritual, and intellectual health. Just as our body and psyche can pose roadblocks, intellect and spirit can impede our best efforts. The symptoms aren't always as apparent as with the flu, but the effects are the same: a scarcity of integrated purpose, coordinated energy, and mission achievement.

GROUNDS FOR CONNECTION + Striving toward balance in all the parts of our being still isn't the whole picture, however. Achieving a mission isn't just about *personal* progress. Indeed, personal progress is merely a foundation for the real reason we're here.

Perhaps you've heard of the "hundredth monkey" phenomenon, an apocryphal idea that attempts to explain what science cannot. The story goes that scientists observing monkeys on the Japanese island of Koshima in 1952 found something peculiar. They watched as one monkey learned to wash sand off its sweet potato before eating it. Over the next six years, one by one other monkeys picked up the same technique until, in the fall of 1958, a good portion of the monkey population was washing its food. Over the course of a few more days, scientists witnessed what seemed like a spontaneous learning combustion. Overnight, practically, every monkey on the island was washing his food. Inexplicably, monkeys on neighboring islands, monkeys who had never shown the ability and had no contact with the Koshima monkeys, began washing their food.

What happened? It's postulated that when a critical mass of individuals learns the same behavior, they gain the power to spread that learning to others, even over great distances. The "hundredth monkey" refers to that one individual whose additional energy turns a loosely affiliated group of individuals into a cohesive unit with the power to effect quantum shifts in consciousness. You're wondering, how is this possible? If we consider the ways we are all connected to each other beyond physical presence, it's not so hard to fathom. Emotionally, spiritually, intellectually, consciously, and unconsciously—we're connected to each other in many ways that are beyond understanding. These bonds make us each a player in a universal orchestra. Even if you can't quite hear the conductor, you're nevertheless playing a part.

Whatever your unique contribution, you're weaving the connections that hold us all together, across generations and through the boundaries of

Relationships that Define Our Mission

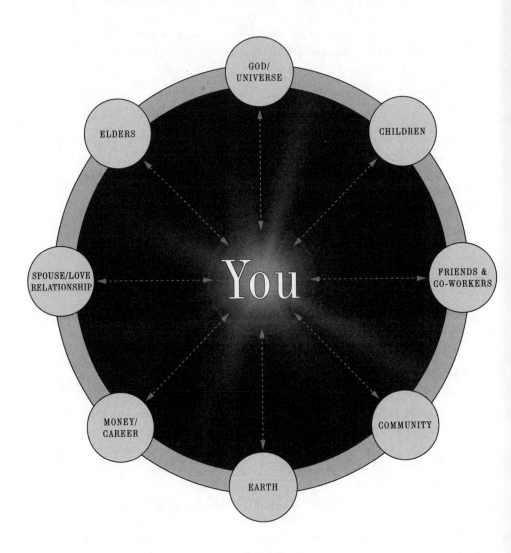

physical being. It's an encouraging notion: the evolution of someone, somewhere else in the world, can help me along my mission path, and I can do the same for someone else.

Determine Your Mission

It's time to determine your mission in life unless you've already got it nailed.

The Big Question: Why are you here? For most of us, this is bedrock. Consciously or unconsciously, the question is under every step and always in the air. But how can you answer it? Determining your personal mission statement is a good beginning.

This idea is nothing new to companies, nonprofit groups, and government agencies. For them, a well-executed mission statement acts like a global positioning satellite. It helps an entire system of employees navigate the waters inside and outside their organizations. It helps an organization define its core purpose so that everyone is clear about the ultimate direction of day-to-day choices and actions.

A personal mission statement serves a similar purpose. It helps focus and direct your life down the road you want to travel. It's an internal compass that serves as a ubiquitous reality check, a benchmark against which everything you do can be examined and tested.

Two explorations can stimulate development of your mission statement: one focuses on your past, the other on your future. Look at them and pick the one that feels best, or use both.

As you answer the questions below, open yourself to a little focused self-reflection. This was crucial for me. Open to messages that were beyond what I could intellectualize for myself, my mission takes on components that come from a higher wisdom. The wisest answers in my life are borne from the combination of imagination, God's direction, conscious reflection, and my willingness to act on what I determine. You may find it helpful to record your responses in a notebook or a journal that you can use to draft your mission and cherry-pick ideas throughout this book.

Exploration 1. Your Birth

This exploration was the first step toward discovering my mission. You'll need a tape recorder and a blank audio tape. If those aren't available, paper and pen will do. This may take you into new territory, and may even feel a little uncomfortable. That's okay. Do as much or as little of the exercise as you wish. You can always come back to it later. I explored my mission with the assistance of my psychologist. You may choose to ask a psychological counselor, spiritual adviser, or close friend to guide you through this, or you can be your own guide.

STEP 1. CREATE A COMFORT ZONE ✦ Find a quiet place, indoors or outdoors, where you won't be interrupted. It should be a haven where you feel peaceful and safe. Keep beside you the tape recorder (or paper and pen) and record every idea and image that comes to mind. By all means trust that they're all worth hearing, and don't try too hard. If you're not used to this type of exercise, you may find yourself trying to edit your thoughts. Resist the impulse. Just let things happen. No one will know but you. Simply follow the instructions below.

STEP 2. RELAX INTO IT ✦ Take a slow, deep breath through your nose and hold it until it's just slightly uncomfortable. With a long, soothing exhalation, let the air go out of your mouth. At the end of that exhalation, hold your breath until it's slightly uncomfortable. Slowly repeat this process five times. As you do so, tell yourself to let go of tension, worry, concern, and distraction. Be as relaxed as possible, letting go of concern about a right or wrong way to do this exercise.

Are you relaxed? If not, repeat the breathing as many times as you like until you feel your body relax. When that happens, take the next step.

STEP 3. RETURN TO THE SOURCE ✦ To return to the past, gradually travel back in time and visualize yourself when you were younger...in your thirties...your twenties...your teens...until you're all the way back to the time you were born. After a brief rest stop, where you do a little sight-seeing, go back even farther, back to a time before you were conceived, before you even had a body. Imagine that you are a spirit somewhere in the cosmos. This may seem strange, but stay with this image.

A most perfect spiritual being approaches you and asks if you're willing to go on a mission to help Earth.

Give your answer.

Once you give your answer, be still and listen.

If you say no, the spiritual being may have a helpful message for you.

If you say yes, either ask or tell the spiritual being what your mission is. How would you help Earth? When answers arrive, record them. Whether you hear these messages directly from God, from your higher inner wisdom, or from your imagination (which may also be directly from God), value them at the appropriate level.

The answers may appear in the form of clear words. Or you may sense something, an intuitive hunch. You may see an image. Messages arrive in many shapes. Stay open, and try not to discount an unfamiliar package.

After each answer, close your eyes again and ask if there's more. Be still again and listen, and repeat the process until you feel finished.

Look at each answer. Are you willing to accept its message? If not, ask yourself why not. If so, ask yourself what stands in the way of acting on it. Listen to your higher wisdom and write down the answers.

You may completely get in touch with your mission, or not at all. If you don't feel full, or if you got a busy signal, check back with the exercise later, or try other methods of relaxation. In your daily life, tune in to messages that have a "mission ring" to them when they appear. Some people get these types of messages just before they fall asleep or while driving. Ask yourself, "What's my mission?" from time to time when you're relaxing— gardening, golfing, rocking on the porch, reading on the beach. Be ready to record your answers.

If answers aren't forthcoming, it doesn't mean you're missionless. It may just mean that your mission needs some more encouragement to show itself. Try the exercise again. Eventually, your mission will become apparent.

TOM'S BIRTH EXPLORATION ✦ My exploration, which formed the foundation for my personal mission (and would be refined through further exercises), yielded this message:

1. I will fill my mind with more spirituality, and I will feed my communication skills with more knowledge.

2. I will not let distractions stop me from growing.

3. I will share with others the gifts I'm blessed with. I want to share caring and loving feelings with others, helping them along, teaching and training, reaching them one-on-one and in groups. My mission, not finding a new mate, is now my priority.

4. I ask my Higher Source and higher wisdom for the discipline to stay the course.

Exploration 2. How I'd Like to Be Remembered

Having gone back in time, you will now travel forward in time, to your death. Imagine that you've died at a ripe old age. Think about the people closest to you. How would you like them to remember you? What would you like them to say about you as they reminisce? What qualities about your life and personality would you like to stand out? What deeds would you like to be defined by?

Record what you would like individual people to say. Be specific and list as many things, large and small, as you can—from idle comments to bold moves to hobbies. My notes from this exploration look like this:

HOW I'D LIKE TO BE REMEMBERED AFTER MY DEATH
  1. He was a loving and caring son, brother, and mate.
  2. He was the best father he knew how to be. He was a friend and mentor to his sons.
  3. He shared knowledge that helped others inside and outside his company move forward, toward what they wanted from life.
  4. He did his best to see goodness in people and sought what brings people together instead of what divides them.
  5. He shared his blessings with others.
  6. He had a sense of humor, had fun, and lightened those around him.
  7. He was caring, loving, and gentle with himself.
  8. He stood up for his beliefs and challenged the powers that be when necessary in the name of the community.
  9. He supported organizations that do good in the world.

Write Your Mission: Possible!

You're ready to build your personal mission statement. Start with a fresh notebook, or create a new document on your computer screen. Using what you learned from one or both explorations, craft your mission statement by answering the question, "What was I sent here to do?" It may be helpful to organize the answer along the lines of specific relationships. For example, what were you sent here to do for your children? Your parents? Other elders? Your career? Your community? Look at each relationship on the circle on page 16 and consider your answers.

These guidelines will help you to write a practical statement you can act on:

1. Be 100-percent honest with yourself. The only personal mission statement you can truly follow and believe in is one that springs from your heart, mind, and soul—a determination that combines discovery and deci-

sion. Think about what you believe you were sent here to do and what you want to contribute while you're here—not necessarily what others think you should do.

2. Just as you found a haven to do your discoveries, find ways to get away from it all while you write your mission statement. We can't appreciate the size of the forest while we're surrounded by trees. While teams can make adjustments midgame, they certainly don't create their game plan in the heat of the action.

3. Your statement can be as long or short as you wish—a sentence or several pages. Inspiration counts more than length.

4. Words may flow the first time, but allow for several drafts. This mission will be the voice of your deepest being and can guide you for life.

5. Resist comparing your mission statement to someone else's. The value of your mission is unique. Everyone's mission, position, and role is necessary and interconnected—no less or more important than anyone else's.

If you're tempted to rush through, consider this: If exploring and crafting an initial personal mission statement takes a couple of hours, it's no longer than a feature film. But since you're beginning to craft the script of your life, those two hours are better spent in a desk chair than in a theater seat. In essence, you're creating a happier ending—and a happier middle—to your own personal movie. The statement may take a while. Take your time, and move through as many iterations as it takes to find clarity.

Once it's complete, duplicate your mission in large, easy-to-read print, like a miniature billboard. Display it above your desk or in any conspicuous spot so that every day you're reminded of what's truly, deeply important to you and why you're here. (If you like, make a wallet-size copy that travels well.)

TOM'S PERSONAL MISSION STATEMENT ✦ Combining my birth exploration, death exploration, and further introspection, here's the personal mission statement I determined:

1. To evolve continually toward a more highly awakened and genuinely loving state of being in connection with my Higher Power and the people around me.

2. To support my evolution through an approach to wellness that integrates body, intellect, psyche, and spirit and to acquire habits and traits that help me become more knowledgeable and experienced so that I can better employ my communication skills.

3. To share love and what I've learned with family and friends by creating personal environments that support growth.

4. To share what I've learned with colleagues by creating business environments that support growth.

5. To share leadership skills with organizations that make positive differences in the world.

6. To live in a manner that respects Earth and its resources, doing my part to ensure that future generations will live on a healthy Earth.

7. To help others, wherever they may be, determine and achieve their life missions.

Synchronize Yourself

Once you have your personal mission in writing, use it to diagnose your current path. When our actions dovetail with our life's mission, power from a Higher Source opens up to us. The reverse is equally true. When our actions are out of synch with our true selves, the opportunities that come our way every day become invisible. I know firsthand that the world feels like an empty place when *I'm* empty. Conversely, when I'm in touch with my mission and higher purpose, opportunities—and the world—are packed with abundance.

That's not to say that things can't or won't happen that don't support our missions. These times are at best disappointing and at worst traumatic. This is when I ask myself if I'm truly tuned in to my mission. Sometimes what our intellect wants isn't what our entire being needs, and it can be hard to tell the difference. Ask yourself again if your wants are focused solely on your own needs, or if they're aimed at a broader purpose—one that connects you with all those in your relationship circle. It's possible we aren't as tuned in as we thought we were. It's also possible our Higher Power is trying to nudge us in another direction, opening doors we may not be ready to step through or even see. As Deepak Chopra explains, there's a universal intelligence at work that has "infinite organizing power." Call it a conspiracy of positive energy. In other words, you will be provided the energy you need, if you simply open yourself to it. Ever since I discovered my mission, this wisdom and energy have been a guiding force. True enough, any progress toward my personal mission moves in partnership with family, friends, teammates, and God. Without them, my hopes would never become reality.

And despite all my blessings, I maintain the importance of sticking to the basic principles that underpin this book. It's essential for me to remain humble—staying on my knees, if you will. For me, continually focusing on personal growth and Self Coaching are lifelong activities essential for staying on a winning track.

The New Bottom Line

It's clear, looking back, that had I spent more time when I was younger in balanced self-development, my trip through the first half of my adult life would have been much sweeter. The problem with putting it off is that time has a way of slipping through our fingers. How often do you hear someone lament, "Where did the years go?" or "Where did my twenties [or thirties or forties] go?" Between the lines, they're saying, "I wanted to do this, and this, and this, but it just didn't happen." When people say this, typically they've failed to get in touch with their personal missions—and if they did tap into their missions, they failed to link them with deliberate, purposeful actions.

What we miss, ultimately, is the chance to experience the full potential of our own lives as well as the connection between our lives and all other life. When they're half on, half off, the range of our relationships are pale reflections of their potential, and opportunities slip by unnoticed.

Odds are that sooner or later most everyone reading this book will get a wake-up call of varying volume. My hope for you is that in these moments of trauma, small or large, you'll snap out of your waking slumber with a splash of growth that moves you. But even if trauma isn't at your doorstep, perhaps you feel that something is missing, that you haven't realized the potential of who you are or who you are meant to be. If that's the case, be proactive. Don't wait until you find yourself on your knees, begging for mercy and guidance. Look out to the horizon, consider what lies ahead, and get started, even if you begin with small steps. The old saw applies: inch by inch it's a cinch; by the yard it's hard. With your personal mission in view, whether it feels distant or close, you can now begin to develop the rest of your winning game plan to put the dream into action.

2

Seven Take-Action Steps
to Manifest Your Mission

WE ALL WANT good relationships, good health, and sufficient income. Some of us also want spiritual abundance, a satisfying career, and a little adventure. Yet many people who want it all never get it, and not for lack of trying. Despite jam-packed schedules year after year, decade after decade, phase of life after phase of life, we're plagued by a feeling that there's not enough time. Step by bitter step, we may end up sadly letting go of our dreams and desires.

As you will see, however, grinding down our passions is anything but inevitable. In fact, by following the right course of action, you can not only halt this process but reverse it. *To do so, you must make conscious connections between your personal mission and the seven steps to manifesting it.*

Like any adventure, a mission is only as good as the provisions you take along on it. Therefore, to manifest your own mission, draw a line from it to your thoughts and actions. Is a house a house if it only exists on a blueprint? Maybe, but you can't live in it. So let's build it, using the Seven Take-Action Steps described in this chapter:

1. **Decide what you want to get and give.** At the end of each year, write down your specific desires for the next year.

2. **Create action plans.** Focus on ways to achieve the goals you listed in the previous step.

Seven Take-Action Steps

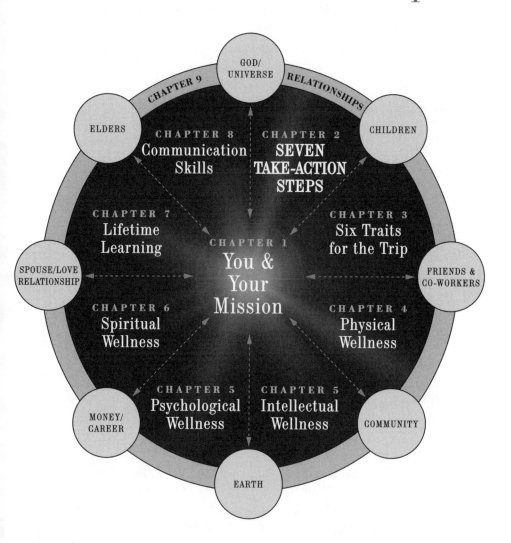

3. **Get organized.** Create an environment that promotes efficiency and achievement.

4. **Integrate the plan.** With schedules and to-do lists, make your plan doable in daily life.

5. **Be time wise.** Provide yourself adequate time to complete key tasks.

6. **Just do it.** Stick to your plan by moving through roadblocks. Getting through fear and doubt are all part of getting to where you want to go. Remind yourself constantly of the desires you identified when you were quiet, grounded, and able to search your heart.

7. **Let go.** Learn when it's appropriate to persist with your plans— and when it's time to change or release plans altogether.

Before You Start

Some people look at the seven steps and think, *Wow, what a lot of work!* But consider the alternative. Most of us need to bottom out in some major way, or suffer through some titanic personal implosion, before we're ready to take up meaningful self-coaching. That's because many people live by the motto, "If it's not broken, don't fix it." It's often easier to settle for what's only half working than to deal with the inevitable discomfort of changing our habits of thought and action. But what's half working is also half *not* working. We wouldn't settle for this kind of performance from office equipment; why should we settle for it in our own lives?

By starting to coach ourselves more effectively right now, we can potentially pre-empt meltdown and save ourselves needless suffering. It seems to me that life is a "pay me now or pay me later" proposition. We can either go through the discomfort of change now or endure the pain of regret later.

So if you're looking at these seven steps and the game plan as a whole and thinking that you'll put it off until next week, next month, next year— please don't. This is particularly tempting for young people who may not even believe that they're vulnerable to the downsides of living an unbalanced life. Though it's true that people often seem more willing to focus on inner development once they reach their forties or fifties (often after a serious wake-up call), it's equally true that people of *every* age are capable of experiencing outer and inner growth—and of reaping its rewards.

As you move through the seven steps, allow yourself to be bold and creative. And allow yourself to make spirit a part of the process. As we move through the linear process of setting goals and setting schedules, some people may be tempted to check their Higher Power at the door, thinking that somehow it's not compatible. But this is exactly the time we can benefit from active sense of spiritual connection. We're co-creating our lives with universal guidance—partnering with the boundless energy of spirit to expand the limited aspects of body, psyche, and intellect. Underlying the structured nature of the seven steps is the limitless potential of spirit. Don't be shy about calling on it.

Be candid when you call on spirit. You can't ask for too much, if it's in line with your mission and your mission is in line with our Higher Source. In fact, most people ask too little. There is a distinct power in asking for something that dovetails with your life's mission. I have learned that when I ask for assistance and truly connect on the right "frequencies," doors open, my energy level rises, my receptivity becomes more acute, and answers effortlessly come to mind. This collaboration with universal order gives action to what couldn't otherwise come into the world.

In 1994 I was the keynote speaker to a group of three hundred Minneapolis engineers. The day before my speech I was blindsided by a flu bug. As I drove to the engagement I was barely conscious, to the point that I had trouble simply walking in from the parking lot. I nearly fainted when I entered the ballroom. I had no idea how I was going to get through my one-hour speech. Then, as I was being introduced, I called upon my Higher Power to speak the words for me. When it was over I couldn't recall the speech, but I did remember a standing ovation. I had simply stood up and opened my mouth; God did the rest.

That doesn't mean we don't have to do our part. I had to ask for help. I had to be willing to receive whatever answer might—or might not—come. I physically needed to get there, stand at the podium, and open my mouth. There's a well-known spiritual teaching that advises us to pray as if everything depended on God, and to act as if everything depended on us.

Perhaps you know the contemporary parable of the man who, for the month leading up to a big lottery drawing, asked God over and over, passionately and deeply, to help him win. After the winner was announced, the man groaned at his loss and asked God why He'd let him down on this one simple, very specific, very important wish. A voice boomed back at him from above: "You could at least have bought a ticket!"

Here, then, is how to buy your ticket.

Step 1. Decide What You Want to Give and Get

Writing down what you want—setting goals, if you like—is a basic strategy that you've most likely heard hundreds of times. Yet a lot of evidence suggests that only a small percentage of people actually commit themselves to writing what they want this year or the next and designing a plan to get it. Deciding what you want to give and get in the immediate future links a long-term mission statement with near-term goals and action. There's a whole lot of talk about goal-setting, but in the end, few people are doing it. At presentations, I used to ask people to raise their hands if they had written down their wants and goals for the year. Rarely more than 5 percent did.

What's going on? If we agree that creating a clear plan is beneficial, what's the roadblock? I think (and I've felt it myself) that people don't write down their aspirations because it makes us think more deeply about what we really want, and that can be scary. If you don't get what you want and there's no written record of it, you can fudge your memory to believe you never wanted it in the first place. You can avoid feeling disappointed about it. You can avoid taking responsibility about what you did or didn't do to get it. By writing down what you want, you're putting yourself on the line. You're getting real with yourself. Yikes!

Writing down your aspirations effectively invites change into your life. You're saying, "I want my life to change, and I'm willing to stick with this process until it happens." But let's be honest. Who really likes change? It's hard, and often it hurts. It means you have to look at other people in a new way. It means you have to look at yourself in a new way.

This may seem like too much to handle. It may seem easier just to take life as it comes, to keep doing and not take the time to reflect. The trouble is that change is inevitable, and if you don't invite the change you *want* into your life, you'll experience whatever change comes your way (sometimes created by other people who are on their own missions). Without a clear map that ties short-term goals to a long-term mission, you'll be limited to reacting to what life gives you instead of working toward the life you want.

Committing your intentions to writing has to go hand-in-hand with surrendering your fear—of failure and of whatever comes next. Some people would call that a leap of faith. Others call it having guts. Either way, putting words to your inner desires is a powerful tool in a winning life game plan.

Writing things down clarifies your intentions. It helps you rank and evaluate them. Moreover, the elementary act of writing deepens your mental impression of what you want. You're employing two senses in the effort—the touch of the pen and paper (or keyboard) and the sight of the words. Add a third sense by saying the words out loud and hearing yourself say them. Thus the simple exercise of writing things down shifts your emphasis from how your life is now to how you want it to be in the future.

Deciding and writing down what you want may at first seem selfish or greedy. But it isn't, really. The words *desire* and *want* suffer from public-relations problems. Wants don't necessarily have to be egotistical, me-type things. Our wants, the mother of our action plans, reflect where we place value and where we find meaning.

It's important not only to identify *what* you want, but also *why* you want it. If I want to grow my company this year purely to gratify ego, that is a wholly different desire from genuinely wanting to provide more guests with pleasant tire-buying experiences and giving more teammates opportunities to grow in a healthy work environment. Keeping that want top-of-mind changes the desire significantly. Healthy desires usually have a positive rebound effect, meaning that by giving, you get, enabling you in turn to give more. Wants can be as much about giving as about getting. Your own wants may include raising a healthy family, teaching important skills and concepts to others, and doing volunteer work or being a new-business "angel."

Write Down Your Wants

Find a quiet and comfortable place where you can be alone, a place where you can clear your head. Keep with you a pen and paper, or a computer—any way to record your desires. Set aside at least an hour (preferably longer) to make your list, and try to do it at a time when you feel confident, grounded, and at ease. It's difficult to be open to higher aspirations when you're panicked or when your mind is racing. You may wish to meditate, pray, walk, or exercise beforehand.

Once you're settled in and feel comfortable, take a thorough look at your personal mission statement. Then go through each of the categories below. For each category, write down those desires that mean the most to you—things you'd like to accomplish or move toward in the next year. Don't be afraid to write down things that seem unorthodox, selfish, foolish, unrealistic, or even absurd. Be honest, and allow yourself to be more than you are now.

Here are the categories I use:

+ spiritual health
+ physical health

+ emotional/psychological health
+ intellectual education
+ family relationships
+ love relationship
+ friends
+ service to wider community and Earth
+ trips/play
+ career
+ money

Under *physical health,* perhaps you wish to lose two inches off your waist or lower your blood pressure by 10 percent. Under *emotional/psychological health,* you may want to list a few alternatives to habits or behaviors that are serving you poorly. Under *family relationships,* maybe you want to improve your relationship with your daughter. Under *career,* you may want that promotion to department manager. Under *service to wider community,* perhaps you want to help at a local food shelf.

As you list your desires, follow these few simple guidelines:

+ Have fun! Approach this just as you did in making out a holiday wish list when you were a kid. In this case, the holiday is the entire year.
+ Make sure the breadth and size of your goals are right for you. Most people fall into two types: the dreamer likes to dream huge, knowing that he'll fall short of his goal but will still feel satisfied with how far he went in reaching for it. The pragmatist gets discouraged if goals can't be reached completely. Know yourself, and set goals that will excite and motivate you based on the way you work.
+ Be specific. Vague moving targets are difficult to hit.
+ Use an outline format or a list of bulleted items. They're easier than paragraphs to read and add to.
+ Make sure your wants are somewhat balanced. Don't focus solely (or almost solely) on money or career. Unbalanced desires tend to lead to a life that doesn't work very well, although in a particular year you may have to focus more heavily on one area over another in order to achieve a better balance in the long run.

+ Make sure the items on your list are something *you* want and not *solely* things somebody else (your spouse, your parent) thinks you should want.

+ Mix short-term goals that can be accomplished in a few weeks with medium-term goals that can reached in a few months with long-term goals that may take a year or more. This gives a sense of ongoing accomplishment that will keep you motivated for the entire year.

+ Balance goals that are really challenging with goals that are more easily attainable. Setting too many big goals may be a setup for failure, and that's a form of self-sabotage. Big goals are necessary, though, to stretch your abilities.

+ Be okay with the idea that you may not achieve all your wants. Rather, ask yourself what you might accomplish that you wouldn't have if you hadn't tried the process at all.

How much you focus on career and financial concerns is entirely your call. Certainly it's okay if money and career are important pieces for you. Please don't feel guilty about desiring success and material rewards. Just remember that they're not ends in themselves, but tools that enable us to do work that reaches beyond the limited scope of career and money—that is, if it affords us the opportunity to work for or speak out for causes we believe in, or to use the material rewards in positive ways. When my company improved in a significant way economically, beginning in 1993, I felt a bit guilty. When I asked my psychologist about this, she said quizzically, "Why would it *not* be okay for people who are doing their best to do good in the world to receive some material abundance? Or do you think money should go only to people who don't seem to be adding value to others' lives?"

It's fine to identify with others or model their success. Just be wary of unhealthy and irrelevant comparisons between others' accomplishments and your own. Beware of valuing certain people more than others because they've got a great résumé or lots of money, or have gotten a lot of press. This just makes us feel inadequate—an understandable response when we sense that our contributions are somehow valued less. Although career and financial success mean something to me, I have absolutely, unequivocally discovered that the truly important things are family, health, psychological and spiritual development, and service to others.

It seems to me that the real story is in all of us tuning in to our unique missions and then doing our best to fulfill them. A person dedicated to helping the less fortunate in life may not have acquired much "stuff." Is this person's achievement less valuable than that of someone who has had significant career or monetary success? How can we judge? Why would we want to? Why not value everyone for *being*—for doing their best based on where they are and the resources they have. Just think of the wonderfully supportive thoughts and feelings we'd all get if we could look at each other and see our uniqueness as human beings, with no need to set ourselves above or below another based on material concerns.

It's not surprising that materially based success is so highly valued in our culture. "In a society that judges self-worth on productivity, it's no wonder we fall prey to the misconception that the more we do, the more we're worth," writes Ellen Sue Stern in *The Indispensable Woman*. Some people who disagree with this dollar-based value are choosing to downsize their obligations so they live under less pressure to make money and have more time for other things. More on that in chapter 9.

Review and Renew

Once your list is done, look it over. This represents what's important in your life. By identifying and writing down what you want out of life in the next year, you've already taken a major step toward achieving it. By simply putting these desires on paper you've consciously begun moving toward your life's mission and marrying your day-to-day activities to it.

Each December I sit down to repeat this process, creating a new, specific list of desires for the upcoming year. As the months and years pass, you will find yourself getting more and more of what your mission draws you toward, living out a life you may not have thought possible.

Each year, when you take time to identify and write your wants, remember these words:

> There is one elementary truth, the ignorance of which kills countless ideas and suspended plans: that the moment when one definitely commits oneself, then providence moves too. All sorts of things occur to help one that would never have otherwise occurred. A whole stream of events issues from the decision, raising to one's favor all manner of unforeseen incidents and meetings and material assistance which no man could have dreamt would have come his way. (W. H. Murray) Whatever you can do or dream, you can begin it. Boldness has genius, power and magic in it. Begin it now. (Goethe)

Step 2. Create Action Plans

The second step to buying your ticket is establishing an action plan that turns your wants into realities. I've found that giving structure to my desires allows me to be more deliberate—more aware, really—in my day-to-day activities. I relax more, knowing that all areas of my life are on track because I've firmly, yet flexibly, decided and planned them.

Next, your action plans will be transferred to your schedule and to-do lists, the critical link between wants and day-to-day life. Any action plan therefore needs to be *specific; feasible and realistic;* and *clearly related to your desires.*

For example, I decided a few years ago to deepen an already good relationship with my parents. They're divorced and live far from my Minneapolis home—my mother in southern Indiana, my father in southern California. My action plan is to phone each of them once a week and visit them at least twice a year. I travel with them at least once a year, and I send cards on Mother's Day, Father's Day, birthdays, and holidays. I also make it a point to tell them how I feel about them. I try my best to leave no loving thought unspoken between us.

Another example: one of my long-standing career desires has been to create a healthy, happy, successful company as measured by specific figures, such as a guest enthusiasm index, a teammate enthusiasm index, a return-on-investment number, and a gross sales figure. One section from my action plan to achieve these goals is the following:

1. Instill and support these desires in my team by attending monthly Head Coaches Team meetings (other businesses call them executive committee meetings), strategic planning meetings, and monthly Store Coaches meetings. Spend time speaking to every class of new hires.

2. Visit Tires Plus stores, spread across ten states, a specific number of days each month.

Write down your own action plans in any manner that works for you. For me, plans work best in outline form—the portion of my life first, the desire under that, and the action plan next. For instance:

I. Relationships
   A. Improve relationship with mother.
      1. Call every Sunday.
      2. Take a week-long vacation in mid-March wherever mom chooses.
      3. Send cards.

    B. Improve relationship with father.
      1. Call every Sunday.
      And so on…

To some people this may sound too structured, too linear. Traditionally, these types of systems have been taught in a rigid and inflexible way, but that's not the way I choose to use them. I build in flexibility and consider my action plans as guidelines, not commandments. They're suggestions and reminders—"mission manifesters." By simply creating these action plans, more of my "wants" become "haves" than if I had never formalized any kind of routine. Also, when I have plans, I'm better able to live in the present moment. I'm rarely thinking about the things I need to do because I know that I have plans that will get them done in the right time.

Still other people may see all this planning and preparing as a waste of time. After all, we live in a nation of compulsive "doers." Why plan when you can *do* instead?

Here's why: because you'll get where you want to go. It's like deciding you want to go from New York to L.A. by car. Waiting for you at the end of the trip is a friend you long to see. If you don't decide which route you're going to take, you could drive in circles for months. You may get there eventually, but meanwhile your friend has been waiting. Your mission is that friend. It's not critical that you get there at lightning speed, but it is important that you give yourself a reasonable chance of succeeding. As John Leach, a Kansas City businessman, says, "If you don't know where you're going, any road will get you there."

Step 3. Integrate the Plan

Now you're ready for the next step to getting what you want—scheduling your action plans. This is the often missing link between words and action. I hear some people object to this as being too confining, too linear. I can understand this. I know I've never wanted to be a slave to my calendar, and I certainly don't want to shut out the serendipitous opportunities that come my way, just because I have too much to do.

Scheduling is less an activity than an art, and it takes practice to get the right blend of flexibility and structure that works for you. Experiment with it. Refine it. Just don't abandon it.

Closely reviewing someone's schedule tells you a lot about that person's priorities. Try taking an objective look at yours. If you find a chasm between what you say you want and what's in your schedule, it's time to bridge the gap. Here's how: I take the items from my list of desires and my action plans and transfer them directly onto my schedule and my to-do list. I do this on a regular basis, each time with an eye toward ensuring that my schedule jibes with those desires that came to me when I was in a grounded and sure state of mind.

As you follow this process, you'll probably discover familiar activities that simply don't make the cut anymore. Don't worry. It's just a sign that you're sorting things out by making conscious choices. Again, if you're thinking this is too systematic, try thinking of the process as a nurturing ritual rather than as a cold system.

The degree of detail you include in your schedule and to-do lists—your appointments, phone calls, e-mails, projects, and daily, weekly, and monthly activities—is entirely up to you. This will determine the physical scheduling system you choose, although price and portability are factors as well. There are as many scheduling and planning systems as there are personality types. The most detailed are by Robbins Research and Franklin Planner™, while the more portable and trendy include Filofax™ and Day Timer™. In the digital realm there's software called Schedule Plus™, and hand-held PDAs (personal digital assistants), such as the Palm Pilot™, are simple to use and small enough to fit in a pocket. These are just a few examples of the many wonderful systems out there. Choose the one that works best for you, or use them as a basis for creating your own personal system.

These systems are all the same in one important respect: it's what you put in them that makes them valuable. If you don't have a system that feels good to you (or, worse, if you don't have one at all), run, don't walk, to the nearest office-supply store. Having a scheduling system that doesn't work is like playing the piano with one hand tied behind your back.

My sons have used the Filofax™ system since they were in high school, and both call it indispensable. I have designed my own. The first element, small enough to fit in my shirt pocket, is my schedule for the year as well as all calls I need to make. My projects file, backup information for upcoming meetings, and other files are in my briefcase or my computer. Other files I use less often are either at my home or work office. The bottom line with scheduling is this: when you commit yourself to writing down things to do that support your desires, which in turn support your life's mission, you increase the likelihood that you'll be able to avoid being sidetracked.

Flexibility in scheduling is critical. Add some slack time to your schedule, so that if Murphy's Law (everything that can go wrong, will) kicks in,
you'll have room to readjust, minimizing the need to feel rushed and
stressed. An important caveat: Never, ever visualize Murphy's Law occur-
ring. Always visualize everything going smoothly—and create a plan to
maneuver in case of choppy water.

Squeezing too much into each moment is unhealthy. Time-management
experts recommend allowing twenty-five percent more time than you
expect something to take. I recommend experimenting with adding anywhere from ten to fifteen percent. You'll quickly see a pattern and realize
how much extra time you need to build in.

I used to schedule my day in such a way that I could only arrive on time
to an appointment if everything went perfectly. One slip in my schedule
affected everything else, because there was no room for slips. I constantly
found myself in a rush. I was walking through airplane doors just before
they closed (or having to beg the gate attendants to let me through after
they had already closed it), and arriving fifteen minutes late. Pumping a little more air into my schedule and a little more heart into my day has made
a big difference.

Of course, the flip side winds up being equally inept. Too much air in
your schedule lands you squarely into Parkinson's Law, that dangerous
maxim which states that work expands to fill the time available. If you
pump up your schedule too much, you can end up blowing all your time on
things that aren't consistent with your wants. As with most things, find a
healthy middle ground. It used to be that I would operate at only two
speeds, lightning fast or syrupy slow. Now I have a third speed I call *steady
as I go*. This pace is far more enjoyable than the other two speeds, though I
still shift into lightning-fast or syrupy-slow modes from time to time. If all
this sounds too rigid, keep in mind that you don't sacrifice spontaneity if

+ you're spontaneous during your scheduled activities

+ you schedule some hang-out time for just being

+ you reserve and enjoy the freedom, when it feels right, to cancel and
  postpone activities and appointments (over-reliance on this one, however, may indicate procrastination or a pattern of self-sabotage)

Step 4. Get Organized

Organizing is planning's beautiful cousin. An organized physical environment clears my mind of clutter and directly boosts my efficiency in quantum jumps. But beware—as with anything, obsessing over order can hang you up in minutiae. Find the middle ground. What follows are four organizing tips to help smooth the waters as you sail through your wants, action plans, and scheduling.

Clear the Field

Keeping a clean, uncluttered desk is a must for me. On my desk I keep a "things to do" stack, from which I give attention to one thing at a time. That way my mind concentrates only on that one piece rather than being distracted by piles competing for my attention. Certainly, many people are able to do just fine with lots of stacks that from the outside look disorganized. What counts is how it feels from the inside. As long as your work environment isn't standing in your way, do what works for you.

Maximize the Home Field Advantage

The idea of a home office is much debated. Whether it's right for you depends on your position and responsibilities and how you feel about setting and being able to live by boundaries between work life and family life. Over the years the quietude of home has afforded me a lot of planning, organizing, and productivity. The key here is to do home office work around home activities rather than in place of them—not during meals, for instance, when your spouse wants to talk, when children want to play, or when it interrupts what someone else wants to do. Discipline here is critical.

My home office has also been helpful when my family is otherwise occupied. These are good times to duck into the home office and peck away at projects, reducing stress by making me more prepared and relaxed in the coming days.

Capture Ideas on the Run

When an idea strikes, capture it. Keep a microcassette recorder handy, or paper and pen or personal digital assistant. Whether I'm at home, commuting, or running errands, I can go back to being fully available to the moment at hand instead of trying to contain in my head simultaneously those fleeting, firefly thoughts. When I'm driving and paper and pencil are impractical (if not lethal), I leave a voice mail for myself: "Tom, this is Tom," I say (to the amusement of whoever's in the passenger seat). "Got a great idea…"

Call a Time-out

Sometimes I declare a shut-in, two or three days out of my schedule when I arrange no appointments, phone calls, or meetings. Nothing. I tell everyone around me about the hibernation. So does my voice mail: "I'm unavailable until next Monday." This is a can't-miss last resort for getting caught up.

If you can't afford the luxury of being completely out of reach for two or three days, try a modified time-out. Look at your situation and decide what you can do to carve out a slice of undisturbed time, even if it's for an afternoon. To whatever degree you can hibernate, do it once in a while. It's a perfect time for important projects that never seem to make it to the top of the stack. It's an opportunity for an efficiency overhaul. Or it's a time to catch up on deferred phone calls and e-mails. As a result, you'll be on top of things and feel that rejuvenating relief of getting to the bottom of the to-do stack.

Step 5. Be Time Wise

No one can afford to overlook the basic skill of time competency. Its value will only appreciate in today's fast-paced, info-saturated age of "initiative overload" and clashing personal and career priorities. If you consider yourself time-challenged, you're not alone. In a 1998 *Wall Street Journal*/NBC News survey of 2,001 people, nearly 80 percent described their lives as busy, or busy to the point of discomfort. More telling still is the fact that surveyors had to call 31,407 phone numbers to find 2,001 Americans with time to answer their questions.

Think of the parts of your life that compete for time: parenting, love relationships, friendships, career, and self-development, to name a few. To make matters more complicated, today we're in relatively uncharted waters given the proliferation of dual careers, changing gender roles, and our increasingly frenetic pace. History doesn't offer many successful models for adequately meeting all these demands.

Time competency, which balances caring for self and others with today's realities, will be one of the most important skills to land what you want out of life. It's the one sure way to protect your schedule against otherwise almost certain sabotage, intentional or otherwise. It is a pure form of self-caring, as well as a form of wisdom. Teddy Roosevelt himself went so far as to say, "Nine-tenths of wisdom is being wise in time."

Put Time on Your Side

Take a close look at what time means to you. Ask yourself if you have enough of it to get done what you want to get done. I often ask this of people, and it's the rare person who indeed thinks he has enough time. The concept and the lament—"I don't have enough time"—runs through most people's heads every day, regardless of whether they indeed have less time than they need. This never-ending loop actually becomes a self-fulfilling prophecy; you don't have enough time because you never believed you would in the first place.

We can experience time differently if we want to. Deepak Chopra heightened my awareness of this in the early nineties, and since then I've made a habit of saying to myself, *I have all the time I need to get done what I need to get done.* As I run my finger down my daily schedule and to-do list in the morning, I visualize getting all of it done. Guess what? By the end of the day I typically *do* get it all done. This method has increased what I'm able to accomplish, and it has increased the joy I take in completing each task.

What we've just uncovered is the magical power of intention. Try it. In fact, consider starting right now by making a verbal commitment to giving adequate time to finish this book over a reasonable period, and visualize its timely completion.

No Time for Time-Denial

Do yourself a favor and jerk yourself out of time-denial. I often hear people complain, "With all the work I have to do, I have time for very little else." The dirty little secret here is that work can be a handy scapegoat. Even if you put in more than eight hours a day, you've still got a lot of time left.

Figure it out. There are 168 hours in a week. If you sleep seven hours each night, you're left with 119 hours. Say you work fifty hours per week. You still have nearly seventy hours left over—close to 60 percent of your waking hours—for other things. Adjust for your amount of sleep and work. Surprised? Owning up to it will free you from denial (a dangerous defense mechanism) and propel you into taking empowering action steps.

We misuse a startling amount of those 119 waking hours. Over time, I've learned not to misuse them as much. Using my schedules and to-do lists as a guide, it's easy to eliminate much of what isn't in line with my action plan, which in turn reflects my wants and personal mission. This gives me more time for things that support what I want to get and give in the world.

Taking Time for Joy

Quieting your mind is another form of time competency. When I'm meditating regularly and in a mindful state, the sense of time scarcity diminishes. My worries about the past and the future lessen, helping me stay where I was all along—in the present. And there seems to be more time because of it. Deadlines don't disappear, but somehow the time expands to fit the work that needs to be done. The time-wise Dr. Stephan Rechtschaffer writes, "Mindfulness doesn't take time, it gives it. We create time each moment we step into an awareness of the present." Lily Tomlin's quip about mindfulness gets closer to the point: "For fast acting relief, try slowing down."

I do my best to enjoy the trip and not let the hectic pace of our world throw me off course. But there are days when competing priorities push this level of awareness farther away than I'd like. It's a tough balance. While I'm getting better, there are still ever more moments I'd like to fully embrace.

If we rush through life only doing—rather than also being and feeling—we'll miss the universal signs that point us down the right road. More important, we'll miss meaningful connections with others. Just before his death, former French president François Mitterrand bemoaned this. "It's sad," he said, "that it's not until the very end that we realize that the marvel is the passing moment." We don't need to wait until death is staring us in the face to realize this. We can realize it today, right now.

The system I've described is about balance, *not* about what you can take, take, take by being a scheduling machine. Take time for your own and others' basic human needs—parenting, romance, friendship, and connection with random people whose paths cross yours.

The importance of making time for others cannot be overstated. Tap into your intuitive sense of when you can brighten somebody's day. Often, it's so minor it appears trifling: a smile to a stranger, holding a door for someone, giving up your seat on the bus. There are literally hundreds of tiny ways to affect others positively and tap into basic human kindness.

Occasionally an opportunity to help someone throws you off your schedule. That's okay. Pastor Kurt Kalland of Minneapolis, Minnesota, says part of our job description as human beings is to be interruptable. Weigh the needs and significance of whoever appears in your life. Your heart and gut are effective guides. Just listen. Success and achievement aren't the ultimate point. The heartfelt path, no matter where it takes you, is a path with rewards beyond anything we can measure.

Remember, time competency is an art and not a tool for sprinting, head down, over whoever's in your way. I regret the instances years ago when I could have taken extra time with my family, friends, and employees. Since 1989, though, I've become more aware.

In 1995 I was supposed to attend a banquet for the Ernst and Young/ *USA Today* Midwest Entrepreneur of the Year Awards. I was a finalist, and I was already running fifteen minutes late when my son Chris, then twenty-three years old, dropped by the house. I could see he was glum. Late as I was already, I stopped everything to talk with him. For the next ninety minutes we talked about the breakup of his long-term relationship. I knew I was missing the social hour and dinner that preceded the ceremony, but I didn't leave until he felt finished. There's no award—and I did win that evening— that could hold a candle to being there for my son. The bottom line is this: Do not let human indifference become part of your time-management repertoire. Human needs must be factored into any time-wise approach.

Beware the Seven Time Bandits

Sometimes the day seems to slip through our fingers without our even being aware of it. Where does that valuable time go? Here are seven of the most common sabotaging time-stealers and how you can deal with them.

TIME BANDIT 1. TOO MUCH TALK ✦ Over-talking, paralysis of analysis, babbling boardrooms—call it what you will, but it can be just as costly as any other systems inefficiency. Imagine this: Each day you may have some thirty conversations over the phone and in person. If each runs four minutes longer than it could, you lose *two hours a day.* Not that this is altogether wrong. It's just that if you find yourself saying, "If only I had a couple of extra hours in the day..." this may be one place to find them.

To make the most of any business exchange, whether in person or on the telephone, I first plan what I'd like to accomplish. I list questions that I want to ask and points I want to make. This makes the outcome of each meeting more positive and productive.

At my company, we use a gentle way of confronting a teammate who's rambling on about a business matter (the situation is totally different if it's a personal matter). With a phrase I learned years ago from efficiency consultant Edwin Bliss, we quickly interject in a friendly, curious way, "The bottom line, Jim?" Without fail, Jim cuts to the quick and within thirty seconds the point is succinctly made. Anyone at the company can be bottom-lined, including me. The one caveat we stress: never bottom-line a customer or your spouse (unless the two of you consider it fair ahead of time).

A variation is the temporary bottom line, delivered in a friendly, caring tone: "Hey, Jim, I'd love to hear more about that project, but I've got an appointment I need to get to. Can you bottom-line it, or should we talk later?" This method is far better than the alternative, which we're all occasionally guilty of: listening and thinking that you're being polite, then stewing about how some prattler is frittering away your time. (Often the prattler is thinking the same thing!)

TIME BANDIT 2. THE PHONE ZONE ✦ The telephone can be either your greatest ally or your worst enemy. It is our single greatest source of interruption. We actually love using it, even though we say we don't. Time flies when we're on the phone. For this reason, I try to keep all my business calls as direct and to the point as possible. Furthermore, maligned as it may be, voice mail is my trusted sentry. I personally leave the following energetic message on my voice-mail greeting: *"Hi, this is Tom Gegax. Thanks for calling. After the tone, please leave a message detailing your needs and desires so either I or the appropriate person can get back to you in a more helpful way. Thanks a lot for calling, and make it a great day."* It's a relatively personal greeting because it's my own voice and I'm being upbeat and friendly. And without fail the message prompts callers to say *exactly* what they need instead of simply leaving their name and number, the dreaded first serve in a game of telephone tennis. When I retrieve the call I either forward it to someone whose specialty addresses the request, or I return the call fully prepared.

Conversely, when I can't reach someone, I leave a detailed message and ask the person to respond on my voice mail. This eliminates phone tag and compresses messages. When I need a synchronous, voice-to-voice chat with someone, I let her know on her voice mail where and when I can be reached. If you're in a job or business involving time-sensitive customer support, however, this is not a wise technique. Overuse of voice mail could cost you accounts. If your phone calls aren't time-sensitive, try setting aside a certain time of the day to return phone calls (and e-mails) so you're not constantly pulled away from other tasks.

In addition, I use my cell phone to transform my commute—fifty minutes round-trip—and other car-bound stretches into useful time. This cuts down on the number of calls I initiate and return at the office or home. That's not to say car phones are great. Besides raising safety issues, they're a minor violation of my effort to avoid doing more than one thing at a time. For safety reasons, I absolutely urge you to follow these tips:

1. Make only calls that don't require you to write anything down or refer to backup materials.

2. Use a speakerphone to keep your hands free for driving.

3. Learn the telephone keypad like the back of your hand so you can dial without taking your eyes off the road.

Another phone tip: when I have two separate people giving me conflicting versions of the same story, I often hook them up for a quick conference call, introduce the subject, and hear them debate the issue.

TIME BANDIT 3. ENDLESS DETAIL ✦ For even better time competency, decide in advance how much time you'll spend on a business meeting or phone call. I sometimes let the person know exactly how much time I have available. That way people condense their points, and you get to the good stuff faster. The 80/20 rule certainly applies: 20 percent of the information can give you at least 80 percent of what you really need to know.

I recall a meeting at which the presenter said she wanted an hour. I told her that since I only had fifteen minutes, she might consider cutting it down to three five-minute increments: five minutes for her presentation, five for questions, five for how her suggestions could be implemented. She talked fast, hit her major points, and stayed within fifteen minutes— with an occasional gentle nudge when I sensed she was in danger of going over.

Whether on the phone or in person, I do my best to think of the task at hand in relation to the big picture—my desires and personal mission as well as a win-win outcome. It's easy to get wrapped up in what's in front of you, and you wind up running a time deficit later, shorting yourself or someone else. Be present and mindful of whom you're with, why you're with them, and how that moment fits into the larger picture of the day and your life. Then act accordingly.

TIME BANDIT 4. TRANCE TV + Television is hypnotic. Literally. Consider the guy who watches TV three hours a day during the week and five hours a day on the weekend, not uncommon for many Americans. These people devote roughly 36 percent of their nonworking, waking hours to TV. Try charting your own viewing habits for a week or two. Weigh the number of hours per week you spend in front of the tube against the total weekly hours you're awake and not working. You may be shocked.

Some people call their TV-watching hours valuable zone-out time. Some people say it makes them feel more relaxed, but consider that sluggish, stiff feeling that may fill your bones when you finally pull yourself up off the couch. Is it really relaxing? Ask yourself whether there are better ways to tune out: tuning in to the people around you, to the outdoors, to yourself.

Back in 1989, as I assessed my wants, I discovered that TV didn't make the cut. For years I didn't watch it at all. Today, I average about five hours a week. The only downside is that I can't relate when small talk turns to TV sitcoms. To be sure, there is some excellent programming out there. With cable-driven channel proliferation and more educational, news, and information-oriented shows, there has never been such a quality-TV bounty. Nevertheless, the fact is that TV can easily be addictive, and real caution is advised here. Determine how much time you're spending watching other people's lives rather than living your own. This isn't about good and bad or right and wrong. If TV is in line with your wants, that's great. But if you're not getting what you want out of your life because you're constantly short of time, then TV habits are another potential place to free up hours.

TIME BANDIT 5. BRAIN MUDDLE + There are some days when you just can't seem to function the way you'd like. Brain-dead. Muddled. Befuddled. Some excuse it by saying they haven't had their first cup of coffee yet. For others, it's just their work cycle. Whatever the case, it's no fun when you need to get your work done.

While most people hit the coffeepot or vending machines to get themselves through, consider these ideas to jump-start your day:

+ Consider working on tasks that require less linear, detail-oriented focus in favor of creative problem solving. If you have the ability to reprioritize your schedule, focus on ideas for solving that long-term budgeting problem instead of balancing the spreadsheet.

+ Ask yourself if your muddle is really a lack of motivation. If it is, it's time to reconnect with your mission. Read it over, look for actions in your schedule that support it, remind yourself that you've already translated it from desire to deed, and draw inspiration from the courage you've already shown. While you're at it, visualize how great you'll feel when your desire is met.

+ Take five minutes for life. Five minutes is enough time to walk outside, to breathe deeply and calmly, notice the sky, say an affirmation twenty times, and let go of guilt that you're not getting enough done today. Refocus on why you're here—not just at work, but in the world. After the five minutes, take a look at your day's workload and reassess your priorities. They may look different to you now. Do what you can. Delegate what you can. Ask for support from your co-workers. Renegotiate a deadline that you know you can't meet. Be proactive about managing your schedule and ask for what you need.

+ Double back and make sure you're doing whatever it takes to maintain an overall state of wellness—such things as eating right, exercising, tuning in to your Higher Power, and getting enough sleep. Make a commitment to yourself to improve these habits in whatever ways you can.

TIME BANDIT 6. BROKEN CYCLES + Many people start projects only to abandon them half-finished; it's often tempting to move on to other things after the excitement of the initial idea wears off. It's not obvious, but unless projects are actually completed, the time and effort devoted to them is generally wasted. However, when you tie a nice red bow on a project, benefits begin accruing.

Few things are more frustrating than a perfectly good project that's shelved without good cause. It's fine if unforeseen circumstances make a project obsolete. Sometimes that's just part of the creative process, especially in the early stages of developing a new service or product. But don't abandon a worthwhile project just because it's in a mundane phase or conversely riding a challenging or labor-intensive wave. There's a certain pain from not getting to see the result of your initiative. If you have this tendency, make a verbal commitment to yourself to complete projects and cycles.

TIME BANDIT 7. THE MEETING MORASS + Meetings can waste the day or, when used right, can be time savers. Through the synergy of many minds working together, solutions can sometimes be reached quicker than by one person working alone. Well-run, productive meetings don't happen naturally, however. Think about how much of your work week is sucked into the void of less-than-productive meetings. Now decide to reverse that void. You can streamline your meeting participation and effectiveness in a number of ways.

First, don't automatically agree to participate in *any* meeting without first thinking it through. Always ask what your role will be, what kind of input they're looking for, and what you stand to learn. Based on your answers, determine how much you need to be involved. (It very well may be none at all, in which case explain, with care and diplomacy, why you don't feel you could add value to the meeting.) If your views must be heard, yet you don't have the time, consider designating a proxy to share your thoughts, or agree to attend only the portion of the meeting that's germane to you. There are, of course, meetings that are important to attend for the full time.

Phone meetings can save you time, too. Before scheduling face-to-face meetings with people away from my office, I ask myself, Can I do this with a telephone conference? I often opt for the phone conference if I already have good rapport with the other person. Certainly there are many things that cannot be done by phone—sensitive people issues, and critical decisions in which total focus is necessary. Yet there is very little done in a business meeting that can't be accomplished just as well via the phone. Handouts? Send them in advance. Fax machines, state-of-the-art speakerphones and video conferencing can make phone meetings more effective than ever before. Of course, the spontaneous whiteboard or flip-chart presentation is impossible via the phone, and the synergistic benefits are often better in person. When people want me to travel to them, I often ask, "What more can we accomplish in person that we can't do by phone?" Typically the answer is "Nothing, really."

When you do attend face-to-face meetings, there are a few ways to ratchet up their effectiveness. Not only do the meetings go more smoothly, but these tips help ensure that you'll need fewer meetings to follow up on all the things that fell between the cracks in the previous meeting:

+ Make sure everyone has an agenda in advance, complete with the amount of time allocated for each item. Also, ensure, or at least request, that presenters distribute complete, succinct handouts, preferably in advance. This reduces the time it takes for participants to get on track with the presenter's ideas, and it prompts the presenter to stay focused.

+ Ensure that the purpose of the meeting, and what you want to accomplish, is clear. Keep this at the top of your mind throughout.

+ Once the meeting begins, gently prod it along if you're allowed to show leadership in that form. When an idea provokes extended indecision, either suggest it be tabled or assign a smaller team to study it and come back with recommendations.

+ Before leaving one item and going on to the next, summarize (if appropriate) what action will be taken to ensure that the meeting's note-taker understands.

+ At the end of the meeting, suggest having each participant's thoughts on the meeting. The nuggets of wisdom that emerge are helpful.

+ Finally, within twenty-four hours after the meeting, distribute or ask if the agreed-upon action steps can be distributed to all participants.

One-on-one meetings have their own unique issues. Most of the rules for group meetings also apply, but here are some other things that I use that can prove helpful:

+ Prepare questions that get to the heart of the issue—expectations, progress, performance.

+ Follow a three-step process I call RAP: create *rapport, ask* questions, and *present* clearly:

  1. **Rapport** begins by taking a little time to reconnect with the other person or getting to know one another if you haven't already met.

  2. **Ask questions** that get to the heart of the matter. Done right, the answers will actually bring out the points that you want made. It's important for whoever you're meeting with to say their piece first. Then they'll be more receptive when you talk. View this not as gamesmanship but as seeking information before making your case.

  3. **Present** your material clearly and succinctly. Provide information, charts, and handouts that support your point.

+ Ask for what you want or need that will provide for a mutually beneficial exchange. This may seem obvious, but I've seen people ace the first two steps and forget, often out of fear, to ask for what they want, need, or expect. Then the meeting is wasted.

Dousing Brush Fires

What to do with those inevitable interruptions that pop up all day long? I face them armed with the Six D's—my secret weapon for fighting flareups. The order of these is very important. Start with the first option. If it doesn't apply, go to the second one, and so on down the list until you reach the level of action required for your situation. Whether it's an urgent voice mail or fax, or a co-worker who suddenly appears at your desk demanding immediate attention, consider these strategies for handling the situation effectively while staying on track with your other scheduled tasks:

1. **Don't do it.** Some things will simply go away if you don't do them, while others will get worse. If "go away" applies, ignore it. Be aware of the tendency to let easy, unimportant tasks distract us from the more important and difficult goal-related items.

2. **Delay it.** Some interruptions will disappear if they're delayed. Remember all those red-hot, urgent voice mails and notes that were left for you while you were on vacation? By the time you got back, despite no attention whatsoever on your part, many of those items had cooled.

3. **Direct the issue to someone outside your immediate work group.** This strategy is useful with many brushfires that will get hotter if they're delayed. Sometimes the problem actually falls in someone else's court—a vendor or a person in a support department. You can often use this third D in your life outside work as well. For example, share household chores such as cleaning and yard work among family members, or delegate them to people you hire.

4. **Delegate it to someone within your work group.** There's no need always to take the heroic, sacrificial, "I'll do it" approach. If the matter falls into someone else's realm of responsibility in your area, which is often the case, put the matter in their lap without guilt or regret. Believe it or not, under-delegation is a serious problem for many managers, even those who think they delegate too much. In his performance review, one of my company's key coaches checked off "delegates too much" as one of his weaknesses. Yet his work group's developmental feedback almost unanimously reported he didn't delegate enough.

5. **Do it imperfectly.** Even when the task at hand turns out to be something only you can do, this strategy can work wonders. We all have had projects that could have been done imperfectly yet successfully. In striving for excellence (or in going from good to perfect), we often use up a huge chunk of time that could be used far more productively in the sixth D.

6. **Do it.** Sometimes doing it yourself and doing it with excellence is the optimal and only way to put out a brushfire. It's easier to find the time for this once you've doused other fires with the first five D's.

Time competency will change your life. Just send yourself positive mental messages, stay out of denial, ward off the Seven Time Bandits, and use the Six D's to handle brushfires. In the process, you can also be both caring to others and respectful to yourself. The more you value your own time, the more others will, too.

Step 6. Just Do It

"Just do it." In other words, do what you know is difficult but necessary. Apologize to someone you have wronged. Make that cold call. Call on a customer who is unhappy with you or your company.

"Just doing it" could be telling someone how you feel about him, or developing a business plan for your new business, or more clearly telling your manager your career aspirations. It could be doing something that's unfamiliar or not one of your strengths. Whatever it may be, remember that a thing's difficulty makes it no less necessary. In fact, it generally makes doing it *more* necessary.

In a way, knowing what's difficult and what's not is a convenient organizing principle. You can usually bet that if something's difficult, it will have a high payoff, it will be related to your action plans and desires, and it will present an opportunity for you to grow by getting outside your comfort zone.

What stops us from doing difficult things? FEAR (sometimes described as an acronym for "false evidence appearing real"), particularly fear of failure. The evidence that fear gives us can appear solid, yet is usually illusory. Often, because of fear, we stop just short of success, punting when we're two yards from a touchdown.

Self-doubt is another attitude that stops us from staying in "just do it" mode. You have every reason to doubt yourself if you're only relying on one aspect of yourself, but if you send in key plays to activate your entire being—body, intellect, psyche, and spirit—the effect is that you'll have access to energy, ideas, and motivation you don't have otherwise.

When I feel myself bucking against something, I start sending myself messages. First, I tell myself that there's no downside to trying (unless, of course, there are safety, ethical, or financial risks). Most of the time the worst thing that can happen is the same thing that happens if you don't try: nothing. Second, I remind myself that I can start by taking small steps one at a time in that direction. Begin writing, look up a phone number, get on the Internet and do some needed research.

Just move things forward. Don't worry about mistakes. In fact, recast mistakes as mis-takes: take 1, take 2, take 3. Do as many retakes as you need. If it works for Hollywood, it can work for you. As my son Trent always tells me, "If you're not falling, you're not skiing." If you're not making mistakes, you're not learning anything.

Avoid the Paralysis of Analysis

A common roadblock to keeping your momentum going is what Edwin Bliss terms "paralysis of analysis," the tendency to overstudy situations. If you find yourself stuck, consider the ramifications of making a decision, and then adjust your time commitment to it accordingly. Move fast on easily reversible situations, slower on ones that are tougher to reverse. For decisions whose ramifications are minimal or can easily be rescinded, be quick and decisive. For decisions that have greater effects or can't be reversed, devote more time to careful study. If you find yourself putting off those decisions that are more difficult, schedule them for your "prime time," that part of the day or week when you're most grounded, focused, and energized.

The Law of Persistence

Part of what helps me to just do it is will. Legendary Green Bay Packers Coach Vince Lombardi had a saying: "The difference between a successful person and others is not a lack of strength, not a lack of knowledge, but rather a lack of will." It is also called persistence. Calvin Coolidge's "Law of Persistence" has been on my wall since I started my business twenty-three years ago:

Coolidge's Law of Persistence

Nothing in the world can take the place of persistence.
Talent will not; nothing is more common than unsuccessful men with talent.
Genius will not; unrewarded genius is almost a proverb.
Education will not; the world is full of educated derelicts.
Persistence and determination alone are omnipotent.

While the references to "derelicts" and "men" are out of place in our day, this is still a priceless and eloquent bit of advice.

Step 7. Let Go

The final step to getting what you want, letting go, is useful when persistence hasn't worked. This step may seem diametrically opposed to persistence, but it is not.

Not every path that you think is the right path will lead to where you think you and your higher wisdom have planned to go. You must be able to recognize when you're on a dead-end road, and be willing to try an alternative route.

Wisdom is knowing when to persist and when to let go. I choose persistence when my aim, after double-checking, agrees with my mission and feels right to my entire Inner Team. When that's the case, my Higher Source winds up giving me more strategies for jumping the high hurdles. On the other hand, I know it's time to let go when, after the double-check, my objective isn't in line with my mission and I start feeling anxious and unsettled. By being in tune with your Inner Team, you can sense the pain and internal thoughts telling you when it's time to let go.

When you're tuned in, you're aware of your environment at multiple levels, and you're more flexible about the cues inside and all around you. These signals can come from literally anywhere—people, things you read, the environment, the back of your neck. We all know the feeling when we get those millisecond glimpses that point the way. Premonitions? Imagination? Smarts? Insight? Foresight? If you're tempted to brush those clues aside, first ask yourself what downside could result from heeding the message. Let go of any preconceptions about the source of the information, and consider it on its own merit.

A slightly different variation on letting go comes from Deepak Chopra's *Seven Spiritual Laws of Success.* The first component of his Law of Least Effort is acceptance. It asks you to make a commitment, such as "Today I will accept people, situations, circumstances and events as they occur." In other words, the moment is unfolding just as it should because everything is just as it should be. Conversely, Chopra writes, "When you struggle against this moment, you struggle against the whole Universe."

The next component in letting go is taking responsibility. Acknowledge that you possess any number of creative responses to *any* situation. All problems contain the seeds of opportunity, if your eyes are open.

When you approach the world as a place of limitless potential, it's not necessary to stick stubbornly to an original plan. When you're receiving signals from within (and without) that you are on the wrong path, let go and watch other doors open. It's been my experience that for every door that closes, another opens. Every ending contains a beginning.

Don't confuse letting go with giving up, however. Take your wants and action plans seriously. Remember, you acquired them by going inside during calm times and getting in touch with how they mesh with your worldly mission.

Knowing when to cast or cut the line will help resolve your internal struggles among competing priorities. Stability, the ability to stay the course, is an important attribute. Together, stability and flexibility give you the deep roots and strong limbs of a redwood tree—and the ability to withstand the ceaseless winds of change.

A Japanese proverb says that "vision without action is a daydream; action without vision is a nightmare." In chapter 1, you found the vision through your personal mission. With chapter 2, you now know how to put it into action. To get the most value from this book, use all Seven Take-Action Steps. With these steps you'll begin getting and giving more of what's important to you in the world. You'll begin feeling a sense of accomplishing part of your mission on Earth. You'll experience the sheer enjoyment of the trip itself. And you'll get more of that most basic and precious of human emotions, happiness.

3

Six Traits for the Trip

ACHIEVING YOUR MISSION—getting where you want to go—takes conscious effort every day. Building on your moves and plays from the day before, you're shifting gears, taking sideroads when necessary, being open to that unexpected, welcoming rest stop. You know where you're going, but on the way, life happens, and you have to be ready to live it.

Manifesting your mission is like planning a road trip. In this chapter we'll explore ways to fuel the trip. It takes a special blend of inner attitude and outer behavior to provide the right mix of fuel for the journey, a blend of traits I've discovered through self-observation and seeing others' success. "COPPSS," an acronym coined by Tires Plus teammate Scott McPhee, makes these essentials easy to remember. The person who embodies them is

Caring
Optimistic
Passionate
Persistent
Systems-disciplined
Spirit-filled

Six Traits for the Trip

The six COPPSS traits combine to precipitate success in life, their combination broadcasting messages about who we are. They don't necessarily come naturally; we develop them over time by habitually reminding ourselves of their value, and then acting on them with conviction.

These "ways of being" begin with "ways of seeing"—orienting your Inner Team in a way that aligns your mission with your actions. Do the right thing, and believe in it as you do. Turn *both* the attitude and the action into habits, and they'll work synergistically to keep you on track. A powerful universal energy will then respond to you in ways that may expedite the accomplishment of your mission.

COPPSS 1. Caring

In our often singleminded drive for success, happiness, and comfort, we sometimes treat people callously. Several years ago I was on a flight from Minneapolis to San Diego, trying to work on a time-pressured project, but the seat in front of me was fully reclined into my lap. At six feet two inches tall, I have long legs. Caring was not at the top of my mind. Feeling pressed for space, I sank my knees (which were already against the seat) just a little deeper to send a message.

A short time later an elderly woman rose with her walker to use the restroom. I was horrified to realize this was the person I had tried to zing with my unspoken message. It made clear to me how uncaring I'd been, regardless of who had been sitting in that seat. Although I typically try to go out of my way to be helpful, this made me see that I can let that slide when I'm rushed or stressed out. I took a long pause to coach myself about the danger of getting caught up in my needs at the expense of others.

A caring attitude recognizes the other person's humanity, sees under the surface, and recognizes a person as someone who has hopes, fears, ideas, vulnerabilities, dreams. Rather than focusing on what this person wants from you, caring focuses first on who this person *is*. The Sanskrit greeting *Namaste* says it well: "The god in me salutes the god in you." After that, wanting to help that person comes naturally.

Some people seem to turn on caring in their personal lives but turn it off in the workplace. Others give their all to coworkers, but are too drained at home to do much more than flop onto the couch. Do we feel compelled to wear a work mask to hide our soft side? Are we afraid people will take advantage of us if we show our humanity? Are we afraid that we'll appear "unprofessional"? Whatever the reasons, what's clear is that being a split personality—shifting from one self at home to a different self at work—can be unhealthy for you and those around you.

We've all seen examples of uncaring behavior in others as well as in ourselves. I'd wager that it never benefits us in the long run. Whether you derive the idea from Newton's laws of motion or from Hindu and Buddhist laws of karma, for every action there is a reaction. Remembering that what we give out comes back to us reminds us to act responsibly when we might otherwise forget. This technique is secondary, however, to our mission-decreed desire to be a positive presence on the planet. Benefiting others shouldn't be predicated on what we'll get in return.

The Big "E"

Caring is born out of a keen sense of empathy. "Empathy," my father would tell me when I was a child, "is the most important word in the English language."

My dictionary defines empathy as "the action of understanding, being aware of, being sensitive to, and vicariously experiencing the feelings, thoughts, and experience of another…without having the feelings, thoughts, and experience fully communicated in an objectively explicit manner." Empathy is a prerequisite to caring. People often don't verbalize their feelings, thoughts, and experiences, so we need to develop empathy, the ability to understand without being told. To appreciate someone else's position, we need to tap into our own emotions and experiences.

Two events helped me get in touch with the real meaning of my father's words. First, my son Chris was hit by a speeding car while riding his bike in 1984. He was in a coma for two days before eventually fully recovering. Then, in 1989, there was my three-ring wake-up call—divorce, cancer, and business crisis. Until I experienced these crises in my own life, I never really understood what other people were going through in their own trials.

Once you know what makes you tick, it's easier to understand what makes others tick—or ticks them off. To some extent we all have this intuition, but when it is developed to a higher degree it becomes a mystical sensibility that allows us to tune in to other people's needs at physical, psychological, and spiritual levels. By consciously developing a deep sense of empathy, we can both feel and act compassionately. Failing to sense others' reality, we can't genuinely respond in a caring way, no matter how hard we may try, whether at home or at work.

Tough Love

Some people deride caring as tantamount to being soft, or even encouraging low standards. This is misguided concern. When the situation calls for it, caring calls for tough love—meeting inappropriate behavior with firm yet loving discipline. As with any caring feedback, separating the behavior from the person is key: the person is lovable; the behavior is not.

When my sons, Trent and Chris, were teenagers, we were out for a family dinner. Trent was in a bad mood and filled his end of the conversation with complaints and putdowns to the point that it disrupted dinner. I decided to take him home and then return to the restaurant. As I dropped him off, I told him, with a passionate mix of anger and caring, "I love you so much, and your behavior is very disrespectful and totally unacceptable. You're grounded." Trent got the message I intended, not questioning my love for him but clear what I thought of his behavior.

It's easy to be oblivious to the cause of disruptive behavior, and focus instead on the result. I act on the assumption that anger masks fear, hurt, or shame. For example, while touring our stores one day, I heard a guest yelling at our store coach. Clearly he was upset. Talking to my teammates, and then to the gentleman, I discovered that we had made a minor error. I also discovered that his reaction rotated on a bigger problem that had nothing to do with the mistake: he had terminal cancer. Because I had once been diagnosed with cancer, I empathized with the source of his fear and, after talking with him a few more minutes, discovered a kind and caring person underneath the anger. We've all had times like this, when things were going poorly and we let a small mistake snowball into a big overreaction.

Making a commitment to be more loving will prompt you to care even when the other guy gets angry—a difficult yet necessary skill. It helps to mentally gaze into the angry person's heart, look at their humanity, and take a deep breath. Count to ten. This method isn't always successful, but it often helps.

Workplace Caring

People generally feel they pay enough for services to reasonably expect a high level of attention. Yet a great percentage say the people serving them don't deliver. In these customers' eyes, the service people don't seem to care.

This doesn't surprise me. When you ask people you interview what they like to do, they commonly answer, "I love to work with people." Yet the common refrain only months after starting a high-contact service position is "These people! They're driving me crazy!" Some, fortunately, still love to work with people even after years of extensive customer contact. People who are altruistic, caring, and service-oriented reap energy from serving others.

Other people—call them the weary workers—find themselves feeling depleted both by serving internal guests (people within your organization) or external guests (customers). When a guest comes in the store or when the phone rings, weary workers may think, *What do they want now!?* The altruist, on the other hand, thinks, *How can I help this person?* Or, *How can we get the best result from this exchange?*

Take, for instance, the caring demonstrated by the Tires Plus Store team in Coon Rapids, Minnesota. Teammates there had heard that a guest by the name of George May lost his dog Ralph in an accident. The entire store signed and sent a sympathy card, and George was touched that somebody cared. The U.S. Postal Service is the butt of many jokes, yet my mailman, Peter Symitzek, is another portrait of caring service. He'll rubber-band dog biscuits to the mail for the two Maltese dogs in my house. One day I noticed Peter's nose pressed against the window, making friendly faces at the dogs. He couldn't see me, but in him I could see caring customer service personified.

How do we maintain an attitude to give and live in service, especially in the midst of our get-it-done-now world? I believe Inner Team wellness, described in the next chapters, lays the groundwork to uncover the caring person inside each of us. Caring is an essential, not an extra.

People simply feel safer, in every sense of the word, when they sense caring in an organization. As the saying goes, "People don't care how much you know until they know how much you care." People who feel safe are more likely to approach you openly. Simply put, caring begets more caring.

Caring is the primary word and concept in the Tires Plus mission statement. To care for guests, maintaining service to others as part of our mentality, reflects the philosophy that Tires Plus teammates do their best to embody. We strive to serve caring to our teammates (employees) and guests (customers) because it's our mission. Everything follows from that. If our products and services are priced correctly and our costs are in line, the service mentality's natural by-product will be enhanced relationships and material abundance.

Caring in the workplace isn't something that can be ordered up from the CEO's chair or distributed like pamphlets at management-sponsored seminars. Instead, caring must come from people's hearts, from people tired of living with two faces. When we really care, everywhere, we generate the best kind of virus, an epidemic of workplace caring.

Caring is a less threatening and less confusing word at the office than the "L" word, *love*. At the office, we're hemmed in by anxieties over expressing ourselves clearly, and we don't have separate words for romantic love and platonic love. Thus the most treasured phrase in the world, "I love you," becomes a landmine in the workplace.

The Greeks called nonromantic love *agape*. Some understand it as a deep sense of compassion or as holding someone in high regard. I experience more and more expressions of agape at my company and in my personal life.

Uncomfortable as men generally are about articulating agape, they sense it nonetheless. Permission to express it recently came from an unexpected place, Anheuser-Busch's half-tongue-in-cheek commercial catchphrase for Bud Light, "Love you, man!" Now I often hear this half-joking and half-serious "Love you, man!" at work. My hope is that *caring* is merely a bridge word to a time when it will be commonplace for the business environment to include expressions of agape—universal, nonromantic love.

Competition with Caring

Competition can be good and perfectly compatible with caring. In its Greek roots, *competition* means to conspire together—helping each other to achieve our best by spurring each other on to greater heights. Ethical, constructive competition doesn't, however, necessitate a win-lose mentality that sees only the egotistical winner or the moping loser. Nor does competition require competing teams, companies, or individuals to be malicious toward one another. That's a case of willpower and competitiveness run amok.

I recall a conference at which the head of the retail practice of a nationally known professional services firm implored the audience to "hate your competitors." I knew this person, and the words he spoke didn't sound like him. After the conference I approached him and asked if these words really expressed how he felt. Having gained a little perspective, he said that he was wrong and regretted his comments. Caught up in competitive battle, he had lost touch with the fact that his competitors are, first and foremost, human beings like him. A different company name on their business cards is no reason to hate.

The business world's competitive environment often conjures up visions of scarcity rather than abundance. Do we need a sense of urgency in business today? Absolutely. Yet, taken to the extreme, this vital element of business success becomes a well of fear, hate, and negativity. Instead of working cooperatively with others, we become dogs fighting over scraps.

I'm no stranger to this zero-sum, fear-based mentality of scarcity. There have been times when it's eaten a hole in me. A few years back, Sears, our Goliath competitor, announced plans to open "off-mall" tire stores in the Twin Cities of Minneapolis–St. Paul, home to my tire retailing company, which at that time had one hundred stores in seven states. Instantly, the stress of losing everything loomed. I feared that my company's healthy market share in the Twin Cities would vanish. After initial panicky weeks of night sweats and a daily blurred vision of the real situation, I leaped into action. Even though we had been preparing for years, I developed a more complete offensive action plan and began to act on it.

And did our market share vanish? On the contrary, the Tires Plus stores *closest* to the Sears-owned stores produced the largest increases of all our stores. Our preparation and action paid off. The lesson here: Trust that there will be abundance. Concern, thoughtful planning, and a bias to action can be healthy. Worry, anxiety, and hate are symptoms of being stuck in the middle of a negative process. Compete, do *your* very best, then wait for the results in peace.

Healthy competition improves the competitors. Competitors model each other's strengths. That triggers change, which develops even more strengths. In this sense, competition is not about wishing bad luck on your competitor. Competitors keep you on your toes and thereby help you better serve your customers, clients, and fellow teammates in a manner that aligns you with your individual and business mission.

Whether the scenario is two businesses competing for market share or two people competing for a promotion, healthy competition fosters a spirit of humble victories whereby no one really loses. There's winning in learning, and there's much to learn in not winning—if healthy self-esteem is present and operating. The old saw "it's not whether you win or lose, it's how you play the game" isn't just a useful cliché for tricking dejected kids into feeling better about defeat. After all, when competition is healthy, the *lessons* of the game are remembered long after the specific performance is forgotten.

Well Done!

We never grow out of enjoying compliments, a vital aspect of demonstrating caring to others. As children we need them to grow, emotional nutrients of sorts. I have vivid memories of beaming inside and out when my mother complimented me. "Good job, Tommy, on cleaning your room!" she would say. As I think back, I can almost hear the words as she spoke them and remember the warm feelings that filled me. Since at one level we're all still kids living inside grown-up bodies, compliments have a feel-good effect that's as powerful on adults as it is on children.

Yet we tend to hand out compliments only a fraction of the times that we see or hear about positive behavior. Why? One key reason is that we don't perceive compliments as powerful because we don't see others react in a way that makes us feel that it registered. Even though people feel the compliment inwardly, our culture typically trains us not to show it externally.

One day some years ago, I asked my assistant, Dorie, to come into my office. I told her what an incredible job she'd been doing, explaining how her performance positively affected the company and how I felt about it. Dorie listened and appeared rather blasé. That's okay, I thought. I just wanted to make sure she knew that I understood her value and appreciated her contribution.

Later that day, one of Dorie's teammates, Wayne, came to me and said, "What did you say to Dorie?"

"What do you mean?" I asked.

"She's absolutely ecstatic!" he said. "She's telling everyone about the compliments you gave her. She's delighted."

While sitting in my office, Dorie didn't beam the way that she or I probably did as children. You might observe the same response to the compliments you give. Our challenge is to see through the exterior and know that inside there's a happy, excited child on the receiving end of your compliments. Be generous and genuine with them.

There are certainly other reasons we give for skimping on compliments. Too busy? It takes only seconds. Don't feel good enough about ourselves to compliment others? Consciously and unconsciously, many of us project on others what we feel about ourselves. By improving our own sense of worth, we can better help others appreciate theirs. If you criticize yourself endlessly, you'll be likely to project that onto others. If you can accept and appreciate your own worth, you'll be more able to recognize it in others. Our ability to give is intimately connected with our ability to receive.

When we don't verbalize those many fleeting, positive thoughts about the people in our lives, we miss incredible opportunities to affirm their wonderful behavior. Just think what could happen if we all began verbalizing those thoughts. Imagine the responses from co-workers, family members, and people who report to you.

You can even compliment those to whom you report. People are often averse to complimenting "the boss" for fear of being perceived as apple-polishers. Yet it's important that we share authentic positives with our leaders. When we do, we increase the chances that their positive behavior will be repeated. Also, your leaders will be more open when you speak about things you *don't* like, and they'll generally be in a better mood. Don't assume that people higher up on the organizational chart don't appreciate compliments. It's one of life's great joys. I know that when I get a compliment, it helps to motivate me and keep me focused on my mission.

For compliments to raise our spirits, they need to be authentic, not manufactured. People know the difference. Any authentic compliment is good. Even better is taking thirty seconds more to tell people specifically what they did well, how it generated positive effects, and how you feel about it. This is more effective than saying, "Good job."

Here, virtually verbatim, is what I said to our Head Coach of Recruitment and Education, Wayne Shimer, after I spoke to a group of brand-new teammates who attended Tires Plus University for a week of training:

> "Wayne—great new people you and your team hired. They exude the COPPSS traits we look for. They'll have a big, positive impact on our company in the future. Congrats to you and your team. I sleep better at night knowing you're in that position bringing talent like that on our team."

Before 1989, I rarely said things like this. My balance is much better now, and yet I want to make more progress. I love to tell people about the positive things they're doing in the world. In giving an authentic compliment, I feel more connected to the good in the world and in that person, a feeling of acknowledging another human being's efforts.

The Littlest Things Mean Everything

Every day presents hundreds of ways to show you care. Offer a smile, a kind word, a gentle (appropriate) touch. Hold a door for someone rather than letting it slip closed. You can give your seat to a weary person standing on the subway. Send support cards to friends going through ups or downs. Caring is doing the right thing when nobody is looking. When I find myself doing a small thing automatically and anonymously—when, say, I pick up an empty can on public property—I feel universally connected.

Caring in everyday ways creates an atmosphere of fairness. It's one of those lessons we learned in kindergarten, but in the business world, fairness goes beyond our financial transactions. It should be involved in every interaction. That's because favoritism and injustice strike a deep chord in people. Our sense of right and wrong is so strong, especially when prejudice brushes up against us, that we'll leave wherever we're treated unjustly, even at the cost of financial security.

The Circle of Caring

Test-drive being less selective in your caring. There can be a tendency to care about family and friends but not about the wider community. For me, it's difficult to genuinely care for some people and push others to the side.

The reverse can also be true. Some people get caught in the trap of caring for a wide range of folks while forgetting their own family. I knew a minister, for instance, who was devoted to his congregation and yet was absolutely absent from his daughter's life. She couldn't understand why she didn't seem to warrant the same attention his congregants did. I know another man to be gregarious and affectionate in public. But when he and his grown son visited me once for an extended spell, I witnessed a cold father. I was unexpectedly thrown into the role of family counselor as feelings spontaneously bubbled up from the two of them. It turned out that the father had given so much to those around him yet had failed to heap the same attention on his family. Don't forget those closest to you who may be desperately seeking your love and attention.

Caring is an orientation that can underlie every thought, every action. Be generous with caring; it's the kind of wealth that grows only when it's spent.

COPPSS 2. Optimistic

In interviews, centenarians almost inevitably mention the same thing when asked for the secret of their long lives: boundless optimism. No matter what their situation, they believe things will turn out for the best. Between the idealism of a picture-perfect life and the realism of life as it is, lies the bridge of optimism. The common thread of life lived into the 100s is that an optimistic life is a life well-lived.

Optimism has been a valuable ally for me for decades, and authentic optimism only in the last decade. The entire year of 1968, the year I graduated from Indiana University, was a lesson in the struggle between idealism and realism and the role optimism plays between them. Both Bobby Kennedy and Martin Luther King Jr. were assassinated that year. The war in Vietnam was peaking. Riots erupted at the Democratic National Convention in Chicago. I was impressionable, and these events made marks deep in my psyche. But they weren't negative marks.

For all the sorrow and despair of 1968, the year produced a lot of positive, lasting change. Kennedy and King were widely revered, and their words and deeds influenced countless millions. Our nation today is less willing to commit ground troops to conflicts in foreign lands, and minorities have more powerful voices in national politics. For me, the message of 1968 was embracing change as a fundamental force for good. It told me, *Be flexible. Don't get too comfortable with the status quo because soon enough it will change. Stay involved. Stay optimistic about what can be achieved and do your part, large or small, for the planet, no matter where you are.*

This is more than garden-variety optimism. The optimism I value is *authentic* optimism. By that I mean trusting that you'll find support in all you do as long as your actions are consistent with your mission. With that kind of optimism in my front pocket, I feel confident that things will work out and that I can turn trying times into bountiful outcomes.

I take optimism so seriously that it's right there in my company's name, Tires Plus. The "Plus" generates positive imagery. Since 1986, the phones at our locations have been picked up with the bright greeting, "It's a great day at Tires Plus. This is_____. How may I help you?" Other companies have begun using similar greetings to spread a positive outlook.

So, what's the big payoff to being optimistic? Call it the double-your-pleasure effect. You reap positive internal and external benefits.

At an internal level, thinking positively transmits "can do" messages deep throughout your intellect and psyche. Consider the power demonstrated by the so-called placebo effect.

Medical researchers often study the effects of new medication on diseases by observing three groups of people. The first, or control, group takes no medication, and the second group takes the new medication. A third group, however, takes what they believe to be the new medication, but is in fact a placebo, typically a sugar pill that has no medicinal effect.

In study after study, placebos lead to positive therapeutic results in numbers that cannot be attributed to chance. Indeed, patients who take placebos generally experience more positive results than those who take nothing at all, and often the effect is as powerful as the real drug. After reviewing the range and power of the placebo effect in his book *Spontaneous Healing,* Dr. Andrew Weil describes the placebo response as "a pure example of healing elicited by the mind; far from being a nuisance, it is, potentially, the greatest therapeutic ally doctors can find in their efforts to mitigate disease."

The placebo effect exemplifies a principle that is a cornerstone of ancient mind-body medicine. What the mind believes, the mind creates. This approach to healing is gaining widespread acceptance both inside and outside the mainstream medical community. And the idea applies not only to bodily wellness but to all aspects of life. Belief and expectation are a factor in creating outcomes.

Optimism also produces external social benefits. Who doesn't like to be around optimistic people, or help them succeed? Whether it's assisting with a chore or helping someone get a promotion or raise, people will push the limit for the authentic optimist. "Smile and the world smiles with you," goes the old saying. People are simply attracted to smiles and a can-do attitude.

Authentic Feelings

Before you can feel and express optimism, you have to get in touch with the source of those feelings. Before I began waking up in 1989, you could say I was optimistic. But in hindsight, frequently it was a rather phony brand of optimism. I was often in denial over my circumstances, my actions, my feelings. If I was sad or fearful, I would paste on a smile and grin right through it. The character Jerry in the movie *Fargo* epitomizes phony optimism. Jerry, a sales manager at a car dealership, only had one way of responding to the greeting "How's things?" "Great!" he'd say, "Oh, you betcha," even as his entire world crumbled around him.

I discovered a similar tendency in myself one day in a group therapy session as I was relating a sad event. When the others asked if I felt happy about what I was sharing, I said no. "Then why are you smiling?" one member asked quizzically.

Trying to hold off the depth of our feelings through a false front is sometimes necessary in the short run, if we just have to "get the job done," or we're not surrounded by people we trust to understand us. In these situations I feel the image of a protective glass shield rising up in front of me. When the meeting is over or the task accomplished, I make a conscious effort to lower the shield and find a way to let out what's really going on. It's often easier to retreat behind the shield than to lower it. It can certainly feel a lot safer behind that protective wall, but in the act of shutting others out, we've also just locked ourselves in.

I'm of the opinion that this tendency to suppress emotions is one of the reasons women generally outlive men. It's no secret that many women tend to express feelings more fully, while men generally are indoctrinated with the macho admonition, "Never let 'em see you sweat." Too often, men wind up smiling right through tears and fears and allowing trapped emotions to wreak all kinds of internal, invisible havoc.

Still, rather than delivering the pat "everything's great" response when a friend asks how you are, look for ways to inject a little authentic feeling.

When things aren't going well, say it. "I've had a few challenges recently," I might say, "but I'm working through them. It's tough sometimes, but I know there's a chance to learn from it. And I know I'll come through this a better person."

Depending on the circumstance, you may want to go into more depth with the person who's asked. Maybe she has had a similar experience you can learn from. Either way, you accept the difficulty rather than denying it, and you open the door to others' help. This is how you learn from friends, family members, and colleagues—the universal messengers.

Avoid Eddie Haskell-ism

The authentic optimist rejects the temptation to tell 'em what they want to hear, a tendency I call "Eddie Haskell-ism," after the neighbor kid in *Leave It to Beaver* who always had a compliment on his lips and an ulterior motive on his mind. "Why, Mrs. Cleaver, isn't it a wonderful day, and, by the way, how *beautiful* you look today..." That's not optimistic but disingenuous, and it only perpetuates dishonest and inappropriate behavior in ourselves and others.

Optimism provides for solving any problem as long as we communicate and look for outcomes through which both sides win. Optimists always tell you how something *can* be done—with a tinker here and a few tweaks there—rather than why it can't. That's the realistic heart of authentic optimism. It's about seeing the potential in everything, not ignoring challenges and roadblocks. It's trusting that events in our lives are lessons— opportunities to learn and grow.

Say your manager asks your thoughts on an idea that's really a stinker. Don't say, "Yeah, boss, perfect plan." Instead, give him a gentle dose of realistic optimism. Say something like, "I see seeds of greatness. Did you consider revising the plan to include more advertising so the product has the opportunity to reach top-of-mind awareness on par with the competitor's product? Everything else looks great." Or say you're approached by a teammate who is criticizing one of your peers. There's a way to be optimistic while still understanding the critic's frustration. Try saying, "I know Jim hasn't been himself lately. Have you asked him how it's going, or if there's any way you can help? He's been a valuable player in the past; I'm sure he can be in the future, too."

Organizations don't need "yes people" any more than they need negative people. Both personalities kill creativity and synergy. What organizations do need, desperately, are people who pick up others by brainstorming for solutions rather than shooting down ideas. That's the mark of a true champion.

Confidence Overboard

Optimism can run amok. In 1991 I had developed a one-day seminar on self-management, and decided to hold the seminar on three different days over a three-week period. My son Trent, who was organizing the process, asked how many people to plan for each day. "We'll pack in two or three hundred each day," I told him. "Are you sure?" he asked. "You betcha!" I said. When the seminar days came, not three hundred, not two hundred, not one hundred, but only about fifty people sat in the cavernous room. For each seminar, I had vastly overestimated my drawing power. The money we lost was the price of my lesson that optimism gives projects wings, but realistic planning gives a project legs.

Negate Negativism

Optimism is constantly under siege from the temptation to belabor what's wrong. Before 1989, I rarely talked about what was right in myself or others. Zeroed in on our losses, I couldn't target our victories. Most compliments people gave me I matched with self-criticism, in effect erasing the compliment. I've come a long way toward improving my ratio of compliments to constructive feedback both for myself and others.

The negative influence of self and others is perhaps the largest obstacle to authentic optimism. Oddly, some people are threatened by positive thinking and by people who drop negative habits or become successful in one way or another. Friends and acquaintances may feel discomfort because you've made progress if they feel they've been left behind. They may even criticize your success. In Australia, they call this "cutting down the tall poppy." I call it poisonous pessimism.

I recognize pessimism in someone who is always figuring out why other people are inadequate. This doesn't make pessimists bad people (I don't see anyone as "bad"); however, expectations do limit the pessimist's world. A joke from Jewish tradition relates what happened when a man asked his rabbi, "Why is it that a slice of bread with butter on it always falls with the buttered side down?" The rabbi had never heard of this before, so they tried it. The rabbi buttered the bread, dropped it, and it landed with the buttered side up. The rabbi pointed and said, "Well?" "But, Rabbi," the man replied, "you buttered the wrong side!"

Whenever possible, surround yourself with positive people, and when faced with negativity, don't let it wound you. Of course it's easier said than done, but with practice I've learned how to deflect negative energy. Let's use the example of someone who's just been handed a huge task of data analysis. He comes to you and starts complaining about the amount of work and the time frame.

If you know the complainer to be someone who is generally a positive person, he may just need to vent his frustration in order to move through it. Allow this, listen, but don't chime in with any encouragement. "Gosh, I can hear the frustration in your voice," is a much better response than, "You're right. Our supervisor is a jerk for not asking you whether you could make the deadline." The point isn't to emphasize the complaint but allow him to express and then move through the feelings. Before too long, I then bring in concrete questions to prompt solution-oriented thinking: "Is there any room in the deadline for negotiation?" "Have you laid out the process with benchmarks and set some achievable goals?" "Is there anyone else on the team who can take part of the workload?" Of course, every situation is different, but by seeking the positive solution or the hidden benefit, you can help people find the optimism they may not be able to find themselves.

Pessimists may try to drag you back into line. In the early days of Tires Plus, a competitor asked me if I would join him and some other Twin Cities tire dealers for dinner. Reluctantly, I agreed. As soon as I arrived, they began barking about how my aggressive marketing was hurting them. If I continued, they said, they would make life difficult for me and my new company. Tires Plus, they said, would soon be out of business. I immediately got up, wished them the best of luck, told them that we all needed to make our own business decisions, and left. I refused to let negativity and intimidation affect me, and my company stayed its course.

If you have a new idea and break out of the pack, be assured that people will tell you how and why the idea isn't a good one. In fact, most new ideas go through four phases: rejection, ridicule, general acceptance, and full acceptance. In the last stage, the early doubters say, "I knew it all along." The weight of the status quo exerts a lot of pressure to conform. Leaders and anyone else who has the discipline to follow an individual path, personally or professionally, will face this obstacle. Too often this pressure is too much to bear, and it slaps people back in line. Pressure to conform to what's "normal" is the biggest hurdle to becoming the unique, optimistic and self-actualized people we're meant to be.

While listening to others is an important way to learn, consider conflicts of interest or biases that could cloud someone's advice as well as their authenticity. Also seek counsel from, and listen more carefully to, the all-knowing voice of the higher self within. Let no one dim your light or rob you of optimism, and you will overcome any obstacle to moving through the seven steps of manifesting your mission.

Laugh Out Loud

If you want to stay lighthearted and optimistic, then don't take yourself too seriously. We can find it tempting to get caught up in events and remain terminally serious. That makes no room for fun, laughter, and their frequent catalyst, humor. Continually serious people who forget to sprinkle their lives with humor become drones. The legendary ballerina Margot Fonteyn said, "The one important thing I have learnt over the years is the difference between taking one's work seriously and taking oneself seriously. The first is imperative and the second disastrous."

People love to laugh and to be around people who laugh—as long as the humor is good-natured, well-timed, and sarcasm-free. I've used humor sometimes in a tense business situation to jolt myself and those around me so that we regain perspective and relieve the stress of the moment. My father, brothers, and sons often use humor in this way effectively.

It's said that laughter is one of the healthiest behaviors we can engage in. Because I don't laugh as easily when I'm stressed out, humor can be a good barometer of my stress levels. PubMed, an online service of the National Institutes of Health, reports studies linking humor to more positive attitudes, higher tolerance of physical pain, and greater longevity. Author Norman Cousins re-energized attention on the healing benefits of laughter when he used humor as a part of his treatment for a painful inflammatory disorder; the effects of daily doses of the Marx Brothers and other light-hearted fare convinced Cousins that humor helped him to heal. He even founded the Humor Research Task Force to support worldwide clinical research to support his convictions scientifically. I prefer, however, not to wait for the proof and take my humor tonic daily.

COPPSS 3. Passionate

Passion is vital to your ability to communicate how you feel about people, yourself, and concepts. People react to you based on the passion of your convictions. The ability to communicate feelings passionately, both verbally and nonverbally, moves mountains. Passion is charisma. Passion is enthusiasm torqued to a level that's undeniable. Used properly, passion can console a distraught child or rally countries and companies around far-reaching causes. One definition of passion is related to suffering—not feeling sorry for ourselves, but feeling the depths in our own lives so that we can feel the depths in others. Passion opens the way to compassion.

The Powers of Passion

Passion springs from far more than the intellect. Coming from our "head only" won't move people. "What we require is the warm embrace as much as the brilliant idea," wrote Rabbi Joseph Soloveitchik. That warm embrace can be actual or sensed. What is it about some people who, with their words and movements, can take us to the ends of the earth?

We generally think it's our words that communicate our passion and convictions. In his pioneering and oft-quoted work in the field of verbal and nonverbal communications, however, Dr. Albert Mehrabian showed that when we communicate about feelings and emotions, the words are the least of the matter. Over half the message (55 percent) is understood through our body language. Vocal tone and pitch accounts for another 38 percent. Just 7 percent of the message is carried in the actual words.

Passion meters hit the red zone when verbal and nonverbal messages are aligned, a match between our words and our facial expressions, our hand gestures and tone of voice. Show me the fire in a monotone voice. Most great salespeople effortlessly strike this balance. Consciously or unconsciously, the power of body language and tone can engender trust of the passionate person.

When we're not passionate about an apology, a product we're selling, or an idea, we're perceived as less than legitimate. If the nonverbal 93 percent of our message is not communicating the spirit of our words, people don't receive, or believe, what we're saying. Left to choose between words and nonverbal communication, people intuitively opt for the latter. Words alone have let them down more often than the tone and body language, which are harder (yet not impossible) to feign.

The great leaders who move us possess that uncommon quality of authentic passion. True enough, many admired public figures have duped their constituencies with passion that was at odds with their passionately stated ideals. The damage is a loss of faith. We're all imperfect, of course, and our leaders live in a fishbowl surrounded by cameras. It's worth pointing out, however, three political leaders who were elected largely because of their passionate rhetoric: Presidents Clinton, Reagan, and Kennedy. Were they acting or being authentic? You be the judge. No matter what you answer, you can't deny that these leaders moved people.

Three Steps to Cultivating Passion

Passion requires that all of your cylinders are firing. So how do you get your cylinders—body, intellect, psyche, and spirit—firing in synch? I suggest three ways.

1. **Embark on a journey to holistic wellness,** as described in chapters 4, 5, and 6. Physical, psychological, and spiritual growth will foster internal connections between your words and your feelings. For me, this step was about cleaning out the internal junk that was creating static. It was a scary step, and I have to admit it got worse before it got better. If you've ever tried to change a tennis swing or a golf stroke, you know what I mean. Dropping any of our old habits can be disorienting and may feel like stumbling through the dark. But improvement is impossible without first letting go of the old. You have to first prune a rose bush before it can bloom. Be brave and watch your passion emerge.

2. **Gauge whether your body language and voice tone are consistent with your words and whether they're appropriate for the situation at hand.** Learning to be aware of this and to align them requires some self-observation. I remember watching one day as David, one of our top coaches, severely reprimanded Ken, a teammate who reported to him. After upbraiding Ken, David forced an apology for his reprimand through a partial grin. Congruency? No way. Ken couldn't hear the apology through David's Cheshire Cat smile. After I showed genuine concern for Ken, I took a few coaching moments with David. He then apologized again, more genuinely.

3. **Observe how others respond to what you say.** Do they really hear you? Do the reactions mirror what you tried to communicate? That speaks volumes about how effectively you communicate. If the reaction is not what you had hoped for, restate your case in a different way. Without that other 93 percent of your communications power, you could be speaking a foreign language. There are classes for regaining your mother tongue. Join Toastmasters. Take a Dale Carnegie course. Role-play. Tell your colleagues what you want to communicate and ask them to give you feedback. Try take after take after take, until your audience picks up a harmony between your words, body language, tone, and the message you're trying to get across.

The effort can be difficult, but it's always rewarding. Your words will be heard. Your ideas will be taken seriously. Your products or services will succeed. Your apologies will be accepted. Most important, your feelings won't stay trapped inside. Acknowledged by you and heard by others, they'll have an outlet.

Be careful not to mimic the classic snake-oil salesperson or the loud, overly animated television announcer. Passion can be soft-spoken and include subtle expressions, pauses, and delicate emotions.

Role-playing can be used as a learning tool to help you gain access to passion, but beware of using it in actual practice. Acting designed to mimic sincere passion is misleading and can have potentially serious consequences. Put the gifts of authentic passion to good purpose. Leave the acting to Hollywood.

Quit Crying Wolf

In our hurried world, many of us are in the habit of juicing our days with drama—crying wolf—as a way of mobilizing our own energy or getting attention from others. That's passion taken out of bounds. Remember the fairy tale about the little boy who continually cried "wolf" when there was none? The one time he truly *was* in danger, no one believed him, and no one came to help.

Chronic complainers and crisis makers begin to feel that no one's listening—and they're right. Their kids and co-workers have tuned them out. When the red flag goes up, everyone else thinks, *Oh, he always says that. It's really no big deal.* If the complainers and crisis makers were more selective about raising an alarm, their children and associates would instead think, *Uh-oh! He doesn't get riled up too often. There must be something to this!*

What's behind this needless drama? Back to our fairy tale, that shepherd boy was lonely and maybe a little bored. He thought crying wolf was a sure-fire way to get attention. But it wasn't a way to solve a real problem or connect honestly with other people.

My habit is to maintain an even demeanor with most matters. When I do show a sense of urgency and the heightened passion associated with it, people realize I mean it, and they respond. You'll find the same to be true. Select your urgent items carefully. My dad, a World War II veteran, says, "That's not a hill to die on." Be selective about when you make a big deal of things, and follow the communication principles in chapter 8. With true passion, you will be heard and people will respond to solve the problem quickly.

COPPSS 4. Persistent

In chapter 2, I touched briefly on Coolidge's Law, which states that nothing can take the place of persistence. That was in the back of my mind in the late 1970s when I overcame five roadblocks that stood in the way of my making a living. Here's what happened:

My first three tire stores in Minneapolis were small converted service stations that also pumped gasoline. The energy crisis was in full swing at the time, and at each store cars were backed up five deep, waiting for fuel. The way service stations got gasoline was through allocations made by the Department of Energy. My own allocation was frightfully low. Meanwhile, I was struggling to meet my payroll. All of this was roadblock number one.

Faced with this, I followed the official government drill and submitted a written appeal for more gas. It was denied. Roadblock number two.

Next I called the Department of Energy's Midwest office in Chicago to request an audience with its director. His assistant tried to shake me: "Because of his increased DOE workload, he isn't seeing anyone." Roadblock number three.

Undaunted, I hopped a plane to Chicago, planning to talk my way into his office. When I arrived, the receptionist put up roadblock number four. She snarled, "He will see no one without an appointment!" I told her nicely that I had tried to get an appointment, to no avail. "I have to see the director," I told her respectfully, and explained that I'd wait for him to come out of his office. I knew he had to come out sometime. Fortunately, I'd seen his picture, so I recognized him when he bolted out of his office and headed for the men's room—roadblock number five.

But I followed him into the men's room, approached him at the urinal and, as he was relieving himself, launched into my spiel. I began by introducing myself and apologizing for the intrusion, then told him in sixty seconds flat exactly why my gasoline allocation was unfairly low. As he zipped himself up, he said, "Okay, kid, get into my office!" I did.

He listened further. My allocation was upped. And the company survived its earliest, darkest period because I blew through five roadblocks. Moral: persistence pays.

Because of the importance of persistence, I'll offer some more examples. In my twenties, when I worked for Shell Oil, I wanted to transfer from employee relations (called human resources today) to a service station field operations position. I was told by my supervisor, "You're not tough enough." I set out to convince him otherwise. I presented my case by telling him that I could take whatever the dealers dished out. After months of persistence, he caved in. I got what I wanted—much to our mutual benefit. My "toughness" was tested right away in my first assignment: an inner-city territory known as one of Chicago's roughest. I was advised to carry a gun.

I didn't. But I did love the job and the dealers, and we partnered for increasing their business to record levels.

Persistence helped in 1976 when my partner Don Gullett and I tried to get a bank loan to start Tires Plus. We were turned down by bank after bank, without exception. Then, at the tenth bank, we presented a proposal that won the loan officer's agreement. If we had stopped at the eighth or ninth, we wouldn't have started our business. You don't punt when you're about to score. Lesson: persist.

"If Anything Can Go Right, It Will"

Persistence is one of the traits designed to neutralize Murphy's Law. The number of crevasses we have to traverse as we proceed toward getting or giving what we want is infinite. As in checkers or chess, we'd better be ready for moves that catch us off guard. My team and I always need to be ready to adjust our offense, depending on what the defense gives us. Keep persisting in the face of adversity. When faced with unexpected, unplanned roadblocks, where do your mind, body, energy and attention go? Focused on solutions? If so, to what degree? Are you "in the zone," or do you lope along with a resigned "okay, I guess this won't work" attitude?

In cultivating persistence, I never think about how something can't be done. I just don't spend any mental energy in that exercise. That sidetracks me from persistence. When a roadblock pops up, it may be tempting to focus on how it will keep you from your goal, and how there will probably be more roadblocks out there. Instead, try focusing virtually exclusively on how to get around the roadblock immediately ahead, and any others like it. This attitude is an extension of optimism, a continuing "go for it."

Shift into Fifth Gear

Persistence is a "won't be denied" attitude, especially during those times that call for it: starting a company, getting a promotion, starting a critical project, or handling an urgent family matter. It's that look in the eyes of people who feel strongly about achieving their wants at a critical time when their path is blocked. Faced with the potential of not accomplishing something I deem critical to my mission, I become so focused and intent that I'm in what athletes and performers call "the zone" or "fifth gear." I go into a state of consciousness where I'm able to engage my Inner Team to access physical, mental, and spiritual energy well beyond what's typical for me. The synergistic effect pushes me into a zone of creativity that lets me brainstorm option after option until a new way of looking at the problem unearths a real solution. Out of the boundless universe in minutes come answers beyond anything I thought possible. Then it's my job to make them real in the world.

Everyone can *access* that level of persistence, but it's one of those rare skills that I'm not sure can be *taught*. Great athletes, from Wayne Gretzky to Michael Jordan, instinctively know when to shift into fifth gear— whether it's the time of game or the time of season, they can't really explain how or why it happens. The same is true with the people in any organization. But when it happens, you can see it in their eyes.

Pitfalls of Perfectionism

I've found that persistence can be a giant double-edged sword. On the one hand, going the extra mile, practicing until you've got it just right, or refining a project to the *n*th degree is how people are able to separate themselves from the pack. More important, though, than needing to stand out as being "better" than others is doing our best to serve those we're here to serve.

On the other hand, persistence taken to the extreme of perfectionism in most everything we do can interfere with happiness. Perfectionism can lead to focusing on what's wrong as opposed to celebrating what's right. This can be frustrating for perfectionists as well as everyone around them. Writer Anne Lamott says, "I think perfectionism is based on the obsessive belief that if you run carefully enough, hitting each steppingstone just right, you won't have to die. The truth is that you will die anyway and that a lot of people who aren't even looking at their feet are going to do a whole better than you, and have a lot more fun doing it."

The inability to congratulate ourselves, relax, and be okay with what we've done is a heavy price we pay for perfectionism. In essence, perfectionism sets us up for falling short. It provides an excuse to attack ourselves no matter what we do, since absolute perfection is impossible. In India in 1996, my mate, Mary Wescott, and I visited a Jaina temple that housed a visible reminder of this point: a priest showed us a support pillar purposely built slightly crooked to symbolize our imperfect human nature. Some Native American tribes purposefully weave a mistake into their rugs, which provides a doorway out of that creation into the next. Perfection would be a dead end; imperfection means that there's still work to be done—and thus a purpose to our existence. What these people know, business culture needs to learn: humans weren't built to be perfect. We were built to strive, again and again and again, never reaching a pinnacle but refining ourselves with each pass.

I started acquiring the mindset of a high achiever when I was young, and I became a perfectionist in the years leading up to my wake-up call in 1989. I felt, accurately or inaccurately, that my company's health was so tenuous that almost any imperfection could put us out of business. But even as my company became much more profitable and financially stable, I could barely let go of the mindset. My perfectionism was what my son Trent calls a "vestigial response"—a trait developed early in life that is no longer needed. Others describe it as a survival skill learned in a time of crisis, which still hangs on long after the crisis is over. I've made a lot of progress in overcoming my perfectionism, yet that vestigial response still sneaks in and requires top-of-mind vigilance from time to time.

The right balance on the perfectionist issue? Don't imagine that you always need to do a task perfectly. But when the situation does call for a flawless personal performance, do the task to your best ability. Persist. Go into fifth gear if it's of great importance. And when you're finished, let it go and wait for the results in peace.

Hang In There

A child of persistence and a close cousin to shifting into fifth gear is enduring or "hanging in there." This trait is important when you're facing extremely stressful events.

In 1983, seven years after starting Tires Plus, we began expanding the number of our retail operations, which were dwarfed by our wholesale division, our core business at that time. The expansion caused our retail division to lose a great deal of money, almost offsetting our entire wholesale profits. Our banker, Jeff Mack, who proved to be a valuable supporter for years, informed me that banking regulators were asking for our loan to be called. It appeared there was no other alternative.

Instead of knuckling under, I worked up a revised, detailed plan that outlined how we could make our fledgling retail division profitable. Jeff got permission to delay the calling of the loan for sixty days. During that period, our retail division turned a profit.

Another example of hanging in there under extreme stress took place in 1991 when I was on vacation in the Cayman Islands with my sons. As we were getting ready to leave our hotel room for dinner, the phone rang. It was my firm's new CPA, John Berg, who over the years became one of my most valuable allies. On this day, John and his firm, Coopers and Lybrand, were just finishing their first audit of the Tires Plus books. Though we were marginally profitable, our fast growth had put us into a highly leveraged situation. We were spending money on new stores faster than we were earning it. We needed more of the stores to mature so that we could begin paying for the initial investment. Any accountant who unconditionally approved our audited statement would, under auditing standards, be stating, in effect, that our company would be able to continue as a financially viable entity. John said he was having difficulty drawing that conclusion under the standards he had to follow.

Convincing John of all the reasons to sign that statement took me an hour. I presented as much supporting information as I could on the company's strategic supplier relationships and budgeted performance, and after lengthy discussion he finally agreed. I went to dinner, trying to shake the incident off so I could focus on my children. I felt as if I'd been wounded in battle.

The short lesson: hang in there. Healthy persistence can overcome countless obstacles. In real estate, the key words are location, location, location. For people who want to manifest their mission, the words are persist, persist, persist.

COPPSS 5. Systems-Disciplined

There's a lot of talk these days about the need for people to be out-of-the-box thinkers, and to think like entrepreneurs and even to be "revolutionaries." There's some truth in this point of view. We don't need "yes people." We don't need to be strapped to the past in our thinking. We don't have to fall in line with everyone else, especially in this age when customers, technology, competitors, and employees are changing even as we speak.

The call for revolution gets dangerous, however, when we ignore the procedures, policies, and other systems currently in place. This creates chaos. And the larger the company, the more chaos created. While some chaos is good and even necessary, plenty of chaos will happen naturally, even when systems are followed closely. Systems provide a common language designed for ease of communication—to ensure that the rules of the game are understood. If everyone is allowed to remake the rules, then chaos goes well beyond a thriving point.

The same can be said about our personal lives. In my earlier days, I often tried to find ways to beat the system, to challenge any rules. In hindsight, I see that playing by the rules produces much less stress and honors others far more.

Ignoring systems generally has an impact on someone somewhere. If a salesperson completes a sales order improperly, this affects the order processors, which affects the customer or client. Completing paperwork becomes a customer-service issue—backing up the promises in the sales call. The same thing applies to properly completing a First Report of Injury to ensure that teammates receive proper followup treatment and worker's compensation. It doesn't matter whether we're a CEO or an entry level worker; we can follow necessary procedures and guidelines so that others won't have to clean up our mess.

While being systems-disciplined, we can still continually examine our policies and procedures. When we find ways to tweak systems and make them more efficient without sacrificing team objectives or customer service, we can speak up for change.

Furthermore, we can make exceptions to systems where flexibility is a necessity. If a current policy or procedure isn't able to resolve a unique customer complaint or client emergency in the spirit of an organization's mission statement, then we need heroes willing to take risks for the client's sake. Wisdom lies in following the system yet sensing the right times to invoke actions outside the normal framework.

So do what you can to ensure that exceptions don't become the norm. Some people ignore systems out of laziness or, worse yet, rebellion and sabotage. This creates unneeded confusion. I compare this situation to what happens when an athlete ignores a play called by a coach in favor of doing it his own way. Unless everyone involved is aware of the change in play, havoc results. Learn your organization's playbook (policy and procedure manual) and give your feedback on which plays are beneficial and which are not. Then go with the play that's called.

COPPSS 6. Spirit-Filled

In March 1998 I was in Paris, France, and had the honor of meeting François Michelin, the seventy-three-year-old head of the company bearing his name. "Wow, you look great," I told him. "How do you stay in such good shape?"

"Spirit!" said Michelin. "When translated into Greek, *pneu,* the French word for tire, means spirit. Air is to the tire as spirit is to the human body." He gave me a big hug. I was absolutely riding on air, buoyed by spirit. How could spirit have such an effect on the physical? It's the understanding I've gained over the last ten years of personal growth that enabled me to grasp what François meant.

In rounding out my discussion of the "big six" traits in this chapter, I come to one that makes the greatest difference, even though the words I use to describe this trait can never do it justice. This trait is being *spirit-filled*. The movie *Star Wars* gave us the term "the Force," as in "May the Force be with you." Others call it a Higher Power or God. For years I didn't realize that François, Obi-Wan Kenobi, and millions of other people were talking about the same thing: spirit, the powerful, Universal Source.

As we approach the millennium, we're entering an era in which spirituality is increasingly important to people. Evidence comes by way of polls and the increasing number of books, seminars, and tapes on this subject. This isn't a fad. It's the resurgence of interest in experiencing spirit.

Let the Spirit Move You

In this book I'll use the word *spiritual* instead of the word *religious,* even though *religious* certainly can, and often does, mean *spiritual*. In checking my dictionary, I was surprised by the origins I found for *religion:* "supernatural constraint, sanction, religious practice, perhaps from *religare* to restrain, tie back." A religion is a vessel in which spirituality can be embodied. Religion is a house; spirit is the air that flows through and around it. Although all religions are intended to be spiritual, not all spiritual practices are considered religions.

In contrast, dictionary definitions of *spirit* reveal a sense of inclusiveness: "an animating or vital principle held to give life to physical organisms...the activating or essential principle influencing a person...a lively or brisk quality in a person or a person's actions." And for *spiritual:* "of or relating to sacred matters." I use the words *spirit, spirit-filled,* and *spiritual* interchangeably.

For one inclusive view of spirituality, consider an idea from philosophers Robert Solomon and Kathleen Higgins, who find three themes in spirituality that they say all religions share:

+ We share our world with other beings.
+ We affect the world and in return have expectations to meet.
+ It's possible that we have a personal essence that continues after death and lives again.

The notion of a personal essence that continues from this life to another existence speaks to the possibility of self-transformation, described in different ways by different religions as *awakening, transcendence,* or *enlightenment,* a concept I firmly believe. The late Joseph Campbell offered another view: "People say that what we're all seeking is a meaning for life. I think that what we're seeking is an experience of being alive, so that our life experiences on the purely physical plane will have resonances within our own innermost being and reality, so that we actually feel the rapture of being alive."

In recent years I've noticed that I feel this aliveness more frequently. This is part of my awakening: coming out of the numbness created by denial, alcohol, the wrong foods, and a myriad of other spiritual tranquilizers. Russian philosopher P. D. Ouspensky taught that most of us move through life in a waking sleep. When I'm in that sleep, I can't tap into my spirituality because I wouldn't recognize it if I saw it.

Common Ground

For me, the word *spirit* includes all sacred beliefs, all religions. Focus on what is *shared* by various religions and sacred belief systems, and be amazed. This kind of thinking guards against exclusiveness.

Although I was brought up as a Christian, I feel a deep respect for all religions and for all human beings walking spiritual paths. I have felt the power of spirit in a Lutheran church and a Jewish synagogue in Minneapolis, at ceremonies of Native Americans in northern Minnesota, at the pyramids in Egypt, at Notre Dame Cathedral in Paris, and in the world's largest Muslim mosque, in Casablanca, Morocco. I felt the power of spirit when I visited Hindu and Jaina temples in India, Buddhist temples in Japan, and aboriginal people in central Australia. I've felt the power of spirit in all of these places as well as in nature and in my own home as I meditate or pray.

The sheer diversity of the world's spiritual paths calls on us to practice tolerance. To me, any belief that condemns people of other faiths is not spiritual; it cannot lead to loving all the earth's inhabitants. Over the centuries, such beliefs have been at the heart of many wars, and we all know that on a smaller scale, in our neighborhoods or workplaces, religious differences have as much power to divide as to unite. I envision a world in which we all learn to honor each other's individual way.

One benefit of our world becoming smaller is a greater understanding of the various religions of the world. Through the Internet, television, and widely available global travel, we have the chance to break down the barriers. We are connected more than ever before. All this gives us the chance to learn and build mutual respect for our varied spiritual paths.

The True Essence of Spirituality

For me, being spirit-filled is about being connected—with myself, my source, my mission, and other human beings. I ask myself,

> *How consciously am I showing up each day?*
> *Am I—body, psyche, intellect, and spirit—fully present?*
> *Do I approach my work with enthusiastic awareness ?*
> *Am I fully connected with my family and friends?*
> *Am I open to encounters with anyone I meet?*
> *Am I approaching life with an outlook that is truly open to*
> *whatever will happen today?*

Before I could begin to feel a sense of being spirit-filled, I first had to wake up and get real with myself. This was a huge challenge for me. I was so used to putting on a mask to play a role and do what would make me look good in the eyes of other people that I could barely grasp what *I* really felt or thought. The result? Disconnection—from myself and everyone around me. I couldn't begin to feel spirit-filled without first taking off my mask and regaining some sense of authenticity in my own life. I feel like I'm early on in this process that will last a lifetime, with new cycles of growth ahead. Elisabeth Kübler-Ross writes, "It's not the end of the physical body that should worry us. Rather, our concern must be to *live* while we're alive—to release our inner selves from the spiritual death that comes with living behind a façade designed to conform to external definitions of who and what we are."

Being spirit-filled is also about sensing a connection to our source, which is both undefinable and indescribable. When I'm "plugged in," I know it at every level of my being. My step is lighter, and a sense of calm comes over me. Purposeful and connected, it changes how I see people and myself in relation to others' humanity.

Our culture teaches us to judge ourselves against any number of measures, and this often leaves us feeling better or worse than others. But when I'm spirit-filled, I see others eye-to-eye, recognizing that at the level of spirit, we're all unique and special. I sense the universal connection between us, and *that* becomes my bottom line. Rather than being caught up in the other person's externals—status, brand of watch, style of hair, type of car—when I'm spirit-filled, my focus goes to who that person is, rather than what he or she has or doesn't have.

When we're spirit-filled, we avoid feeling or acting as if we're better than another because of appearance, material wealth, or any other circumstance. Such comparisons lead nowhere. We're all human beings on a unique assignment from our Source, and life is about doing our best in that assignment. There's no universal scorekeeping system that ranks material success over any other mission. I agree with Margaret Mead's view: "I personally measure success in terms of the contributions an individual makes to her or his fellow human beings." There are so many wonderful ways to serve our families, organizations, communities, world, and universe, and *every* path is vital in its unique way.

Actually, focusing primarily on the pursuit of material wealth is a sure way to pull us off a spiritual track, and history has shown clearly that material wealth is not a prerequisite for being spirit-filled. In fact, quite the contrary. I used to feel that I'd focus on God when I had more time and after I got that promotion...after I made my first million...when I'm older and can't do the fun stuff...While some of these comments were tongue-in-cheek, it's good to realize the hidden message: "I don't have time for spirituality until my world is in perfect order and I don't have much else to do."

But it's not possible to put the world and our material concerns in perfect order. If we wait for that day, we'll wait in vain. Even when you think you've got it made, things have a way of turning upside down. That faulty game plan became apparent to me in 1989, when, in spite of my previous best efforts, my relationships, finances, and personal health were somehow in worse shape than ever. The sense of security I had formerly taken from things "out there" had vanished, revealing my lack of a spirit-based security "in here." It was a painful lesson, but it has stayed with me: material concerns without genuine spirit are a dead-end road.

Challenge yourself to face your own barriers to being spirit-filled. Spirit isn't a luxury. It nourishes us, like the air we breathe or the food we eat. Whether you can afford only a bowl of soup or a banquet, you can be spirit-filled.

To live as a full human being, spirit can't be put on a shelf and taken down when convenient. It's also not a bargaining chip, portrayed in the poignant comedy *The End*. Sonny, the principal character, swims out to sea with the intention of drowning himself, but after some time he realizes he doesn't really want to die. Now far from shore and with a renewed will to live, he realizes that he may not make it back to dry land. What follows is a long plea to God that is both hilarious and sobering. "Please, Lord, I'll give you fifty percent of whatever I make! Just make me a better swimmer!" As the shore draws near, however, he amends his bargain, "I'll give you ten percent, Lord! I know I said fifty percent, but ten percent isn't a bad start!"

The message is clear. Start where you can. Being spirit-filled comes more easily from the smallest honest step than from all the grandiose promises in the world. The only real prerequisite? *A willingness to hear when spirit answers you back.*

Spirit Goes to Work

In the past, spirit in the workplace has virtually been an oxymoron. It seems that there are usually one of two radical courses: one discourages thinking about or discussing anything even distantly related to spirit. The other involves an organizational leader who pushes, either explicitly or implicitly, a particular religion or set of spiritual concepts along with implied "shoul-das" or "oughtas." In the workplace, organized groups that follow a particular spiritual path can create a backlash among workers who are not involved. This serves to divide the workplace rather than unite it.

The middle ground, which we attempt to occupy at Tires Plus, is the freedom and even encouragement for teammates *to feel spirit in the workplace in the manner that feels right to them, while allowing others to do the same.* With the love, caring, and connectedness we've talked about earlier, everyone can find his or her own spiritual space while not stepping on anyone else's toes. Rather than bringing something specific into the workplace, it's about creating an environment where spirit can come out, because it's already there. Listening to employees, allowing them freedom to express their ideas, and demonstrating caring are a few of the ways spirit can emerge in the workplace.

Spirit in the workplace is also about an emphasis on service to other employees and customers. It's about staying aligned with spiritual values. Poet and Nobel laureate Rabindranath Tagore says it better: "I slept and dreamt life was joy. I awoke and saw life was service. I acted and behold service was joy."

Whether you're serving an external or an internal customer, a service-to-others mindset will result in win-win solutions. I ask our new hires, "What if you cared so much about our guests [customers] that you had a feeling of doing 'volunteer work' [yes, they do get paid here] by making it a better day for each human being we touch? Put a smile on each guest's face. Let's be in the business of distributing caring as well as tires, wheel alignments, and brake jobs." That's also a way of expressing that spirituality in the workplace.

Being spirit-filled creates a desire for balance in your life at work and at home—and accepts that it's an important and continuous process to build that bridge between your personal mission and your organization's mission. There are times, however, when you may need to go into fifth gear to meet a deadline, when you may need to work an extra shift to service your clients. Most people don't mind hard work—in fact it can be invigorating and the rewards can be great—as long as you feel the extra effort is in line with both your personal mission and your organization's mission.

So what does it mean to be a spirit-filled worker? It's not something you can measure with a gauge, but by a person's actions. Apart from loving and caring, spirit-filled behavior (in or out of the workplace) includes striving to demonstrate competence and forgiveness and giving apologies, compliments, and constructive feedback. It also embraces empathy and an awareness of those times when we can share our thoughts and feelings on a deeper level. Not pushing, not preaching, but rather responding to specific needs or questions.

I don't go around prodding people to be spiritual. Rather, attempting to model it (albeit imperfectly), I work to create a nonjudgmental, inclusive environment for it, and I do my best to answer questions honestly and share what's worked for me. It's a slow process, and it works better that way.

Does this spirit-at-work thing sound risky? What's the downside? Visualize what would happen if you permitted yourself more of these thoughts, feelings, words, and actions with co-workers and customers. As many people actively seek ways to discover more balance at work, a new form of leadership is also emerging, resulting in part from the growing presence of women in high-level management positions. This new leadership melds intuition with logic, blends nurturing and caring with adherence to high standards, and places feeling shoulder-to-shoulder with intellectualizing. The new rallying message: Coach people as *people,* rather than managing people as *things.*

Many Voices, One Message

Just as spirit-filled behavior can happen anytime, anywhere, spiritual lessons can arrive in many forms. Avoid judging whom you can receive these messages from and whom you can't. Spirit doesn't check anyone's credentials, bank account, or social status before making itself heard.

My father told about his experience with one of these messengers of spirit—a repairman who came to the house to fix a vacuum cleaner. As he left, he handed my father a note that read, "Good morning, this is God! I'll be handling all your problems today. I won't need your help. So have a nice day!" Feeling touched by spirit, Dad's load was lightened that day, and then he passed it on to me. Lessons can come from anyone at any time. In fact, the least likely people often have the greatest message to give. I've received spiritual teachings on a subway, in a field in India when talking to a brickmaker, and standing in line waiting for a movie. Open your heart and listen.

Own Your Mistakes

If you're not being honest with yourself, it's difficult to open yourself to spirit. Owning mistakes is an important step in being able to face yourself and others with clarity. Whether a mistake is large or small, nothing is more irritating to others and harmful to you than covering it up with denial or excuses. Despite any elaborate list of "reasons why," people generally see through them to the truth.

Owning your mistakes reveals your humanity, and allows you and others to be cleansed and move on. Instead of resisting the discomfort of the people who were affected by the mistake, you're empathizing with the pain you've caused them. The three steps are simple but critical:

1. Own the mistake.

2. Apologize sincerely.

3. Talk about how you're going to do things differently in the future.

Owning your mistakes shouldn't be used as a tactic to put a favorable spin on events or to get a desired reaction. People usually know that what's done can't be changed. They do, however, want to hear an apology and know how events will be different in the future.

I saw a great example of this from Pete Selleck, COO of Michelin America Small Tires. At a 1998 meeting of key North American Michelin dealers, the participants came loaded for bear. Michelin's ability to deliver a good percentage of their products during 1997 and up to spring 1998 was dismal. In setting up the agenda, Pete knew that the poor supply issue had to be hit head on, honestly, and humbly. Further, he knew that to encourage discussion and focus on solutions to the problem, he had to quickly get beyond the frustration that the dealers felt.

After kicking off the conference with a brief introduction, Pete made this the first topic of the two-day meeting. He told the dealers that the company's supply performance was unacceptable to them and to Michelin. He explained why the problem existed, and he took full, personal responsibility and ownership for the failure. He apologized, in a heartfelt way, for the deleterious effect this situation had on the dealers' ability to serve their customers. Only then did he explain what Michelin would do to solve the supply issue in the future, and ask for their support in implementing the corrective actions.

That's spirit at work. While François Michelin proudly looked on, Selleck got a rousing ovation. Had he missed any of the three steps (own it, apologize, and propose corrective actions), he would have been boiled by these dealers who had come to vent. And while it was not the *reason* Selleck made the apology, the *result* was that there was nothing to be gained by hammering him more than he'd hammered himself. And no one did.

You could say that Selleck apologized in order not to lose customers. Rather than discount the positive result by assigning it a cynical motivation, I prefer to focus on the good that comes from genuine apologies.

Apologize from the Heart

Authentic apologies for our wrongdoings creates a healing effect for everyone involved. When I don't apologize for a situation that calls for it, I feel weighed down on an energetic (emotional and spiritual) level and often on an intellectual level as well. It becomes that nagging task on the to-do list that never gets done.

Apologies at any level can take on extraordinary meaning and power, from the criminal who shows genuine regret and remorse to a president who sincerely apologizes to a nation. The key to an apology is that it's authentic and heartfelt; an insincere apology is obvious to everyone. Have you ever heard yourself say, "Gosh, what are you still mad about? I apologized!" Did you? Maybe the other person just isn't ready to accept it. Or it could be that you weren't completely sincere. When you apologize, check to see if your tone and body language align with your words.

Ifs and *buts* render an apology only minimally effective. An apology conditioned with, "If my actions upset you, I'm sorry," or "I'm sorry I spoke in that tone, but I was upset with you," isn't really a full apology. This basic, universal rule gets broken by everyday men and women as well as by people in the public eye.

Get in touch with your role in the other person's discomfort and own that role, fully and unconditionally. Consider this: "I'm sorry I spoke in a way that discounted you. You deserve better than that. I'm really sorry." If your tone and body language (especially facial expression) mirror those words and your heart is in it, then your apology will usually be healing for you both and accepted by the other person. "Please forgive me" is a powerful addition. Even in those times when the other person can't accept your apology on the spot, you've created a bridge between the two of you for the possibility of forgiveness. Maybe tomorrow. Maybe next year. The point is that you've opened yourself honestly.

I try to approach every encounter with the thought that if I never saw this person again, would there be anything unsaid or unresolved? If there is, I do my best to say it. Many people understand *carpe diem*—"seize the day"—to mean "go for the gusto" or "enjoy every moment." But I understand it to mean "take the moment and say what needs to be said." Don't leave it for tomorrow. Make the apology. Express your love. Don't leave unfinished today what you might not be able to finish tomorrow.

An acquaintance of mine has been unwilling to speak to his grown son since his son revealed that he was gay. They've not spoken for years. It weighs on both of them, yet the words are not forthcoming. I wonder what would be lost by at least trying to bridge the gap?

There are so many times in life when we can't be where we'd like to be: a parent in another state having a birthday, a sick friend in another country, a daughter who calls you at work to tell you about something that happened at school. You wish you could be there, but it's not always possible. We can only be in one place at one time. That's the nature of the world. But what if we made a commitment to make the best of that one place where we are—to apologize, praise, guide, or celebrate when the chance comes along? It doesn't make up for the regret of not being present in those other places, but you've done the most you can. Owning mistakes gives your spouse, children, and business associates an effective example and increased level of permission for them to be equally honest with you.

Forgive and Release

On the other end of an apology is forgiveness. "I forgive you." Whether you say it to another or to yourself, or listen as someone says it to you, those three words have power to release resentments and open the access door to spirituality. Resentments can potentially harm the person you resent on either a direct or subtle energy level. If we value caring, connection, and being spirit-filled, we won't harbor grudges. Rather, we'll share our thoughts and feelings in a healthy, respectful way, forgive, and move on.

Carrying grudges and refusing to forgive are ever-present anchors that weigh us down—always there inside us, an endless detour to feeling truly loving. *A Course in Miracles* says, "The unforgiving mind is full of fear and offers no room to be itself; no place in which it can spread its wings and soar above the turmoil of the world. The unforgiving mind sees no mistakes but only sins...rising to attack.... Yet it regards its judgment of the world as irreversible, and does not see it has condemned itself to despair."

I use visualization to promote forgiveness. Any place and at any time of day it's possible to access this technique. Simply look inside yourself and think of someone you resent, for whatever reason. Visualize that person. Now visualize a warm light around that person. Surround that person with forgiveness. The next time you have the opportunity, signal your forgiveness to this person either directly with words or indirectly in your mind, depending on the situation and what you're able to do.

Fearlessly Honest

Finally, being spirit-filled is about making right choices and being fearlessly honest. I cringe when I think about the years when my children were growing up and I would occasionally understate their age so I could save money on movie tickets. That's not the kind of model I want to be. Today, if I discover that a salesperson has given me too much change, I simply give it back. Not to return it would feel like pulling the plug on my spirit, a big disconnect. To set my values aside to fill my pocket is at best a short-term gain. We get what we give. Whether you call it the Golden Rule, karma, or any other name, it's a universal law in the game of life.

Engage the Spiritual Warrior Within

One common misconception is that acting in spirit-filled ways (nurturing, caring, honest, authentic) is the same as being a doormat. Just think of Martin Luther King Jr. or his spiritual progenitor, Mahatma Gandhi, to dispel this notion. Part of being spirit-filled is having a spiritual warrior inside us. I'm not speaking of waging battles with guns or about "hating" competitors. Rather, spiritual warfare is speaking up about day-to-day concerns and causes that you feel strongly about. Being a spiritual warrior is about being tough and loving at the same time, firm yet soft, confident yet humble.

This surprises some people who equate being spirit-filled with being a pushover. Rather, being a spiritual warrior implies the courage to take unpopular stands. In fact, spirit demands that you not walk away from a situation that needs you, especially when other people stand to lose if you don't act. For the spiritual warrior, however, battle is a method of restoring a healthy order, not an end in itself.

King made this point in what was to be his last Sunday-morning sermon: "On some positions, cowardice asks the question, is it expedient? And then expedience comes along and asks the question—is it politic? Vanity asks the question—is it popular? Conscience asks the question—is it right?"

Riding on Air

How will we notice as spirit begins to permeate the workplace and our personal lives in a deeper way? A sense of inner tranquillity is a giveaway that spiritual practice, inward and outward, is manifesting in your world. In chapter 6 you'll read more about potential ways to enhance spiritual wellness. In the meantime, here are some useful road signs for recognizing when you're already moving toward it.

ROAD SIGNS TO TRANQUILLITY

+ Smiles appear. Those that were there before become wider.

+ Dangerous curves no longer seem so dangerous. You have a sense that you can handle whatever lies ahead.

+ You feel a sense of adventure about where you're going.

+ You start to notice the scenery in ways you didn't before.

+ You don't feel guilty about stopping to rest.

+ You enjoy being on the road with other people. Instead of traffic being a burden, you think of the other people on the road as fellow travelers.

+ You stop worrying about why other people are the way they are. Instead you start exploring and wondering why you are the way you are.

+ You feel less need to judge other people and instead approach them with openness.

+ You appreciate other people for their uniqueness, ready to learn from them.

+ You notice that you feel grateful and happy more often.

+ You accept your own unique mission—no better or worse than anyone else's—as a vital connection to your Universal Source.

Put COPPSS in Your Game Plan

Caring, optimism, passion, persistence, systems-discipline, and spirit-filled—a game plan that includes these traits is six steps farther along your mission road. As constant companions, COPPSS traits support your Inner Team—body, intellect, psyche, and spirit—and help you develop into a person with the stuff it takes to pursue your personal mission. Guiding you toward greater balance at home and work, COPPSS traits help smooth out the rough road that can cause a breakdown short of achieving your mission.

4

Fit for Your Mission:
Physical Wellness

IF YOU'RE LIKE most Americans, you consider yourself well if you don't feel sick. Sure, it would be nice to shed ten pounds or knock a few points off your blood pressure. And, of course, you could do without the occasional headache and back pain. But for the most part, you wake up every morning assuming you're going to make it through the day in one piece.

In the years before my three-ring wake-up call, I thought I was well enough. To be sure, stress was a constant drain, and I cycled through many bleary-eyed days following too much too late the preceding nights. But I'd always find a way to carry on.

Still, I began to wonder, was this really my personal best? I suspected that my decisions weren't as clear-headed as they could be. I began questioning whether my relationships with family, friends, and colleagues were what they could be. A feeling washed over me that I was missing something. But what, exactly, was I missing?

Physical Wellness

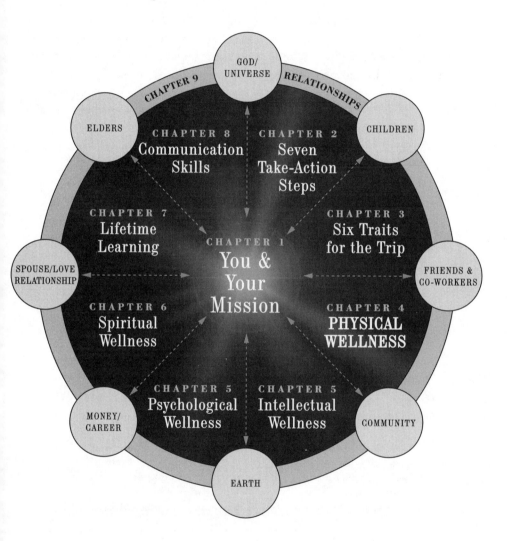

Tapping the Source of Whole-Person Wellness

When I hit the wall in 1989, my assumptions about wellness changed forever. Divorce and a business crisis raised deep questions about my psychological and spiritual fitness, and cancer made me rethink what it meant to be physically fit. Balancing this against the ways I used my intellect, I began to realize that what I was missing was a connection between these essential aspects of self: body, intellect, psyche, and spirit. I was missing what I came to know as my Inner Team.

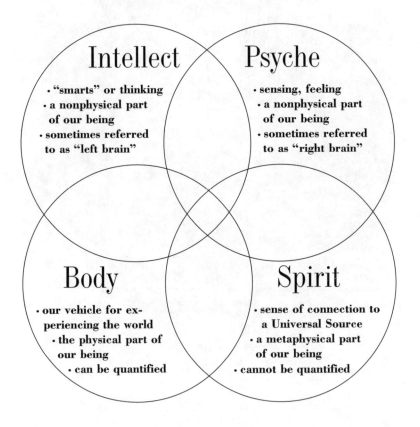

At the time of my wake-up call, I didn't have a team but rather four players who didn't know each other and didn't communicate. While intellect ran most of the plays, spirit and psyche often sat on the bench. My body kept energy flowing, yet this go, go, go effort never led to real wellness. Here's how I could picture my state at that time:

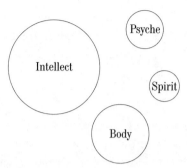

Without a winning game plan, my body, intellect, psyche, and spirit didn't stand a chance of functioning as a whole. As I moved through the period after my personal crash, developing key wellness strategies for each aspect, here's what began to happen:

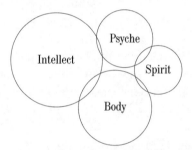

Integration. Greater balance. Clearer connection. I began to see and feel the results of an inexplicable synergy—a quantum leap in wellness that comes when our inner aspects are in synch. Here is how this looks in the ideal:

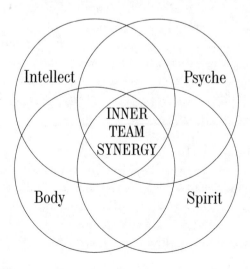

Inner Team synergy is of course always in flux and never completely in balance. Self-coaching strategies aren't about perfection, but about equalizing the attention and care we give each aspect of the Inner Team. And by strengthening one, all benefit.

Body on Board

After my wake-up call and the resulting growth, this inner synergy only seemed obvious. Perhaps I was naïve. I'd always assumed that I had time to reach my goals, that the future was an endlessly spinning potter's wheel on which I could mold my body and mind. A malignant tumor, however, said otherwise, ready to erase my future and dissolve my dreams.

To my endless thanks, surgery swiftly disposed of my tumor. But that wake-up call still echoed in my ears, telling me my old ways of thinking had reached their limits. I started reading books and talking to experts about nutrition, traditional medicine, alternative medicine, emotional health, psychological health, spiritual health. I sought mentors in Dr. Deepak Chopra and John Robbins, author of *Diet for a New America*. I joined the regional boards of the American Cancer Society and American Heart Association and plunged into their research. These storehouses of knowledge opened my eyes to the ways that I could roll back the boundaries to bring a higher level of wellness into my life.

My thinking shifted, and like a gosling following a mother goose, gradually my behavior followed suit. I learned that physical fitness, which I had always considered the main component of wellness, was only part of a wellness matrix composed of nearly every aspect of a person. To redefine the wellness equation, I had to drop some long-held beliefs. What is physical wellness? What does "being in shape" mean? It's more than suffering through "weekend warrior" aches and pains, or chugging megadoses of vitamins to offset a bad diet. Clearly, personal wellness is as systemic as Earth. Just as chaos theory's butterfly effect shows that a butterfly fluttering its wings in Tokyo can cause a hurricane in New York, clearly each of my actions either built up or chipped away at my physical foundation.

Target: Fit for Life

In the wake of cancer recovery, my new fitness habits would become part of a lifetime wellness plan. I began to consider my wellness as being like a bank account: poor food choices, lack of sleep, emotional tension, and other life stressors were withdrawals, while deposits were made with exercise, supportive relationships, healthy food choices, and other positives. With more deposits than withdrawals, I had enhanced energy, crystal-clear thinking, and deeper serenity to keep me on my mission's course—greater motivators, in fact, than the fear of a cancer curtain call. Moreover, I knew that it wouldn't do to recover from cancer, find a new relationship, and rescue my business only to resume my previous lifestyle. I had to approach life anew. I had to raise my wellness bar, which meant that not being sick was no longer enough. I deserved better for and from myself—to say nothing of what I wanted to give the people around me.

The Wellness Team

Through my entire life, the paradigm that the body was a machine had made the most sense to me. Simply fuel the engine, ensure that the gears mesh smoothly, and voila!—for as long and as far as I desired, my machine would run like a well-tuned Mercedes-Benz. Certainly our bodies are impressive high-performance machines, but this analogy cheats the true nature of our beings, which is more than the simple sum of our parts.

Instead, think of your body as one of four players on your Inner Team. The other players on Team Wellness include your intellectual, psychological, and spiritual health. Linked hand in hand, they constitute complete health; you need them all in the game to play your best. Not a moment passes when every part of your being isn't enhancing (or detracting from) every other part of your being. While exercising, you're not just engaging your body; you're also affecting your intellect, psyche, and spirit. When analyzing a new business plan, you're not just using your intellect; your body, psyche, and spirit are also involved, supporting your intellectual functioning through a relaxed synergy of alertness, openness, and perspective.

"But I Don't *Feel* Sick . . ."

The idea that I was not well would have been hard for those around me to grasp. After all, they saw me exercising regularly, eating a relatively healthy diet, and rarely taking a sick day. To their way of thinking, since I didn't look sick, I must have been well.

Not exactly. If you rarely change your car's oil, you might drive for months—years, even—and see no mechanical problems. Inside, however, your engine's dying a slow death, and one day it will leave you stranded. I've often wondered why many of us pay more attention to our cars than to our physical and nonphysical bodies—which carry us through this life's trip. Americans keep their cars for three to ten years. The body, intellect, psyche, and spirit need to last a lot longer than that.

Because it's difficult to define, wellness can be easy to ignore. Defining it as the absence of disease is a start. But on the other hand, it's rather like saying you've won a tennis match even though your opponent never showed up. If your body shows no sign of disease, it may feel as if you're not losing. But staving off losing isn't the same as winning. I discovered that prior to 1989 I had been waiting on an empty court for disease to show up. When it did present its challenging face, I had two options: either forfeit the game or devise a winning wellness game plan.

I was unwilling to forfeit. But suddenly I found myself calling on players I didn't even know I had. In some ways it was embarrassing to admit that I had never called on half of my Inner Team, that in fact I didn't even know they were patiently waiting on the sidelines. Translated to the business world, this was unlike me. I would never allow half of my workforce to remain unmotivated, yet for years I had ignored half of my own inner force.

Over the long haul, forsaking wellness is a road paved with sad statistics. Beyond missing the day-to-day benefits of increased energy, focus, and presence, there's the trauma of long-term damage. Given the nation's current levels of wellness, it's predicted that one in three Americans will die of heart disease, while another one in four will succumb to cancer. Many of these deaths will come early, costing years of potential life. On top of that, many who die of these diseases, along with many who do not, will suffer unpleasant treatments and endure years of reduced quality of life. Few of us are safe.

The Unnatural Nature of Disease

Given that humans can live longer than one hundred years, why don't more of us make it to that advanced age? Considering the dramatic increase in chronic and lifestyle-related diseases during this century, it would seem that most of us "disease out" before our bodies wear out.

Health is a state that our bodies naturally seek, while disease is an unnatural state. Our bodies' healing systems are constantly at work, in countless ways, rebalancing and recalibrating the chemical and electrical messages that keep our bodies in tune. From a scabbing scratch to a mending bone to muscles that ache one day and stop aching the next, our bodies have the astounding power to heal.

Your immune system, in fact, is at this very moment heading off disease before it starts. Cancer cells, for example, reside in everyone. But for the most part the body's immune system arrests the renegade cells before they can do too much damage. It's when the immune system coughs, pings, and misses a beat that a cancer cell breaks through the net and grows unchecked. In a perfect world, our immune systems would function flawlessly. Unfortunately, that ideal is often strained by genetic predisposition and environmental factors, and by leaving wellness on the sidelines instead of putting it front and center.

Playing Your Odds

It's as if homicide had been decriminalized. Our two major killers, heart disease and cancer, have become so common that many people are resigned to them as simple consequences of aging. *Yet heart disease and cancer do not have to be natural by-products of aging.* As the other great killers in history have been dramatically reduced during the twentieth century, heart disease and cancer have increased in importance, becoming two of the top three causes (along with accidents) of lost potential years of life. Both diseases are heavily influenced by lifestyle and environmental factors that are within our control.

In 1996, heart disease and cancer combined killed 1.3 million people— almost twice as many deaths in one year as the total U.S. casualties for all wars of the twentieth century. The National Center for Health Statistics asserts that if all forms of major cardiovascular disease were eliminated, our average life expectancy would rise by almost ten years.

Bringing It Home

Something has got to give. While researchers work on medical solutions, we can work on another front much closer to home. Growing evidence shows that nutrition and lifestyle play a part in the incidence of disease. *The U.S. Surgeon General's Report on Nutrition and Health,* issued in 1988, asserts that what we eat affects our risk for several of the leading causes of death for Americans—causes that account for two-thirds of all deaths each year. To quote from the report, "As the diseases of nutritional deficiency have diminished, they have been replaced by diseases of dietary excess and imbalance—problems that now rank among the leading causes of illness and death in the United States." The federally funded National Cancer Institute says that in men and women combined, 35 percent of all cancer deaths are diet-related.

And if this still seems too far from home, consider that many ordinary doctor visits are related to reactions to everyday stress, symptoms including headaches, back pains, upset stomach, shortness of breath, high blood pressure, and weight fluctuations. Stress raises blood pressure and makes the heart work harder, contributing to the dangers of cardiovascular disease. Adding more stress to psychological and physical well-being, one in three American men and one in two American women claim to be on a diet at any given time. Even so, according to the National Institutes of Health, 55 percent of the adult American population is overweight or obese.

The moral to this statistical story? Much of the "diseasing of America" is caused by factors *within our control.*

Free Agent: DNA

Some would say that despite lifestyle factors that we control, we remain prisoners of our genes. We've all heard about marathon runner Jim Fixx, who died of a heart attack while running. Those who like to discount the valuable contribution of exercise to overall health use his story as an example of someone who, despite exercising couldn't overcome a family history of heart disease. Those people often omit, however, that Fixx lived to fifty-two, nine years longer than his father, who had died of a heart attack at forty-three. John Fixx, Jim's son, says, "We know that Dad believed absolutely that running added life to his years, and we in our family know it also added years to his life." While Jim Fixx couldn't completely reverse his genetic legacy, he overcame it in significant ways.

We can't just blame our genes for the dramatic increase in certain diseases. After all, our genes haven't changed that much over recent generations. We each come into the world with a unique DNA signature, but winning or losing is often determined not by what you're dealt but by how you play your hand. Though genetic tendencies are predetermined, their outcomes are not. Unless triggered by environmental or dietary factors, negative genetic tendencies can lie dormant for a lifetime. So while we can't yet change our genes, we can play our hand well through positive management of day-to-day eating and exercise habits, environmental factors, reaction to stress, and psychological and spiritual health.

The Long and Short of It

Improved physical wellness yields benefits both today and in the future. Here are few of the positive effects people experience:

SHORT TERM

+ Increased physical energy and mental clarity

+ Better sleep patterns

+ Serenity and improved stress management

LONG TERM

+ More productive years, adding years to your life and life to your years
+ Fewer "lurking" diseases springing from an accumulation of bad habits
+ More normal weight levels
+ Fewer injuries associated with loss of physical wellness in later years

From a business standpoint, physical wellness is good for the bottom line in terms of improved morale, greater productivity, fewer sick days, and lower health insurance rates because of better claims experience. The costs of preventing disease pale in comparison to the costs of treatment.

Living Well

It's human nature to imagine that we'll live forever. But that illusion eventually gives way to resignation. As Bob Burr, an old friend of the family, once said with a chuckle, "If I'd known I was going to live this long, I would have taken better care of myself." It's as true today as when Mickey Mantle made that line famous. Health is not just about *quantity;* it's also about *quality.* Living more years means little if you can't live them well.

What's enough to wake us up? For some people, a desire to feel better is enough to motivate change. For others, a brush with disease clears the air real fast. For still others, the daunting death and disease statistics are enough. For me, all three merged into an ominous motivator I couldn't ignore.

There are people, however, who believe the Grim Reaper will never find their front door. American pop culture, with its extreme sports and bottomless appetite for synthetic fountains of youth, celebrates risk and youth to an extent that doesn't exactly support the idea of weaving healthy patterns into the fabric of our lives. Workers in all financial strata and workplace scenarios feel the pressure, as do stay-at-home parents. For those on a traditional corporate track, the hard-driving, fast-living, deal-making, ladder-climbing, stress-stuffed lifestyle is hard to buck, especially when the model of success in the workplace appears to demand those values.

In the end, of course, you have to decide what's right for you. Perhaps you consider the price you pay for your lifestyle to be small change. You are your own head coach; that's your decision. If you see room for improvement, then the ideas in this chapter, as well as in the next two chapters describing wellness of intellect, psyche, and spirit, can point you in directions that you may have never considered.

You're the Coach

We were taught to put our health in professionals' hands, to trust blindly in the wisdom of the people in the white coats. Sure enough, we benefit from the knowledge of these trained professionals. But that's no reason to abdicate responsibility for your own health. With the explosion of information about wellness, we've never been in a better position to take control of our health—through diet, exercise, and stress reduction, to name a few ways of achieving this.

Of course, if you break your foot, it's no time to go to the bookshelf. But after you come home wearing a cast, thumb through books on nutritional supplements that help bones heal faster. Look at stretching exercises that keep you in shape while you're on the mend. Do what you can. Actively team with health professionals, both traditional and alternative practitioners, rather than docilely expecting them to hand you a cure. Participate in and lead your own health, and coach it as you would any other crucial part of your mission.

It used to be that the only way to assess your matrix of health risks was to go to a physician. Now some companies and health-insurance programs offer risk-assessment tests that you can take as often as you like. Those tests factor in lifestyle as well as genetic predisposition, and allow you to watch the scores improve as you reach new benchmarks. Check your health plan and ask if it offers a health-risk assessment test you can use to motivate your own improvement.

I've honed my wellness habits over the course of thirty years, with a substantial leap in the last ten years, and I'm still tweaking my plan. Some lifestyle changes result in major improvement, while others have had more subtle effects. But whether during periods of major growth or steady maintenance, I now have the balance to respond to situations that require both action and reflection. Moreover, sharper thinking and better intuition have improved both my personal and professional judgements. These assets propel me through the Seven Take-Action Steps that help manifest my personal mission.

Without wellness, I can't play my COPPSS traits, neither feeling nor living the habits that support me on the mission road. I don't feel caring, optimistic, or passionate, no matter how hard I try. Nor do I feel persistent, systems-disciplined, time-wise, or spirit-filled. When I'm not at the top of my game, I tend to spend more time on easy, low-priority things, and I'm daunted by important duties, often riskier and uncomfortable. As my high school basketball coach, Chuck Hurley, used to tell me, "Fatigue makes a coward of us all."

Time for a Health Check

A few questions for you: Do you have a health benchmark? If so, are you satisfied with it? Are you willing to venture into new territory where you might discover new wellness? If so, perhaps you need to give yourself a checkup and chart a plan to get where you want to go physically. Life is a marathon, and sprinters burn out. To accomplish your mission, you need to be in shape for the long haul. You need to know how to deal with the digital age's daily—often hourly—rate of change and ceaseless, competing demands.

If you're ready to get on the road to greater wellness, start from right where you are, right now, and wind down the road in a positive direction. At its core, physical wellness comprises four elements:

+ Food, water, air (what we take in)
+ Exercise (what we work out)
+ Sleep (passively renewing our bodies)
+ Supportive bodywork (actively renewing our bodies)

The specific lifestyle changes you do or do not make are your call. They're not designed to make you look a certain way, or to push you into a box of prescribed habits. I offer these ideas as a compass to point you to a level of wellness that can bring you greater health, life enjoyment, and mission fulfillment. You decide which habits will best help get you there. It's not about "shouldas" and "oughtas."As you read this chapter and the following ones, consult with experts outside and within—health professionals you trust and your intuitive, wiser self. And keep moving.

Fuel Up for the Journey

Our bodies depend on three main sources of fuel. Food gives us energy and other nutritional value. Water keeps us hydrated, transports the nutrients and is a key to balanced metabolism. Air provides the oxygen we need to metabolize the energy from the other fuels.

Fuel Yourself with Food

I was in my early thirties when I came across *Please, Doctor, Do Something!* by Dr. Joe Nichols, then-president of the Natural Foods Association. Until then I had eaten the typical American foods—Big Macs with extra cheese, pizza with extra sausage, and Colonel Sanders extra crispy. Nichols argued that the typical American's food choices were anything but healthy, which he supported with acres of data. I read that book from cover to cover and then sat back for a long moment. I clearly saw myself in those pages. I was twenty-five pounds overweight, stressed out, having a hard time summoning energy. What was a guy to do? I could deny what made obvious sense, or I could take a risk and try his advice. The more I pondered it, the more I realized I had nothing to lose.

I stopped eating some things altogether—sugar, fried anything, red meat, white bread. It was a radical change from my previous habits. But it would prove to be only halfway toward the food plan he recommended, the one that wound up being my ticket to physical wellness. Still, I shed twenty-five pounds in a few months, and my energy level increased. I felt much better. I wasn't sick, I reasoned, so I must be well.

Ten years later I discovered the cancerous lump on my neck, and suddenly I understood what it meant that a well person has many hopes and a sick person has only one—to be well. Sure enough, cancer motivated me to reevaluate what I ate. Even though business and personal cues told me it was time to evolve further in my way of eating, it still took a leap of faith to believe that something as simple as what I put in my mouth could be an important part of a better life.

At a weeklong t'ai chi retreat in 1989, I was given the first taste of a new way of eating. On the first day, the organic vegetarian menu barely had any taste. I missed the chicken and milk that were my usual staples. As the week unfolded, however, the food we were served tasted better and better. As my taste buds woke up, so did I. On my return, I gave my refrigerator an interior makeover and replaced some of my regular foods with nourishing noshes. It had never dawned on me that simply eating foods from the earth—vegetables, fruits, grains—instead of processed, packaged foods, would help me feel more grounded psychologically and spiritually.

The Fuel of Champions

Call me gullible, but there was a time when I trusted that the food on supermarket shelves and bistro menus was safe beyond question. The next time you're waiting in a checkout line, scrutinize the label ingredients and nutritional value of what's in your basket. Check out that "healthy" frozen dinner or your tried-and-true canned soup. You may get a real education.

Our culture generally values the *taste* of food first, *convenience* second, and its *nutritional payoff* third. You know the question: Do you eat to live, or do you live to eat? America rewards hard work with indulgence. Focusing on what tastes good, however, ignores an important part of the equation: food's effect on us once it clears our taste buds and winds its way into our stomachs. The good news is that there's a consummate balance—you can enjoy good taste *and* the nourishing effects of food.

To begin moving toward that balance, remember the most basic reason we eat: to nourish muscles, bones, blood, organs, and other tissues. Nourishment depends on both your body's ability to process food and its ability to absorb nutrients. Thus, two questions become important: Are you feeding your body foods rich in valuable nutrients? And is your body physically able to make the best use of those nutrients?

Increased Efficiency—Decreased Nutrition

Profound shifts in American food production and choices have impaired our ability to give our bodies optimal nutrition. Many feel that changes in the array of available foods have been nutritionally compromised in the name of bottom-line efficiency. Consider these changes in food consumption:

+ Whole grains, previous generations' traditional staff of life (accounting for up to 50 percent of the diet), now account for only a small portion of what we eat. And the grains we do consume are mostly refined, bleached, and stripped of their nutrients.

+ Beans, our traditional source of protein, are now primarily used (along with grains) as food for stock animals. Ironically, by converting these beans and grains into meat, we lose 80 to 90 percent of the nutritional value.

+ Meat, poultry, eggs, and dairy products have replaced whole grains and beans at the center of our modern meals. These foods have nutritional benefits of their own, but many Americans rely too heavily on them. A diet drastically higher in saturated fats—a major culprit in heart disease—than humans have traditionally consumed is the result.

+ Sugar and sugar-related ingredients are ubiquitous. It used to be considered an infrequent luxury, but today sugar is a staple in many Americans' diets.

+ Pound for pound, many of today's vegetables and fruits deliver less nutrition. Artificial preservation techniques and increased use of chemicals have produced camera-ready cucumbers and telegenic tomatoes twelve months a year, and longer storage and transport time have brought exotic foods closer to home—at a price. While crop yields are increasing and spoilage is decreasing, the question remains:

How much have these production improvements compromised nutritional content?

+ More foods contain increasing levels of synthetic additives. Without even realizing it, many of us make chemical fertilizers, insecticides, preservatives, and artificial colorings part of our daily diet.

+ Highly processed foods make up a major part of what we eat—a direct result of our busy, convenience-conscious lifestyles. The basis of these foods is often white flour, fat, sugar, or a combination of all three, since they keep well on the shelf and appeal to the widest range of consumers.

The full impact of these changes has yet to be quantified, but we do know of the mortality rates of heart disease and cancer and the increase in obesity and diabetes during this century. Remember—according to a report by the U.S. Surgeon General, a startling two-thirds of all deaths are affected directly by improper diet.

Addiction and Compulsion: We Are What We Eat

Addictive and compulsive behaviors, rampant in our society, have a rebound relationship with our diet. The catch-22 is that what we eat affects the way we think, and the way we think affects what we eat. In addictive and compulsive cycles, the body and psyche are trapped in a dance of unhealthy choices that perpetuate rather than break the vicious circle.

To greater or lesser degrees, many Americans currently battle addictive or compulsive relationships with food and drink. Specific food choices can change the physiology of some addictive-compulsive cycles, enhancing mood and eliminating some of the biochemical triggers of unhealthy behavior. Food affects our mood, and our mood affects our ability to make healthy choices for ourselves. Correcting internal chemical imbalances can reduce cravings and impulsive feelings, and provide a solid foundation for psychological and spiritual work. This combination points to successful steps forward for those struggling to alter addictive and compulsive behavior. Breaking addictions to unhealthy food choices is one of the most powerful things we can do to improve our health and embody our true spirit.

The Troublesome Trio

Certain food choices that are popular with many Americans are often associated with compulsive behaviors. Sugar, alcohol, and coffee (as well as nicotine) can be particularly troublesome. No wonder. Take a look around. They're *everywhere*.

SUGAR: SWEET SURRENDER ✦ Who doesn't love sugar? Whether it's a crème brûlée to cap the celebratory dinner, or a midafternoon Snickers, we associate sweets with rewards. And who doesn't deserve a reward?

I'm a reformed sugarholic. I felt absolutely addicted. When I was a child, my breakfast routine was dipping chocolate chip cookies into hot chocolate. In my twenties, I wolfed down entire pans of hot, half-baked brownies. I loved sugar, but it didn't love me back. After the initial high, I'd crash, becoming moody and irritable. It wasn't easy to hide. The standing warning around my company back then was, "Tom's just had sugar! Steer clear!"

Like caffeine, sugar gives you a short-lived burst of energy. World War I soldiers knocked back packets of the white stuff to pump up their aggression immediately before charging out of their foxholes into battle. Sugar alters mood by affecting blood-sugar balance and shocking the stomach and pancreas. Sugar is also believed to weaken the digestive system and is linked to a number of health issues including tooth decay, diabetes, and obesity. Statistics show a drastic increase in our consumption per capita: from forty pounds of sugar annually per person in 1875 to 152 pounds per person in 1998. Even if you don't think you eat much sugar, think again. Only about a quarter of our sugar consumption comes from sugar we add to foods. The rest—all 114 pounds per year on average—comes through sugar that manufacturers add to factory-made food.

How does sugar affect you? As for me, I discovered that my susceptibility to sugar was a form of anesthesia. It seemed to keep me numbed to real emotions. We humans are such adaptive creatures that I couldn't even see the haze I'd created despite years of pounding my body with marginal nutrition and the ups and downs of sugar and alcohol. Feeling anxious? Calm me with a glass of Scotch. Feeling sad? Zip me up with chocolate.

Like the guy who's oblivious to how dirty his windshield is until it's been washed, I had no idea how poorly my body handled sugar until I stopped eating it. Sugar cravings can spring from eating too quickly and too much, or from eating refined foods or excessive protein. The first way I found to overcome intense desires for sweets was to eat a healthier overall diet. Initially, the tough part is enduring the adjustment.

Sure, I missed the taste of sugar at first. But within a matter of weeks my taste buds and physiology adjusted to my new, stable diet, and my sugar cravings tapered. These days, when I have a craving for sweets, I pick up a banana or slather some apple butter on toast.

Inevitably, people's thoughts turn to sweets in midafternoon. It's logical enough to look for an energy burst to punch through the workday and into dinnertime. Instead of turning to sugar, though, consider some other ways to boost energy—and nip cravings in the bud.

+ Have some fresh fruit.
+ Take a short, brisk walk.
+ Breathe deeply for five minutes, focusing on relaxing and affirming a higher state of wellness for the coming hours.
+ Substitute brown rice syrup, fruit butters, or fruit juice.
+ Drink a cup of tea.
+ Drink a glass of water, flavored with a lemon slice.

In the end, most people feel that the incredible pleasure of eating sugar— studies of chocolate show that it produces the same ephemeral "sense of well-being" as marijuana—outweighs the downside. If that's the case for you, enjoy sugar with a positive attitude and ask your body to process it the best way it knows how.

ALCOHOL: BUZZ IN A BOTTLE + I used to be what we called a social drinker. During my twenties, Johnnie Walker Scotch was my drink. In my thirties I moved to wine, a few steps up from the Thunderbird of my university days, drinking three to four glasses three to four days a week. I drank in the name of having fun and shedding the day's stress. As a friend used to say, "Have a drink. Get a little personality." At cocktail parties, my inhibitions came down along with those of everyone around me. Suddenly we felt more connected. But the connection lasted precisely as long as the buzz. The warmth and depth waned along with the next day's hangover, causing me to question the integrity of my own emotions and those of my drinking mates. I distinctly remember hearing one evening, "Tom, you're such a great guy! A friend for life!" The next day the same person looked at me as if I were a stranger. I finally realized it wasn't me who was connecting with people. It was the booze.

The seduction of the social scene was only part of the story. The kicker was the hangover that lingered for twenty-four hours afterward. To the casual observer, my hangovers were subtle. No pounding headaches and no serious difficulty getting to work on time the next day, despite restless sleep. Once there, however, I could not think as clearly. Sound decisions took more effort. The upshot was that I operated at less than 100 percent for much of the work week. I couldn't see that after every hangover my Inner Team struggled to remember the plan and usually got back in the game just in time for the next bottle of Chardonnay to put them on the bench again.

Ultimately I discovered that drinking wasn't the problem. The problem was that what I wanted and got from alcohol only lasted as long as the buzz. I had to learn to find warmth, intimacy, relaxation, and fun through other, more lasting means. Now I occasionally have a glass of wine, but I feel fine not having a drink in my hand even when everyone else does. In the fall of 1998, I realized how much my thinking had changed from those earlier days when a fellow passenger on a flight asked the attendant for a screwdriver. He was thinking vodka and orange juice. I was seriously wondering, Phillips or flathead?

I was fortunate. Though I had a compulsion for alcohol, it was never an addiction the way it can be for some. Addiction has different dimensions and difficulties than compulsions, but the goal to overcome either is the same: find a way to make your decisions consciously rather than let the alcohol make decisions for you. Through the help of twelve-step support programs, a higher power, or other proven methods, everyone can make a play to put alcohol in its place.

COFFEE: GRIND ME UP ✦ Coffee—that is, really good joe—is the fashionable microbrew of the millennium. In fact, in many ways the coffeehouse has replaced the trendy bar as the place to see and be seen. A Starbuck's on every corner, a Krups espresso machine in every office, gourmet grind in every fridge—it's practically impossible to avoid the black gold of worker productivity, a reputation earned for its stimulating, eye-opening qualities. But like its troublesome siblings, coffee carries nutritional baggage that's obscured by the glow of its cultural cachet.

Besides the highs and lows that go along with a shot of caffeine, coffee inhibits your body's ability to absorb such key nutrients as calcium. To nobody's surprise, caffeine is addictive, stimulating your central nervous system. In large doses, caffeine can cause insomnia and palpitations. Got a weekend headache because you haven't had your usual morning java? You've got coffee withdrawal. While some people place coffee right alongside oxygen as the only life preserver for a stress-filled day, coffee in fact compounds stress by creating a self-perpetuating wired-tired cycle. Getting off the wheel takes conscious effort.

If you'd like to cut down, try tapering off with a half-leaded/half-unleaded blend for a few weeks before going completely caffeine-free. Going cold turkey will usually yield headaches for a few days to a few weeks.

Teas, including herbal varieties, are budding, hip alternatives to coffee. I've come to love caffeine-free herbals like chamomile and peppermint. For a happy medium, try black or green teas, which have various degrees of caffeine but fewer of coffee's nervy side effects. Black and green teas are also rich in antioxidant compounds that may play a role in helping to prevent the growth of tumors and reduce some factors in heart disease.

CHOOSE CONSCIOUSLY ✦ Now reconsider your relationship with the troublesome trio of sugar, alcohol, and coffee in light of their powerful effects. Sure, in the right moment each can be appropriate, even salubrious. On a regular basis, though, odds are they will not serve you well. If you fall under their influence, consider it a warning light on your personal dashboard signaling an internal checkup. Notice how well your body handles them and the degree of side effects and risk you're willing to accept. Becoming conscious of the effects of these pleasures can motivate you to change, but if you feel that eating a Hershey bar, sipping a Stoli martini, or snuggling up to a cappuccino are worth it, then by all means indulge. Enjoy them with the clear mind of conscious forethought.

Empower Yourself

For all the downsides I mention, in our statistics-cluttered world you can find a figure to support just about any food or drink there is. That's the malleable nature of statistics. Beware of relying on them. The accumulation of evidence from multiple studies yields a fuller picture. Approach all wellness information—including what you read here—with both openness and circumspection.

Following the claims and counterclaims about various food choices can be confusing, if not a lesson in conundrums. What's clear is that dietary choices and biological reactions are as diverse as snowflake patterns. Take into account your particular needs and any genetic predisposition to particular diseases so you create food habits tailored to your own life plan. For instance, I eat a primarily plant-based diet, but I wouldn't recommend it for everyone. What I will suggest, however, is that it serves everyone to learn more about individual nutritional needs and the upsides and downsides of their food choices. Explore new foods. Try eliminating others. See how foods taste over the course of weeks as your tastebuds adjust to the changes. With the right information and an honest self-evaluation, you have a better chance to make choices that are right for you.

As I learned more about food and nutrition, one question stood out: Why hadn't doctors educated me better? The problem, I learned, is that physicians (unquestionably among the hardest-working professionals) find difficulty in playing a role in preventive wellness, specifically with dietary changes. First, take the amount of time that hospitals and HMOs allow doctors to counsel patients on disease prevention. It's a rare instance that it happens at all. Second, incentives for doctors to help people prevent disease are rarely built into hospital management systems. Basically, doctors don't get paid to help people *stay* well; they get paid to help people *get* well when they're already sick. And, third, nutrition has a very low priority in America's medical schools; many haven't required even a single course in nutrition. Help is on the way, however, through a younger generation of medical practitioners who are demonstrating an increased interest in nutrition; they will make the difference.

Still, huge challenges remain. Dr. Jim Calli, my close friend, is a cardiologist. No slouch, Jim earned his medical degrees from Johns Hopkins University. As I've nudged him with nutrition discussions, Jim has looked for books on the subject at the American Heart Association's annual cardiologist's conferences. At the 1995 conference, among the thousands of books available, he said he could find not one about nutrition—even though diet is recognized as a primary cause of heart disease by experts and by the AHA. I've shared with him the nutritional information I find, which he wishes were more readily available through "official" sources. I believe more education for doctors and the public on healthy eating (including how to prepare foods and where to get them) needs to share the spotlight with research dollars. Given the contributing dietary factor in a high percentage of diseases, aren't we overlooking an important part of the cure?

I know that these physicians could better benefit their organizations (to say nothing of their patients) if the American medical elite gave doctors more time with patients, more rewards for keeping patients well, and more nutrition and wellness education. The American Medical Association, as well as our nation's medical schools, insurance companies, HMOs, and hospitals, would do well to heed the father of medicine when Hippocrates wrote, "Let food be thy medicine." Dr. Mitchell Gaynor, head of medical oncology at New York's Strang Cancer Prevention Center, says, "We've seen the future, and the future is food." Until the future arrives, we as lay-people need to be proactive about our nutritional needs instead of assuming that what our doctors *don't* tell us can't hurt us. Again, the diseases that result in 66 percent of all deaths each year are caused or exacerbated by diet. Don't wait for our institutions to get up to speed on this. Misplaced trust can be deadly.

Empower yourself. You don't have to be a prisoner of genetics, or of grim statistics that predict our chances of contracting a fatal disease. Ask your health professionals about nutrition, and don't stop until you find someone who takes the role of nutrition seriously and respects your views and curiosity. Begin with your medical doctor; there is a small but growing band that's becoming nutritionally aware. But don't stop there. Chiropractors, dieticians, nurse practitioners, doctors of naturopathy and homeopathy, and other health-care professionals—all of these people are potential fonts of knowledge. Natural foods stores typically sell good nutrition books as well as offering healthy cooking classes. Browse bookshelves, electronic and otherwise. Check the Resources section at the end of this book for specific starting points.

Your life may depend on it. And what you model may very well influence the eating and health habits of your children and others around you. The positive effects ripple out further than you imagine.

Shift into Gear

Some people make dietary shifts gradually, while others prefer the "cold turkey" route. If you choose to change, take the route that's best for you, and make it a change for life. Build your habits in a way that they fit you like a glove—so comfortable that they're second nature.

Not sure where to start? Here's a step in the right direction, some dietary guidelines based on recommendations from the American Cancer Association, similar in some ways to the American Heart Association's recommendations. For their exact recommendations, contact the ACA or the AHA for a full brochure. These represent doable, sound approaches that can increase your level of physical wellness.

1. Choose the majority of foods from plant sources.

   + Eat five or more servings of fruits and vegetables daily (a serving is about one cup).

   + Include grain products in every meal (rice, pasta, breads).

   + Choose whole grains rather than processed grains.

   + Choose beans as a low-fat, high-protein alternative to meat.

2. Limit your intake of high-fat foods, particularly from animal sources.

   + Replace fat-rich foods with fruits, vegetables, grains, and beans.

✦ Opt for baked and broiled foods rather than fried foods.

✦ Select nonfat and low-fat milk and dairy products.

✦ Among packaged, snack, convenience, and fast foods, pick those that are low in fat.

3. Limit consumption of meats, especially those high in fat.

✦ If you do eat meat, select lean cuts.

✦ Eat smaller portions.

✦ Choose beans, seafood, and poultry as alternatives to beef, pork, and lamb.

✦ Select baked and broiled preparations rather than fried.

My Food Plan for Life

Here are the food choices I've made to keep my own wellness on track:

REGULARS AT MY TABLE

✦ **Whole grains,** including brown rice, millet, oats, and whole-grain breads and pastas

✦ **Beans,** including tempeh (from soybeans) and veggie burgers

✦ **Condiments/oils,** including tamari (for spice) and olive oil (a heart healthy oil)

✦ **Soups** including my favorites, carrot, miso, and onion

✦ **Sea vegetables,** including nori, arame, and hijiki

✦ A wide variety of **fruits and vegetables,** in salads and side dishes

✦ **Natural fruit sweets,** including raisins and apple butter

✦ **Organic and natural beverages,** including bottled water, carrot juice, herbal decaffeinated teas, and fruit juices

OCCASIONALLY AT MY TABLE

✦ Fish, cheese, eggs, and butter

✦ Nuts

✦ Alcoholic beverages

I AVOID

✦ Processed, prepackaged products with refined sugar, refined grains and flours, hydrogenated oils, artificial coloring or preservatives

✦ Red and white meat

+ Most dairy products
+ Coffee, soft drinks, milk, tap water
+ Salty, fatty, and sugary condiments and sauces

THE ORGANIC ADVANTAGE + Other than when I dine out, I eat organic fruits and vegetables. By organic, I mean foods that haven't been treated with pesticides or fungicides. Recently, organic agriculture has become a fast-growing industry in its own right. This is an important shift, not only for the health of people, but also for the health of the land and of small farmers who've been squeezed by factory farms. Organic ag is a niche that the industrial farms are ill-equipped to fill.

There's no shortage of doctors, scientists, and health administrators who discount concerns over pesticide proliferation. But it's important to note that they base their claims on the short-term effects of a single pesticide in a single piece of fruit or vegetable. That, they claim, is not a dangerous amount of toxin. However, their methodology prompts important scientific questions:

+ What are the long-term cumulative effects of pesticides on our immune systems and our bodies' ability to heal?

+ What happens when two or more common pesticides on separate vegetables or fruits are ingested together? Studies show that dangerous reactions can result.

At the forefront of this discussion sits the renowned Dr. Andrew Weil, endeavoring to connect pesticides with the modern epidemic of breast cancer and immunodeficient disorders. Having contracted cancer and watched its incredible rise, as well as the rise of other diseases, I can't help but wonder how the accumulation of chemicals employed in food production has affected our well-being. It wasn't so long ago that the EPA and USDA both permitted the use of DDT on U.S. food crops. Lacking conclusive evidence either way, I eliminate the potential risk by buying organic produce whenever possible. Many people also consider free-range poultry and hormone-free beef healthier alternatives. Unfortunately, these products cost somewhat more than the conventional variety, a situation that will change as more and more people vote with their feet and support these chemical-free products.

Take Down the Roadblocks

Does this sound like too much change, too fast? Certainly, most people are attached to their current diet, just as I was attached to sugar, alcohol, meat, and milk. We learn our dietary preferences in youth. By adulthood, our taste buds are indoctrinated. Factor in the emotional ties to our favorite comfort foods, and it can seem impossible to change the way you eat. Even so, many adults do change their diets. And you can, too, if you wish.

HEALTHY EATING AT HOME ✦ It's easier to control what and how you eat at home, because you have control over what's in your cupboards and refrigerator. My partner, Mary, and I buy groceries—organic whenever possible—at local food co-ops and markets that specialize in healthy foods. Some of the big grocery chains are establishing larger natural food sections, which I applaud, yet they generally focus more on packaged products than on fresh, organic foods.

HEALTHY EATERY EATING ✦ When dining out, ask around for restaurants that advertise healthy menus. More and more restaurants recognize this growing niche, and respond with expanded menu choices. In almost any restaurant, I can piece together a healthy meal—salad, soup with vegetable stock, grilled or broiled fish, fruits, vegetables, rice, beans. Ask for these foods even if you don't see them on the menu. It's a rare restaurant that won't whip something up to order. Even in the rare instances when the menu is barren of healthy choices, I don't stress out. Instead, I simply eat the best food available and visualize my body converting it into friendly fuel.

HEALTHY EATING AT WORK ✦ The office is one of the most difficult places to eat right. Every other desk holds a candy dish. Coffeepots are full and steaming. The vending machine is stocked with what everyone knows are empty calories, but that turn irresistible when three o'clock rolls around.

As if your day-to-day duties weren't enough to preoccupy your mind, work is where you must actively be possible hard to find good eating choices. Though the following suggestions may not be possible in every setting, the underlying attitude works anywhere. Be proactive. Know where the healthy choices are during every part of the day. Otherwise, you'll be caught high and dry with the hungries and no place to go but the vapid vending machine.

+ Request that your office's vending machines be stocked with at least a few low- or no-fat and low- or no-sugar selections, as well as apples, bananas, and oranges in place of some of the candy bars if possible.

+ Talk about your food preferences with the manager of the company cafeteria. Some still believe that low-fat means yogurts and salads.

+ Bring your own lunch.

+ Create a lunch cooperative. Find co-workers with similar tastes and rotate responsibility for bringing lunch.

+ Store boxes of your favorite teas at work. Minus a source of heated, bottled, or filtered water at work, bring a thermos from home, or ask your office manager to install a water dispenser.

+ While traveling, get healthy, local recommendations from the hotel staff.

THE ZEN OF EATING

+ Eat sitting down, and take time to enjoy your meal. A slower pace gives your brain time to register when your stomach is full. If you eat too fast—or in front of a television—your fork will outrun your brain and you'll wind up overeating.

+ Thoroughly chew your food, which helps your digestive system metabolize food (I'm usually the last one to finish eating at my table).

+ Cultivate a positive state of mind. By taking your mind off stressful events and focusing on the nourishing aspect of what you're eating, you aid your body's ability to get the good from your food. There are times when I eat lunch at my desk, although I prefer not to. When this occurs, I strive to take two minutes of relaxed breathing before eating. This allows me to take a mental step away from the moment's concerns, and take in food with a better attitude. Then I get back to business with an air of well-being.

Super Supplements

To push the well-being envelope even further, I take a variety of nutritional supplements—vitamins, minerals, trace elements, and herbs. By no means would I recommend substituting supplements for eating healthily. I use them to offset the extra stress of our polluted world and a sometimes intense schedule. Look at them as insurance that keeps your immune system humming.

There are hundreds of helpful supplements on the market, and consumers are beating a path to them. Between 1994 and 1997, sales increased from $8 billion annually to $12 billion. Not too long ago, the American Medical Association deemed vitamin and mineral supplements a waste of money. Their position has changed, and they now endorse vitamin and mineral supplements for those with specific dietary deficiencies—and in this day and age, I believe that includes most of us. Remember, your nutritional requirements fluctuate depending on stress levels, age, physical activity, diet, and gender. Though it may be tempting to trust the generic advice in FDA-mandated food labels or in the boilerplate Recommended Daily Allowances (RDAs) of vitamins, minerals, and trace elements, your situation may benefit from a customized approach that includes a wider range of RDA and other supplements.

Beyond the RDA supplements, including vitamins B, C, and E, folic acid, selenium, calcium, and magnesium, the shelves of health retailers grow more crowded by the month with herbal and whole-food supplements. Some have migrated from the traditional medicine chests of other cultures, particularly Chinese medicine. The FDA tightly restricts manufacturers' claims of benefits, but with a little homework, you'll find the information you need to decide what's right for you. Just as you wouldn't take a prescription drug without quizzing your doctor about the upsides and downsides, you'll want to get the whole story for yourself on herbal and whole-food supplements. Check the Resources section of this book for a quick start, or head to your local health-food stores. Some of the more common supplements you'll find are St. John's wort, echinacea, goldenseal, *Ginkgo biloba,* saw palmetto, valerian root, astragalus, ginseng (Korean and Siberian), kelp, coenzyme Q-10, omega-3 fatty acids, spirulina, and acidophilus.

Ready or Not

Ready to turn some of these ideas into action? Here are a few ways to get on the road:

+ Read and ask experts for advice about your specific needs.

+ Cut out a chunk of time—a retreat, or a health vacation—to formulate and focus on your dietary goals, as well as give your taste buds a chance to adapt. It's easier to start new habits in unfamiliar settings, where you're more open to change.

+ Give your refrigerator a food makeover.

+ Ask friends to accompany you to restaurants that serve menus in tune with your new dietary goals.

+ Build in support. If you have a friend who's making similar changes, share information and encouragement. But be prepared to stay on track if your friend derails.

+ Try a structured program, such as the one laid out in Dr. Andrew Weil's *8 Weeks to Optimum Health*.

+ Don't underestimate the power of old habits. Be ready to forgive yourself when you slip—and enthusiastically get back on track.

+ If you find yourself unable to get a healthy offering at a restaurant, relax. Eat the best option, even if it's off your plan. These are the seductive moments that try your dietary will, that can seem the perfect excuses to fall off the health wagon and order the richest thing on the menu. Hang on.

+ Have fun with this. Leave behind the "shouldas" and "oughtas." Make a change only if it's right for you. If it doesn't feel right, continue supping just the way you are, with a loving heart and a positive attitude.

Fuel Yourself with Water

Like Earth herself, our bodies are more than half water. Hard to believe indeed—since we don't go sloshing through the day—but water is the vital link for all our bodily functions. Oxygen, nutrients, hormones, and chemical messengers ride the water chutes through our bodies. Like messages in a bottle cast downriver, our vital organs send communiqués to each other via the water in our cells. Digestion and metabolism as well as lubricated joints depend on water.

Every day, the average adult processes about two and a half quarts of water by way of respiration, perspiration, urination, and elimination. Stress, disease, injury, exercise, and excessive sweating can dramatically affect this output. That can be dangerous. A shortage of water winds up causing the body to turn on itself, unleashing the poison of stalled waste products. Impurities in the blood increase, and our kidneys yell "help!" Moreover, when we don't get enough water, our bodies kick into drought mode and shunt most water to such vital organs as the brain, lungs, and heart. This saps less vital parts, including skin, nails, hair, bones, and joints. The net effect is that we experience an energy shortage, which leads to imbalance. Without an adequate water supply, the body, basically a battery of water cells, has no way to efficiently and thoroughly produce, store, and transmit energy.

To maintain healthy hydration, drink water between meals. A good rule of thumb is to drink half your weight in ounces of water daily. A man who weighs two hundred pounds, for example, should drink at least one hundred ounces of water each day. Healthy skin, hair, and fingernails and toenails are one barometer of adequate water intake. More insidiously, though, improper hydration manifests itself in lost performance, cloudy thinking, illness, and disease. The reality is that a lot of Americans suffer from chronic dehydration. As F. Batmanghelidj, M.D., the author of *Your Body's Many Cries for Water,* says, "You are not sick; you are thirsty."

Water, Water Everywhere

With countless water choices, it's sometimes hard to know what's best. I drink filtered water at home and bottled water elsewhere. In the United States, water supplies are mostly free of disease-causing germs, yet they're not necessarily free of toxic chemicals from industry and agriculture. More than one-third of all community water systems have been cited for not meeting EPA water-safety standards. More than two hundred toxic chemicals have been found in water supplies nationwide. Whether you choose filtered, bottled, or tap water, know what you're drinking and feel good about its important role in helping your overall wellness.

Water, Nine to Five

Now you have another reason to gather around the water cooler. A cooler that provides healthy, good-tasting water is a great ally against workplace stress. To dress up the experience, keep a nice pitcher in your office and toss in a few slices of lemon or lime. Keep a special water glass at work that reminds you of the life-giving power of this basic beverage.

In the course of a busy day, it's easy for me to forget to drink enough water. My solution? I carry a water bottle with me and sip on it throughout the day, refilling from the filtered-water coolers at home or office.

I also drink water that's either room temperature or warm. The United States is one of the few countries in the world that primarily drinks fluids iced. Some say that refrigerating our insides with cold liquids stresses our stomachs and digestive systems. While there is no clear answer in the matter, I figure that living in Minnesota gives me enough exposure to cold; I don't need to drink it, too.

Fuel Yourself with Air

You've witnessed the scene many times. Shaquille O'Neal stands at the free-throw line ready to shoot, or Venus Williams sways at the baseline, ready to eat the next serve. First, though, both pause and take a long, deep breath.

Done right, breathing can be a useful stress reducer and energy producer. In the United States, breathing isn't generally considered a health practice. We simply assume we do it right. Hard as it is to imagine, most of us don't. Our natural breathing, generally speaking, fills a small percentage of our lung capacity. That doesn't even account for stressful situations, which tighten muscles and raise anxiety, causing breath to become shallow.

Think about it. You can go without food and water for days, but how long can you go without air? It's the element most necessary to produce energy—and promote survival. When the brain is starved of oxygen, damage is practically immediate. Without breath, you can't think; and although your brain accounts for only 2 percent of your body weight, at rest it consumes 20 percent of the oxygen you breathe.

Light Up and Cough

A deep breath of clean air is one of life's simple pleasures. Smoking, an addictive cousin to sugar, alcohol, and coffee, is one of the most common ways people prevent themselves from enjoying the benefits of a pure lungful of oxygen. Smoking is a prime cause of lung cancer, the leading cause of cancer death in America. It's a testament to nicotine's addictive influence that despite these statistics, an estimated 46 million Americans are tied to the pack.

Like any other habit, smoking can be overcome and replaced with a new habit—*not smoking*—as testified to by the more than 44 million adults who have successfully quit. Through various means—behavior modification, nicotine therapy by prescription, and kick-the-habit-cold-turkey—many are taking steps toward clearing the air and breathing deeper as a result.

Check In . . . and Out . . . and In . . . and Out . . .

In Asian cultures, studied breathing is viewed as a vital health practice. Breath implies more than the mechanical act of drawing air in and out of the lungs. It's the juncture of being, somewhere between physical, nonphysical, and metaphysical. Established instructors of meditative relaxation techniques teach breathing as an empowering art form. Disciples of some of these traditions spend years studying how to breathe. In yogic traditions, breath is a vital link between mind and body: no breath, no vitality; no breath, no life.

The first step to understanding your own breathing pattern is simply to notice how you breathe. Like the rings of a tree, which record temperature and rainfall fluctuations and other influences, every breath you take reflects minute changes in your psychological and emotional states. Stressful, angry moments produce shallow inhalation and vigorous exhalation. Fearful situations prompt rapid, ragged breathing. Laughter invokes deep, relaxed, open breathing. Once you've noticed these patterns yourself, you can work with them consciously to cue your body in to a state of relaxation, counteracting momentary stress and the cumulative effects of tension. Try it the next time you're tense. You'll find that you can move to a state of calm by consciously breathing deeply and regularly.

Note your breath, right now. It only takes a couple of seconds. First, focus on your breathing. Just observe the full cycle of your inhalation and exhalation...

What changes did you notice just by concentrating on your breath? For one, you're probably breathing more regularly now. You may have even taken a deep breath without even trying to. Feel how your breath glides through your mouth and nose, through your throat and into your lungs. Is the flow smooth? Is your throat relaxed? Now take another deep breath. Notice whether it feels easy, or if your chest or stomach is tight. Notice how a deep breath fills not just your lungs but, more important, expands your diaphragm and belly and relaxes the rest of your body. Tense muscles don't take oxygen as well as relaxed muscles. Breathing deeply, and consciously releasing muscle tension in your body, triggers a domino effect that helps your entire body rebalance itself.

For optimum benefit, a lot more practice is required to learn breathing patterns that get the most from each breath. Yet anyone can observe his daily breathing patterns; that alone is a beginning step to relaxed breathing and better health. Just noticing my breath at spots in the day triggers deeper breathing, one of the most easily available de-stressors there is. It opens the door to staying more relaxed in the here and now, and aware of what's going on around and inside me.

Air Raves

It's 3:00 P.M., and you need an instant energy boost. Before pressing button 5B on the vending machine to release that candy bar, take a few minutes to energize with breath.

Put one hand on your stomach and the other on your chest. Which rises more fully when you inhale? Your stomach? Great! That's pulling more oxygen into your lungs. Now close your eyes and breathe slowly through your nose. With these full breaths in motion, simply notice your cycle of inhalation and exhalation. Concentrate on the rhythm, and let it find a relaxed pace. Open your eyes and continue the breathing. Still need the candy bar?

Try breathing more fully. Self-awareness will, in itself, take you a step toward balance. What a great tool we have in our breath; it's a readily available resource, convenient, requiring no appointment and no permission. It's always right there with you. No equipment or batteries required. And it's one of the healthiest things we can do for ourselves.

Exercise

We're an idle lot, compared with our ancestors. We drive four blocks to the corner grocery. We use moving sidewalks, escalators, elevators. A few sidewalk blocks is the most we'll walk, and we climb stairs only when there's a fire drill. No longer forced to hunt for our food (thank you very much), we buy it at the grocery store or eat at a restaurant. Instead of working as farmers or manual laborers, we sit in front of computers at desks, where the heaviest thing we lift is a telephone or a stapler. Our children watch videos, play computer games, and hang out in malls, diversions that have only recently become available. Add to that the couch-potato syndrome of watching TV, a preoccupation only a couple of generations old. We don't even have to move anymore to change the channel. "Surfing" (an ironic metaphor for such a static pastime) with the remote control does the trick. The upshot? Less motion. Less exercise. Less fitness.

A Pushup a Day Keeps the Doc at Bay

None of this would be a problem were it not for one thing: Mother Nature knows that we need regular physical activity to keep limber, to increase and maintain bone mass, to extend heart and lung efficiency, to activate chemical balance, and to enlist our immune system.

Exercise helps the body process more efficiently the 5,300 gallons of oxygen it inhales daily. Exercise maintains and improves muscle strength and tone. During the first ten to twelve weeks of initiating an aerobic exercise program, your heart rate decreases by one beat per minute every one to two weeks.

People who exercise moderately even have fewer infections. Exercise sparks natural highs thanks to endorphins, brain chemicals containing pleasure-inducing properties similar to opium. Exercise programs are also prescribed for sufferers from depression. The increased blood flow, endorphins, and resulting chemical rebalancing offer relief that seems magical to me. Exercise's role in longevity and disease prevention is crucial and indisputable.

Great as these benefits are, they're not the reason I exercise. I run and play basketball because they clear my head and fill me with enthusiasm to play my mission each day. When I'm low on energy, exercise recharges me. It also relieves stress. A vigorous workout restores perspective and helps me release concerns that had seemed deserving of worry. Sure, some concerns need attention, but they don't have to be a reason to stress out.

Likewise, the mind is always sharper after a workout. Decisions are made easier by exercise. I've also noted that when I'm not exercising regularly, whether because of injury or illness, I'm not nearly as caring or tolerant with others. Better sleep and weight control round out the incredibly positive effects of exercise.

Feels Great, Less Filling

The leading question: Given these benefits, what would keep you from regular physical activity? Lack of motivation? Well, not if you understand the above benefits. Package these effects of exercise in a pill, and list its benefits on the package, and you've got a Viagra-sized seller. But it's not available in pill form. It takes time and effort.

Like many people, I reflexively do informal cost-benefit analyses on things I choose to spend time doing. Every other day, I spend about sixty minutes on a combination of aerobic exercise, stretching, and weightlifting. Those three or four hours each week (a mere 3 percent of my waking hours) provide a great ROIT (return on invested time); their benefits far outweigh the time cost. The way I figure it, each session produces forty-eight hours of feel-good benefits, plus the healthy by-product of stronger immune, cardiovascular, nervous, and muscular systems.

Just to test its value, I've experimented now and again, for two decades, with spending those three to four hours each week doing something other than exercising. It's a disaster every time. Life's stress eats me up; I lose my serenity, my energy and clarity, my mental agility. And at the end of the day, I don't even end up saving time. In fact, it costs me time. It's not hyperbole to say that without regular exercise I would not be walking the planet today. Life's voluminous challenges would have done me in long ago.

Pace Yourself

These are all-or-nothing times. Some people actually tell me that if they're going to exercise they'll go full out or not at all, and they don't exercise because they can't fit into their schedule a daily, two-hour workout.

Lifestyle extremism makes fertile ground for failure. The fact is, you don't need to be extreme to profit from exercise.

Jogging twenty minutes every other day, for instance, works fine for me, while I find running marathons to be over the top. Whatever you do, do it because you love it and it's right for you. You needn't have your own cot at the health club in order to reap benefits. You'll notice a change simply by giving over twenty minutes, every other day, to aerobic activity, combined with forty minutes of stretching and weight-bearing exercises. If strenuous aerobic activity isn't your thing, find a level of activity that is—walking, dancing, biking, or gardening.

Getting Started Again

If you've been a stranger to exercise, and haven't had a physical recently, you might start with a complete physical. You can use this baseline information to measure your progress as well as ensure you're ready to start back—slowly but methodically. According to the Consumer Product Safety Commission, nearly 96,000 people were rushed to emergency rooms in 1994 because of workout-related injuries, many of which were caused by out-of-the-ordinary demands on the body.

Getting motivated to exercise is often a huge roadblock. If you don't exercise regularly, you won't feel like exercising. Once you start regular exercise, you'll be more likely to keep going. You can turn the vicious cycle of inactivity into a victorious cycle of exercise with a commitment to "just do it." I was active throughout my twenties, but laid off for a few years in my early thirties. When I began again, I tried jogging and found that despite a previous athletic lifestyle, I couldn't run more than a few blocks without exhausting myself. Not to be denied, I ran, then walked, then ran again and walked again, until I completed my circuit. This I did every other day until, with each successive outing, I increased my stamina. It wasn't long before I was running the full twenty minutes, 2.5 miles, without walking or stopping.

Choose Exercise You Enjoy

It's simple. If you enjoy what you're doing, there's a pretty good chance you'll keep doing it. Now apply this natural law to exercise. What I enjoy most is basketball; I was born and raised in Indiana, so it's sort of a congenital condition. What do you enjoy most? Running, tennis, racquetball, biking, swimming?

Sharing these healthy pastimes with loved ones and friends is an endless source of motivation. Whenever possible I double my pleasure by exercising with my sons; with my partner, Mary; or with friends. Be careful not to let this become a roadblock, however. When their schedule doesn't jibe with yours, go with yourself.

Hang in There

Weekend warriors are the best candidates for injury. Try your best to maintain consistent activity, avoiding long gaps if possible, and be mindful when you return to exercise after a layoff. Basketball was my primary exercise—one-on-one or five-on-five pickup games, corporate league games—until age forty-six, when my love for roundball was trumped by the convenience of home exercise. Soon I found, however, that I dearly missed the game I'd played since I was a youngster. At fifty, I took it up again. It was difficult, needless to say, and even reentering the game slowly left my legs throbbing with pain. No problem, I thought. Just part of the program of recovering the game I used to play. Then, one night while playing, I hyperextended a finger. Not long after that healed, I sprained my right ankle. That healed and I trudged back on the court. Months later, as I worked myself back into shape, I sprained my other ankle. The second injury was frustrating. The third shattered me.

I was at a crossroads. Should I call on persistence, or should I let go? Logic and better judgement said it was time to hang up my high-tops, but basketball has a magical, invigorating effect on me. It's a kind of moving meditation. During treatment on my second sprained ankle, I said to my practitioner, "Guess I can't go full out?" "You can go full out," she shot back, "just not fully out of control."

I got the message. I can continue playing hoops, as long as I stay within my limits. Persistence was the course. My comeback would continue apace, despite the fact that I'd lost quickness, vertical leap, and shooting accuracy. It felt as if I was back to square one, but I refused to bow to the typical lament, "I'm too old to *play*."

For too many people, aging is like speeding ever faster by a series of signposts that name all the things they love but must give up. I choose to see aging as a process of gaining new strengths while acclimating myself to others that may simply require some adjusting. The wisdom I gather with time helps me compete in different (and smarter) ways than I played when I was younger—on and off the hardwood court. Be selective about the way you see your future. Thoughts are powerful. Focus on the strengths that age is giving you, rather than mourning lost youth. Yes, it's challenging when the twentysomethings on the court yell, "Hey, Pops, look out!" And I still enjoy playing one-on-one against my older son, whom I'd always beaten until I turned forty. Nowadays I can't touch him—for now. Be clear—don't let anyone else tell you you're too old for anything, especially when it comes to getting in the game. That's nobody's call but your own, and you'll know when it's time to hang up the jersey in favor of some other enlivening activity.

S-t-r-r-r-r-e-t-c-h

That battery of injuries brought to mind an important principle: Always balance aerobic exercise with stretching and strength training. Stretching before and after a workout maintains muscles' flexibility while strength training (free weights, Nautilus, Cybex) tones muscles. Both drastically reduce your chance of injury. Weight-bearing exercise also helps prevent osteoporosis, a growing risk as we age. In addition, stretching staves off the stiffening usually associated with advancing age. My eightysomething mother sings the praises of her daily stretching routine, and I know firsthand the agility-boosting benefits of daily yoga.

Use your body's wisdom to tell you where you need to stretch. Stretch to a point that your muscles begin to hurt, then back off a notch. Hold this steadily, breathing deeply, for twenty seconds. Exercise physiology, like other disciplines, is constantly being developed and refined, so don't assume that what you learned in your college phys-ed class is still current. Get updated recommended routines from health-club professionals, or use the books on stretching and strength training listed in the Resources section of this book.

Exercise Anywhere

No one said that finding and sticking to a regimen is easy. I divide my time between a home gym—a treadmill, stationary bike, weights—and a fitness club ten minutes away, where I play basketball. Home workouts give me the flexibility to exercise when and where I need it, and the club offers the support of like-minded people, a great motivator.

Being on the road is another, often challenging, issue. When traveling, I pack my workout gear and try to stay in hotels outfitted with fitness rooms. Failing that, I run outdoors. And when weather thwarts even that, I run the hotels' carpeted hallways (as quietly as possible). Many hotels have swimming pools, and most cities have a park where you can run or take a brisk walk, or rent a bicycle or in-line skates.

Make a Date and Don't Be Late

Make wellness part of your year-long action plan, then schedule it on your calendar the same way you would a business meeting or doctor's appointment. This is an appointment with yourself, so give it the same importance you would a meeting with your most important client. That is, don't miss it. When I'm tempted to blow off an exercise appointment, indeed I pretend I am meeting a client and I put one foot in front of the other, put on my workout clothes, and get moving. The club's atmosphere, music, and positive Self Coaching ("Good job, Tom! You got here! Now let's get to the warm up...") plop me right into the groove. Before I know it, I've glided from languor to post-workout high energy.

The only times I skip a workout are when I'm sick, injured, or extremely low (not just a little) on energy. I interpret those signals as messages from my body saying it's time to rest and renew. Even if I'm not feeling well, I often stretch or do some gentle form of movement. But I get back to my usual routine as soon as possible, typically within a day or two.

Exercise at the Workplace

No joke. You don't have to wait until you're home or at the health club to exercise. Even during the workday, you can energize yourself with exercise.

+ Take a brisk ten-minute walk during your lunch break. Ask colleagues to come along so you can double your pleasure, and reap the benefit of their motivation on those days when you're low on energy.

+ Climb stairs instead of taking elevators.

+ Keep at hand a chart or book of exercises you can do at your desk. Knock them out for five minutes during the morning or afternoon. These same exercises can also translate to airplane trips or long car rides; you'll arrive more refreshed.

+ Stretch, stretch, stretch. Especially if you work at a computer, every forty-five minutes stand up, walk around, and stretch your arms, wrists, neck, and shoulders.

+ Encourage your company to do anything it can to promote physical activity among employees. At Tires Plus headquarters, our workout facility houses a treadmill, stationary bikes, weight machines, and other exercise options. Our outdoor basketball court and Ping-Pong table are great for impromptu games. Health fairs a couple of times a year broaden teammates' access to a variety of wellness options, while the company-sponsored basketball team, which I play on, participates in a local league. A spring fitness challenge encourages first time exercisers to get involved and helps motivate those whose commitment to exercise has sagged.

+ Ask your human resources department to sponsor a yoga or stretching class.

Enjoy a Lifetime Habit

Physical activity promotes well-being and longevity in ways nothing else—not drugs, not supplements, not surgery—can match. At ninety-nine-years old, Olympic gold medal winner Leon Stukey advised, "Be involved, be on the move, and do not give up until the end of your life."

Whatever your routine, make it a lifetime habit. I envision playing basketball until I'm around sixty-five, tennis till I'm around ninety, and brisk walking and golf until...? By then, I'm sure there'll be new sports or exercises to keep my limbs lubricated and moving. You know the saying: Use it or lose it.

Sleep

The next piece of the wellness puzzle is sleep, which has a major impact on clarity of mind, energy, and serenity. Certainly I get through days preceded by inadequate sleep. We've all been there, and we all know that on those days even small things seem to take great effort. Our moods, relationships, work—all of it—suffers. Insufficient sleep disturbs our bodies and minds in ways we don't fully understand, but we sure know what it feels like.

Few people realize how much sleep they need, and how little they get. James Maas, sleep authority at Cornell University, says that losing as little as an hour of sleep nightly over the course of a week is the equivalent of pulling an all-nighter and shaves 25 percent off an individual's productivity. The National Commission on Sleep Disorders Research, created by Congress in 1989, reported in 1992 that Americans today get 20 percent less sleep than our counterparts did one hundred years ago. The commission estimated that the cost of lost productivity, accidents, and impaired decision-making related to sleepiness in 1990 alone was $15.9 billion.

How Much Is Enough?

Sleep requirements vary from one person to the next. Some need ten hours, the average nightly knockout for Americans prior to the advent of electrical lights. Others, like Bill Clinton, author Harvey Mackay, and superpreneur Martha Stewart, get by with four or five hours. I operate best on seven hours a night. No matter what the dosage, to be fit and well we need more of what good rest gives us—a higher-functioning immune system, a renewed and rested body. Otherwise we're left with the fallout of poor sleeping habits— irritability, low energy, and a cloudy mind.

How much sleep do you really, truly need? After all, just as sleeping too little leaves you groggy, so too does oversleeping. As you practice the other wellness tips in this chapter, you'll naturally begin to understand your real sleep needs. If you're still not waking up refreshed and ready for the day ahead, experiment with other factors in your life until you find your ideal sleep equation.

Early Bird or Night Owl?
Are you an early bird or a night owl? Early birds rise with a song in their voice and a twinkle in their eye. Owls, on the other hand, stay up late and grow happier and sing louder and louder as the day progresses. To the degree you can follow the pattern that most closely matches your natural rhythms, so much the better. Me, I'm an owl, and while I can't always follow an owlish schedule, I'm aware of my natural rise in energy late in the morning and into the afternoon until it peaks late at night.

Guarantee a Good Night's Sleep
Stress is a common sleep filcher. Those workday thoughts that don't evaporate when you hit the sheets wreak havoc throughout the night. Pinpointing stress sources and breaking them down can produce night after night of sound sleep. For techniques on relaxation, meditation, and emotional and psychological health, the next two chapters set forth everything that's helped me sleep well. One of the simplest techniques, though, is to take fifteen to thirty minutes to wind down in bed with some calm reading. Then observe your breathing, and try to relax rather than sleep. Before you know it, you're out.

The power of affirmations and positive suggestions is useful for creating a state of restful, healthful sleep. Sincerely telling yourself "Tonight I'll sleep deeply and wake up renewed and ready for the day" can open your mind to an expectation that soon manifests itself into reality.

Darkness, quiet, and a comfortable bed are essential for a good night's sleep. While the physiology of sleep is rather mysterious, scientists do know that our body chemistry changes when we sleep. Controlling environmental factors is easier at home than on the road, of course, but even in unpredictable surroundings you can tote sleep-facilitating eye masks and ear plugs. Reducing or eliminating caffeine in your diet, especially in the evening hours, can also help you saw more logs.

Regular sleep patterns are like solid drummers; they keep things in synch. The tendency of some is to burn the candle at both ends during the week and sleep double-time on the weekends. But that only trains the body further in ruinous rhythms. While occasional sleep irregularity is inevitable, regular sleep habits pave the way to long-term wellness.

Finally, if you've tried all this and still can't sleep well, try herbal assistants or aromatherapy oils like lavender. I have, on rare occasion, and found serious success. Of herbal sleep aids, valerian root is my first choice because it's milder than other sleep aids.

Power Up on a Nap

The nap has a bad rap in America. Used wisely, it's a great form of rest that can be beneficial. I can instantaneously go from sleepy and dull-minded to alert and fully awake after a ten- or twenty-minute catnap. I've found creative nooks in which to do this—on a couch in my office, in a meditation or massage room in my headquarters, on an airplane, in a car (only, of course, riding passenger side).

In *The Art of Napping,* William Anthony, a professor of psychology at Boston University, writes that the "United States is a nappist society, prejudiced against the siesta because of the country's drive to produce." Many Americans hold the mistaken belief that napping and productivity are strictly at odds with one another, when, in fact, a nap can be a great productivity-enhancing procedure. Two keys are not sleeping so long that you fall into a deep sleep (generally after twenty or thirty minutes) and planning a fifteen- to thirty-minute period after you wake to return to peak alertness. The "power nap" is a quiet, growing trend in corporate suites, although it remains somewhat tainted by the false appearance of laziness. History holds the best evidence: No one ever called nappers Winston Churchill and John F. Kennedy slackers.

Sure, it's often difficult to find a nap space at work. But maybe it's not impossible. If you do find a private nook or cranny, and your supervisor supports the idea, sometime test-drive a ten-minute nap instead of taking a coffee break.

Supportive Bodywork

Nerves, muscles, and bones duly serve every day, and while in turn a winning life game plan supports them with exercise, good nutrition, and sleep, there's even more we can do. Supportive bodywork—therapies that directly affect the physical body—used to be the province of the fringe or the famous. Now it's estimated that more than half of all Americans have used these types of complementary therapies to enhance their wellness. Massage, acupuncture, acupressure, osteopathy, chiropractic, and physical therapy are just a few of the methods of bodywork that are growing in availability and acceptance across the country.

The Stress Effect

It's no secret that stress is a national epidemic. But stress, it should be recognized, is actually a natural part of life. Any time we're confronted by change (which is constant), we experience stress—the body's reaction to any demand placed on it, regardless of the source. How we react—whether we consciously manage the stress or let it rule us—determines whether it becomes a growth opportunity or a health threat. Completely eliminating stress is unrealistic. Managing and reducing stress, though, are realistic.

Stress physically affects the body in a manner that sends ripples through our emotional, psychological, intellectual, and spiritual "bodies." Short-term stress is familiar. Someone unexpectedly jumps out at you and your heart races, your muscles tense for flight, your gasp expands your chest, which becomes tight. Over the long term, that physical response can become the status quo. Sitting at a computer day after day, your shoulders tend to feel more like a rock formation than a part of your body. Then, when confronted by a co-worker or a family member who angers you, you'll likely take shallower and shallower breaths, tighten your chest, and fold your fingers into a fist without even realizing it.

Without conscious relief, these daily stress cycles accumulate and activate externally—back pain, headaches, jaw ache, stiff neck, muscles so tense you can barely move. This happens so gradually that many people simply adapt to the pain that accompanies these unnatural physical states, oblivious to the freedom of motion they've lost—until injury sends a wake-up call.

When we're young, our bodies have a tremendous ability to recover from stress, whether it's long hours at a desk or a nonstop lifestyle that burns day into night. As we age, though, our bodies require more time and help to recover from the same stresses. Whatever age we are, most of us can benefit from learning how to recognize the signs of chronic tension and how to release it. This is when modes of bodywork can make the difference.

Stress Check

Take inventory of your body, and find where you store tension. Be aware of your head, face, and neck. Scrunch up your forehead, and then relax it fully. Roll your head from shoulder to shoulder. Feel tense? Take a deep breath and release the tension wherever you find it. Move your awareness down your body, to your shoulders, arms, hands, chest, upper back, lower back, legs, ankles, and feet. Does your level of tension change depending on whether you're at home or work? The morning, afternoon, or evening?

When I first started my own personal stress check, I discovered that I not only tensed in reaction to an event—I also tensed in *anticipation* of stress. There were days when I was all armored up, even before I had any reason to be. We don't wear real armor against threats, the way they did in medieval times, so we protect ourselves with tensed bodies and hyper alert minds. Body language (crossed arms, a stiff back, a rock-hard jaw) and emotional defensiveness that says "that's not possible" and "don't you dare ask" before we've even heard the question are ways we shut out and shut down. While we're acting out of perceived need for self-protection, we end up shutting out the potential for new experiences and a deeper connection with others, as well as the chance to live our emotions honestly.

After regular chiropractic, energetic bodywork, and massage, my neck turned from a washboard into a pliable, relaxed circuit between my head and heart. As the deep muscle knots in my chest relaxed, my breathing became deeper, and I felt as if real armor fell away from my heart. What a weight off. The years of stress that had strangled my muscles began melting away, opening the door to emotional and psychological changes that complemented the methods discussed in chapter 5. Feelings became more immediate and clear. I felt more caring to the people around me. I felt plugged in to my Higher Power. As the numbing armor fell away, my Inner Team stretched themselves, and I was able to feel more fully than I had in years.

Our bodies store and hold emotional and psychological memories more literally than most realize or understand. While great progress can be made with traditional psychological approaches, I've found that bodywork can also facilitate the healing and release of nonphysical challenges. Consistent bodywork, in fact, makes a clear connection to my emotional, psychological, and spiritual well-being easier to maintain and grow.

Bodywork Bonanza

Methods of bodywork focus on various types of pressure, stimulation, and manipulation of muscles, soft tissue, and bones. Below is a short list of some of the more available types of supportive bodywork. To learn more about what will best suit your needs or to find a reputable practitioner, ask for recommendations from friends, check with professional associations, do research (the Resources section offers some starting points), or check with local wellness directories.

+ **Chiropractic** focuses on whole-body wellness through manipulating the spine; often combined with muscular treatment.

+ **Osteopathy** focuses on correcting body mechanics through treatment of muscles and bones.

+ **Massage** (Swedish, Esalen, neuromuscular, deep-tissue, sports) stimulates circulation and enhances healing in specific ways depending on the technique.

+ **Acupuncture** stimulates energy flow by applying thin needles to specific points on the body.

+ **Acupressure and Shiatsu** are techniques of finger pressure massage to stimulate energy flow.

+ **Structural integration therapies,** such as Rolfing, Alexander Technique, Rosen Method, Feldenkrais Method, and Trager, facilitate more natural and greater freedom of movement through various combinations of muscular, skeletal, massage, and psychological techniques.

+ **Integrative therapies,** such as CranioSacral Visceral Balancing and Reflexology, are touch techniques that affect specific points in the body to stimulate the body's own rebalancing abilities.

Three-Minute Massage

I augment a weekly massage from a therapist with a three-minute self-massage every morning just before showering. Adapted from Deepak Chopra's "Seduction of the Spirit" workshop, I've used it for several years as an energizing ritual almost every morning. This massage releases tension, increases circulation, and improves skin texture. (For more on this routine, see Chopra's *Perfect Health.*)

+ Using sesame oil, almond oil, or another massage oil you prefer, pour a tablespoon of oil on your scalp. (If you prefer not to put oil on your hair, you can do this part of the routine as a dry massage.) Using the flat of your hands (not your fingertips), vigorously massage in the oil. Cover your entire scalp with small circular strokes, as though you were lathering shampoo. Move to your face, temples, and ears, massaging more gently.

+ Apply a little oil to your hands and massage your neck, front and back, then your shoulders.

+ Vigorously massage your arms, using a circular motion at the shoulders and elbows, and long back-and-forth motions on the long parts. Don't forget your hands, palms, and between your fingers.

+ It's important to be less vigorous when you get to your torso. Using large, gentle circular motions, massage your chest, stomach, and lower abdomen. Use straight up-and-down motions over the breastbone.

+ Vigorously massage your legs just as you did your arms—circular at the ankles and knees, straight back and forth on the long parts.

+ With a dab of oil, vigorously massage your feet. Be careful not to slip if you're doing this in the shower, and don't forget your toes.

Bodywork at Work

The more connections you make between what your body needs and the right remedial bodywork, the more ways you'll discover to integrate wellness in the workplace. Does your body feel loose when you come to work only to tighten within the first few hours? Ask yourself, Is there something about my environment that I can change to reduce stress?

People who work at computers commonly encounter posture challenges. If that's your case, try adjusting your chair so you're looking straight ahead, not up or down, at your screen. Make sure your arms form a ninety-degree angle when typing. If this isn't possible, invest in an ergonomically correct chair, or request one from your supervisor. When you consider that many of us spend as much time sitting at our desks as we do sleeping, a chair that helps rather than hurts is a no-brainer benefit. Try a footrest to elevate your feet and discourage crossing your legs. This helps maintain healthy circulation in your legs.

Keyboard mavens often encounter problems with forearm and hand tension. Maybe you need a better wrist support for your keyboard. Articulated keyboards that flex in the middle can help. Relief can sometimes be as simple as taking more frequent breaks to stretch. Rapidly opening and closing your hands fifty times, or shaking your hands loosely, can greatly improve energy circulation. If you're on the fly, in and out of cars with briefcases and other luggage, do your back a favor and pack light, and distribute weight evenly among your luggage. If you're a shoulder-strapper, remember the 10 percent rule: the weight your shoulder supports should be no more than 10 percent of your body weight. A few visits to a chiropractor and a massage therapist for an out-of-whack neck may reveal the culprit to be the time you spend with your head craned over bracing the phone against your shoulder. The remedy is as simple as a hands-free headset. Look around your workplace. There are ways to change your environment so that it's kinder to your body.

Physical Wellness—Within Reach

As you become more aware of your bodily needs, you'll discover more and better ways to answer them through better fuel, exercise, sleep, and bodywork. It's never all-or-nothing—a great thing to remember during those inevitable blips. It's also not about what others think is best for you. Self-knowledge begins with embracing your own body in all its potential and with all its flaws. That leads to self-love, living and moving forward with the body helping the rest of your Inner Team help you feel the best you can—whatever that means for *you*.

Changes can be implemented gradually or quickly. It's consistency over the years that yields the real benefits. For me, the perks of greater physical wellness aren't about a dream of physical immortality or endless youth, but rather the added quality miles I have to spend with family and friends and accomplishing my mission. And the subsequent energy, clarity, and tranquillity are great traveling companions during the game of life.

5

Fit for Your Mission: Wellness of Intellect and Psyche

THANKS TO PHYSICAL wellness, one member of your Inner Team is now firmly in the game. Now it's time to take a look at teammates associated with the mind: intellect and psyche. Because these aren't weighable or measurable bodies made of atoms, it may be difficult to grasp what it means for them to be "fit." But as you'll learn, you'll know it when you feel it.

Many go through life acting and reacting, pulled by our instincts, habits, and desires, or listening to what others tell us is the right way to think or to feel. For a lucky few, this pinball approach to life leads to peak experiences and happiness. The rest of us, however, need deliberate direction to optimize our intellectual and psychological fitness.

The Healthy Intellect

The dictionary defines *intellect* as "the power of knowing as distinguished from the power to feel and to will." The digital age chants the mantra "Knowledge is power," and indeed knowledge keys open doors (in the inner world as well as the outer) that cannot be accessed otherwise. A telling sign that the Industrial Age has given way to the Information Age

Intellectual Wellness

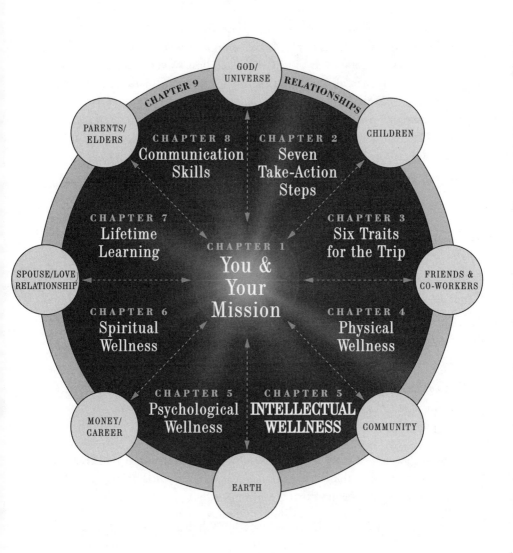

emerged in 1991, the first year that companies spent more on communications and computing gear than on mining, construction, farm, and industrial equipment.

Consequently, at every turn, our heads are bombarded with TV news, radio talk shows, the Internet, books, magazines, newspapers, seminars, audio tapes, videotapes, DVDs, PDAs—endless waves of digital and analog, zeros and ones, all designed to bring us more information faster. As the millennium overtakes us, a critical mass of people is standing up to ask the obvious: Is all this information a boon or a burden? How much useful data is wasted because we simply don't have the energy or headroom to take it in? How many broadcasts do we see without really grasping?

Tackling Overload

The words, facts, and figures crashing over our lives inspire an out-of-control, overwhelmed, sense of overstimulation. The burden of that crush of information is a huge factor in creating stress and burnout, two major job hazards that have come of age in the last two decades. It's estimated that one issue of the *New York Times* holds more information than the average seventeenth century English citizen encountered in a whole lifetime.

People's ability to *understand* information often lags behind their ability to *get* information, and too much too fast, it turns out, leads to confusion. "Data smog" is the term that author David Shenk coined for it. "Data smog is not just the pile of unsolicited catalogs and spam arriving daily in our home and electronic mailboxes. It is also information we pay handsomely for, that we crave—the seductive, mesmerizing, quick-cut television ads and the twenty-four-hour-up-to-the-minute news flashes. It is the faxes we request as well as the ones we don't; it is the misdialed numbers and the drippy sales calls we get during dinnertime; but it is also the Web sites we eagerly visit before and after dinner, the pile of magazines we pore through every month, and the dozens of channels we flip through whenever we get a free moment."

Only in the last fifty years has information overload even appeared on our landscape, creating a gap between our evolutionary ability to process information and the necessity to make sense of the media maelstrom. The models of the world that many of us were raised on don't always hold up in the face of constantly shifting paradigms. As a baby boomer, the intellectual habits I picked up in school couldn't possibly prepare me for the technological changes that bring the world to my Minneapolis doorstep every hour of every day. Inevitably there's a breaking point. The question becomes, How do we get out from under the churning waves and up on top of the surf, where the view is clear, the ride smooth? Part of the answer is the crucial connection between having the information and understanding what can be done with it.

One woman attends a time-management seminar, returns to her workplace, stashes the seminar materials deep in a drawer, and goes back to doing things the way she's always done them. Another woman at the same seminar arrives at work the next day, reviews her notes, singles out a few ideas she learned the day before, and puts them in play. People can be quick to mention how many seminars they've attended, or how many magazines they read. But what's germane is how many ideas they glean and actually turn into meaningful life change.

America is awed by those who can inhale vast quantities of information and regurgitate it at will. What's actually useful, though, is the ability to convert that storehouse of information into knowledge. That happens only when we act on the information in daily life. And when that experience is consistent with our mission and wants, the result is wisdom—the stock-in-trade of successful self-coaching.

Information that can't be converted into knowledge crowds the mind like excess baggage. Learning to discern and discard it turns information into "exformation," a term coined by Danish science writer Tor Nørretranders. Think of it as mental housekeeping, a way to keep the decks clear for incoming landings that you need to get you to your next destination.

Passion of the Intellect

Intellectual passion is one of the greatest forces shaping the world. Sometimes derided as nerdy, intellectual curiosity nevertheless is innovation's gestation pool. Before you fashion something new with your hands, you must first behold it in your mind's eye. The longing to match internal vision with external invention is as ancient as it is modern, something I understood when I saw the pyramids of Egypt, built with intellectual passion and ingenuity as much as with sweat and stone. "Passion of the intellect," wrote Leonardo da Vinci, "makes the fruit of sensuality." Moreover, intellectual curiosity is a component of charisma, and it's a habit that will keep you sharp into your later years. Florida resident Eleanor Wishart, for example, attributes her mental clarity at the age of ninety-two to her passion for duplicate bridge, a game she has played nearly every day since taking it up in earnest at the age of seventy-nine. There is also most certainly a spiritual component to the intellect as well. People who have had near-death experiences commonly return to life spiritually awakened and fueled by a vastly increased hunger for knowledge and desire for intellectual pursuits.

There's no shortage of food that nourishes the intellect. The danger is in gorging on intellectual eats at the expense of emotional, spiritual, and bodily health. Most of us, in the natural course of our day, spend a great deal of time on intellectual pursuits. Even then, we need to ask ourselves if we're tapping our full intellectual power. Within that answer lies another piece of the information-management puzzle.

Half-Brain-Think

For years I focused on the linear, logical strength of intellect. What is sometimes referred to as "left brain" thinking was essential for meeting the morphing challenges of my growing business. Every three years or so, the company would outgrow my ability to lead it. Each time I came upon a new cycle, I had to ratchet up my intellectual skills in organizational strategic planning, problem solving, communicating, and delegating as well as other skills that were more personal—goal-setting, planning, organizing, time competency.

These structured approaches often fueled the tank that kept me on the road. Likewise, they would sometimes make me cough and sputter. I began to wonder what I was missing. I discovered that part of it was the other half of my intellect.

Whole-Brain-Think

Like too many businesspeople, I never considered myself a creative person. Instead I saw myself as a straight-ahead thinker. The word *creative* brings to mind painters, musicians, sculptors, designers, not businesspeople. Then one day I was telling a friend about my drawing a Tires Plus organizational chart. Instead of the usual structure of hierarchical boxes, the chart is a floating series of concentric circles, like ripples in a pond all emanating from a common source.

Rather than the typical from-the-top-down attitude, the chart suggests a center-outward approach. "Wow," he said. "What an incredibly creative idea. How did you think of that?"

How indeed? I'm certainly not the first to re-envision an organization's relationship with its employees and customers. By finding the answer, however, I tapped a part of my intellect that went much deeper than simply putting together known quantities in order to get another known quantity. Logical thought says one plus one equals two. Creative thought says one plus one can be whatever you want it to equal. Logical thought too often narrows possibilities, while creative thought expands them. At the end of the day, a combination approach will illuminate the best solutions.

To greater and lesser degrees, everyone has access to both ways of thinking. As unwritten law seems to dictate that creativity is left to the artists, while the business of business is given over to the creatively challenged. Obviously it's not that simple. Just as an artist may employ principles of geometry to construct his paintings, we can use creativity as a tool in business.

If you've always thought of yourself as solely logical, as I did, wake up your intellect's creative side. Soon the freedom to try new things will be yours. Now, instead of "processing information," I think of *composing pictures* with information. In problem-solving with my Tires Plus teammates, I often use a white board to visualize the paths and options we could take to get from our issue to potential solutions. Listing positives and negatives along each path helps us reach a creative solution faster—and sometimes the answer isn't one path or another but a fusion of many.

Without adding creativity to your problem-solving recipe, it's hard to make a cake that captures the shifting tastes of tomorrow's world. Conversely, without a little organization on the creative side, chaos will ensure that you're distracted and your message is muddled. You're better served when you call on your whole intellect.

Shhh...I Can't Hear Myself Think!

Are you ready to call on your intellect? Now the question is, can it hear you? With millions of information bytes running through your head every day, your intellect is hardly stagnant. You know the feelings. Frantic thoughts put sleep just out of reach. You wake up with your mind racing. You find yourself talking to someone and thinking about something else. Allowing thoughts to run roughshod leads to a lack of focus that can hurt both work and relationships.

Quieting your mind is the first step toward regaining focus and calling on the full power of your intellect. With today's hectic pace, this may seem like a luxury. But it's a necessity. Unless you get out of the forest in order to see the trees, burnout may be only a spark away.

I let go of my racing thoughts by stepping into one of three different levels of relaxation. The first level involves relaxing activities like a day at the beach, dinner with friends and family, playing a board game, walking, traveling. These things give my body and mind a partial reprieve from the stress loops I've developed over a variety of issues. These reprieves, however, are only partial, because even during a walk or a board game, I'm still churning thought after thought—which inevitably includes the current source of stress: *I'm really nervous about that presentation I have to give tomorrow. I shouldn't have responded to my teammate that way this morning...*

For more direct relief, I move to second- and third-level relaxation. The second level is what I call moving meditations, practices that can ease a person into a relaxed yet mentally alert state. Deep breathing, yoga, basketball, running—all are my moving meditations. My sons, for instance, have their own moving meditations: Trent plays the mandolin and basketball, while Chris plays the piano and runs. Others choose gardening, hiking, or fishing for mental tonic. Think of an activity that puts you into a relaxed state of mind, and then schedule it into your week.

Directed relaxation, such as still meditation (to be discussed in chapter 6), is the third level. Others find that guided visualizations, biofeedback, and hypnosis are effective avenues for slowing and focusing the intellect.

Taking a mental break through any of these levels of relaxation yields many benefits. First, like our physical body, intellect performs better after it's had a breather. Second, relaxing a racing mind clears the airwaves for messages from others—from loved ones, from your wiser self, from your Higher Source. In other words, you hear others more clearly, which makes you more present with them, and you hear your own internal wisdom more clearly, which helps you make better decisions. A still lake more clearly reflects the sky. When the lake is disturbed, the sky is distorted.

Care and Feeding of the Intellect

So how do you rev your intellect? The day-in, day-out grind of our familiar patterns wear ruts that can make us stale. Refresh your mind by exposing yourself to subjects and ways of thinking that you aren't normally asked to. Here are a few suggestions (consult the Resources section of this book for more):

+ **Learn something new.** Take courses on subjects you've always wanted to learn about. Challenge yourself to think in new directions, not just the same-old-same-old.

+ **Play games to stay alert.** Crossword puzzles and board games are great mental aerobics, not to mention a lot of fun. My partner, Mary, completes the *New York Times* crossword puzzle nearly every day, and we love word games like Boggle.

+ **Suspend decision-making.** When stuck on a problem, let go of the need for a solution for a set period of time. Taking the pressure off frees up your creative mind and gives your wiser self room to get through. Suspending the urge to make decisions quiets the voice of criticism that might otherwise step in and choke your wellspring of creative solutions.

+ **Quiet your mind.** Relax. Breathe deeply. Count to one hundred. Repeat a short, calming phrase twenty times. Take a short walk. Do whatever it takes to decelerate your cycles of thought and shift your awareness.

+ **Change your surroundings.** Clean your desk, hang up a new picture, or move the furniture. If you have a chair in your office where guests sit, try sitting there a few minutes observing the view from the other side of the desk.

+ **Do something that you're not good at,** or something that will make you look silly. It was helpful for me to begin letting go of ego and its associated desire to stay on the ground of familiar activities. Keeping ego in check frees the creative side of intellect.

+ **Appreciate your efforts.** Opening yourself to new learning can be both energizing and humbling. Congratulate yourself for taking the risk.

+ **Do occasional burnout self-exams.** If you're in an unshakable funk, or if you're constantly overwhelmed, intellectual health may feel out of reach. But it isn't. Ask for the help you need from professionals, peers, family, and friends.

Jump the Hurdles with a Fit Intellect

You'll find other intellectual fitness tips throughout chapters 2, 7, and 8, and no doubt you're exposed to innumerable ways of expanding intellect in the course of your average week. Of all the members of your Inner Team, intellect is spotlighted the most by virtue of our meritocratic society. Even so, the balance between intellect's logical and creative sides often leaves something to be desired. Although you may have a powerful intellect, consider the potential of a *fully* functioning intellect.

An intellect firing on all cylinders propels a person in an approach to the world that is more passionate and less fearful. The magnetism of structure and strategy, of logic and creativity, can launch us into an intellectual state well beyond our normal limitations. In those magical moments, everything is possible.

The Healthy Psyche

Psyche, vessel of emotional and psychological wellness, is the third member of your Inner Team. The dictionary defines *psychology* as "the science of mind and behavior." As the center of thought, emotion, and behavior—unconscious as well as conscious—psyche is the endlessly fascinating part of us that translates inner thoughts into outer behavior. Understanding psyche is in large part understanding the game of life.

How we think and feel about ourselves guides the way we act. Just as a coach sets a strategy before it can be put in play, psyche sets certain inner patterns that manifest in the plays of day-to-day life. Our level of psychological wellness determines in large part the quality of our relationships and our work, and thus the quality of our lives.

Freud defined mental health simply as the ability to love and work. Psychologist Daniel Goleman asserts that in the workplace it's not IQ that determines an outstanding worker but what he calls "EI"—Emotional Intelligence—which includes such aspects as self-control, empathy, inspiration, and cooperation.

For me, psychological well-being is a firm handshake between healthy thoughts and feelings on the inside and positive behaviors and habits on the outside. When in this groove, I act out of a desire to fulfill my mission rather than play games for attention or power. I can observe myself and see how my actions either hurt or help me and others. Then I can make course adjustments to keep my well-being on an upward track.

As a word, *psyche* is associated with soul, self, and mind. Its origins are more expansive, however, carrying associations from ancient Greek and Sanskrit that conjure up ideas of soul, breath, and elemental life-force. It's a foundation that builds a bridge between intellect and spirit. For brevity's sake, I'll use "psyche" as shorthand for the psychological and emotional aspects of who we are.

The verb *psych,* as used in the phrase "psych up," means "to make psychologically ready especially for performance"—in, I might add, the game of life. In the psyched-up state, we perceive roads of insight on ourselves that weren't otherwise obvious. Instead of sleepwalking through life, psychology shakes us awake to be more conscious of every passing moment.

For years I tried to intellectually outmaneuver the emotional pain of unhealthy relationships and disconnection with my inner nature, not to mention a higher source. Contrary to the assumptions I held prior to 1989,

Psychological Wellness

a quick intellect cannot make up for stunted psychological and emotional growth. Sooner or later, emotions undermine intellect. My maneuvers ended with the crash described earlier, which in many ways was a good thing. A better understanding of my psychology and behavior has spurred growth in every other area of my life, including intellect. What took some time to understand is that by suppressing my psyche's development, I was unwittingly retarding my Inner Team's full development.

Why did I spend so much energy avoiding this aspect of my life? Simple. While my intellect was familiar turf, my psyche and emotions were dark, unexplored caves. The rules of intellectual pursuit don't necessarily work in the realm of psychology. Even though it's a part of me, encountering my psychological side was at first like touching down in a foreign land whose language I didn't speak.

Do you have personal behaviors or attitudes that are blocking your winning game plan? Do you believe that your key plays could be more successful if only...? Are there others in your life whose behavior you'd like to understand more fully? The ideas in this chapter explore the potentials of psychological growth and education. Whether applicable to your own life or as a perspective on others around you, learning about the dynamics of psyche can help us appreciate the awe-inspiring dimensions of being human.

Sources of Psyche

Our behavior grows from soil chock-full of elements—genes, social and economic environments, and the influence of parents, siblings, and peers. Fascinating debates rage over the relative influence of these factors, but most psychologists agree that combinations of these forces etch indelible behavior patterns, some beneficial and some we could do without.

When behaviors today stand in the way of your mission, change can begin by identifying their source. A behavior's origin reveals volumes about what influences our lives today and points to healthier behavior for tomorrow. But no matter who or what planted the seed of a behavior, we can change the course of it through our own decisions today. Cultivate it? Prune it? Uproot it? If a behavior doesn't serve us, regardless of where it came from, it's our choice to change it. Change, not blame, is the name of the game.

According to child-development experts, much of our self-concept congeals by age six, when we're utterly dependent on others. A child's impressionable young mind is fertile ground for people and the environment to impress lessons and habits. Consider a child's size and strength relative to an adult's. Consider how little access a child has to physical and emotional nourishment—unless others offer it. Children can't kick back in a coffeehouse or find a new relationship if things aren't working out. And parents come equipped for their jobs with the legacies of their own parents. Family patterns are often as deep as all the generations of a family tree, bringing good and bad along with each new growth.

Peers also have a definitive influence on shaping a child's behavior and attitudes. Some kids are virtually raised by their peers, while others bond less with those their own age. We can all relate to wanting to fit in with a group, hoping to be considered cool rather than a fool. Especially in the early years, when identity and self-confidence are developing, kids may adjust the way they think, dress, walk, and talk to copy the peers they admire and magnify certain parts of their own personalities.

Emotional Replays

Don't underestimate the power of parenting, however. Even with peers, the values and principles we learn in the families we grew up in often guide us unconsciously toward choosing certain peers rather than others. We also often interact with our peers to some degree based on the behavior we learned from our parents and siblings, depending on age and circumstance.

Consider that adults have many options when it comes to getting what we need; a baby has only two: to cry or, exhausted if he doesn't get a response, to quit crying. This same cycle—the call for help and the resigned "I give up"—sometimes acts itself out in adult life, if on a more subtle level. How many people complain that their husband or girlfriend never listens? "When I ask, I get no answer—so there's no use in asking." I learned from Brenda, my psychologist, that if in a relationship we ask for what we need and we're not heard, we often either withdraw from the relationship and search elsewhere for what we need, or we abandon our emotions altogether, suppressing the need behind the pleas.

Any number of psychological challenges—blue moods, overwhelming stress, fear of failure, low self-esteem, inflated ego, compulsive behavior—begin with the basic emotional disconnection that some experience as young children. Regardless of whether we're still conscious of these early impressions and their psychophysical effects, our bodies and minds store them. They become prisms through which each new situation is evaluated and acted upon. At first I was blind to the fact that the defenses I constructed in childhood didn't work in my adult life. For example, as a kid I developed a smiling defense—"everything's just fine"—to shield myself from issues too big for me to confront. Once I was older and had more resources to deal with the issues, I still found myself with that smile pasted on, years past its usefulness. Many people inadvertently carry behavior based on outmoded frames of reference into situations that call for very different responses.

As adults, many of us begin to look back on our childhoods. If you look long and hard enough, what you got in abundance and what was strictly rationed become clearer and clearer. This is the crossroads of change where we can reroute and head down a road of healthier possibilities.

Roadblocks to Self-Discovery

I know the fear. Taking a step down the road of self-discovery sounds like it should be easy, but caught between what was and what might be, the future can look dark. On some level, it may seem easier to let our inadequacies lie, hiding them as best we can, hoping people won't notice.

But right in back of the fear was the pain of behavior that stood in the way of my mission. As scary as moving forward seemed, the thought of turning back was worse.

Intellectual Rationalizations

Why is it so painful? Distinguishing and remedying harmful behavior often obligates us to come face to face with the past and events that aren't exactly a walk in the park. This is when people tend to play the intellect card. "Hey, I don't need this shrink stuff," people will say. "I have plenty of ways I can solve this. I just need to strategize better. I'm the master of my universe." Intellect can be crafty. I know. I intellectually outmaneuvered my emotions in the short term, only to be trumped in the end by my psyche and its cache of ill-serving behaviors. We can only outthink emotions for so long. As the saying goes, pay me now or pay me later. I wish I'd paid earlier.

Spiritual Rationalizations

Some people try to bypass psychological issues and go straight to spirit, hoping that God will solve everything. "Let go and let God" is the common refrain. That sounds good, to be sure. But if it isn't reinforced by our efforts, we may be back to asking God to help us win the lottery even though we haven't bought a ticket. Put simply, God won't do for us what we can do for ourselves with God's help. Uplifting spiritual feelings can mask the psychological pain of our dysfunction for a while, but sooner or later it may be no more beneficial than hiding behind intellect.

I don't believe it would have been possible for me to begin to know God if I hadn't begun to know myself more fully. That meant taking responsibility for who I was, emotionally and psychologically. For me, psychological clarity was a prerequisite to—not a result of—being more spirit-filled. To my way of thinking, I'm not spirit-filled if I confuse surrendering personal problems to God with dumping the responsibility to face my own roadblocks.

Not My Fault!

When my rationalizations didn't cut it, I always could find a scapegoat. "Ultimately I'm not responsible here," I'd say. "It's not my fault." Then who *was* at fault? Parents? Colleagues? The neighbor? The position of the sun in the astrological chart? The economy? God? At work, managers and supervisors are fat targets. There's no end to people and excuses at our disposal if we want to pass the buck. In modern office parlance, it's called "blamestorming." But if we accept anything less than our full responsibility, we blow the chance to educate and upgrade our psychological well-being. Our psyches can shift blame, but we can't shift responsibility.

As I studied my behavior, I began to clearly see my role in rocky relationships, both personal and business. Without question, tangos take two. I used to tag any psychological insight with, "Wow, I wish *she* would have heard that," rather than accepting that I was the one who needed that insight. Gradually I learned to resist the urge to shift the inquiry away from myself and onto what I couldn't control (other people), and keep the spotlight on what I *could* control, namely my own behavior. That's where real change begins. As I changed, people responded differently to me. The treacherous tangos I was locked into began shifting as I changed my tune. Doors of progress opened, and I became closer to some people and let go of others.

The Comfort of the Familiar

We are creatures of habit. What's familiar to us out of repetition, even if it's unhealthy and causes pain, offers a strange shelter of comfort. Many of us get attached to negative patterns, not because we believe they're nourishing, but because they keep us on familiar ground. Change, even if it's for the better, always travels alongside the potential for discomfort. Fear of the future, guilt about the past, feeling imprisoned by vanity, selfishness, desires, conceit—all of it can lock us into pernicious cycles. Fear engenders more fear. Guilt is always set to spew another internal lecture. And ego always wants more. If we stay in these negative cycles just to preserve the comfort of the familiar, we're left with no time or energy to jump the ruts and find the grooves.

Too, Too Strong Is Sometimes Wrong

One of the tallest roadblocks standing between you and help may be...you. It's a familiar fact that people are often raised to believe that asking for help, especially emotional or psychological help, is a sign of weakness. Perhaps it's the particularly American imperative of rugged individualism or the "never say you don't know" mindset. Whatever the cause, admitting that we don't have all the answers strikes a blow to the core of many people's self-worth. In fact, this is the first step to seeking a deeper psychological strength.

The brittle thinking that keeps us from asking for help is macho at best and dangerous at worst. After years of believing I could do it all, I discovered that I couldn't reach in without reaching out.

Expanding—Not Shrinking—Psyche

It's a curious paradox. People have teachers and mentors for their bodies, intellects, and spirits, but many cringe at the notion of psychological guidance. In fact, advice is a booming growth industry of the future, full of business consultants, motivational speakers, spiritual and religious advisors, personal trainers, cooking instructors, and golf pros. Yet there's an unmistakable change of tone when someone considers the advice of a "shrink." Despite being home to some of the most cutting-edge psychological education in the world, America still suffers from a cultural prohibition against seeking that type of advice and counsel.

Dismissing the benefits of psychology because I don't have a serious mental illness is similar to saying that I don't have to see a doctor because I don't need surgery. Psychological challenges come in all shapes and sizes. Some people, it's true, are victims of serious mental conditions, but the vast majority of people who could benefit from psychological education each year have milder issues that, while generally not as life threatening, are still no less deserving of attention.

In order to reach peak wellness in every area of my life, I needed to shift gears from reactive crisis management into proactive, preventive education.

That includes treating my psyche. Varying degrees of education can profit anyone. There's no shame in seeking help, whether it comes from browsing the health section at the bookstore, jumping online into a Newsnet health forum, or taking a few hours on the couch.

A Damaged Car Won't Fix Itself

"A damaged car won't fix itself," says Earnie Larsen, a Minneapolis-based behaviorist. A car with a dented fender stays a car with a dented fender until the dent is pounded out. It's true, after a while you don't even notice the dent. It becomes part of the car, like the curve of the hood or the color of the paint. A look around reveals other cars with dents. Soon you begin to believe that that's how cars were meant to be—dented. Don't they come off the assembly line that way?

The point, obviously, is that we can become so used to our dents that they become indistinguishable from our character. We operate with them whether or not they help us. Rather than fix the dents, we frequently ignore them or work around them, sometimes torturously—whatever it takes to avoid arduous change. But the cost of stasis is inevitably greater than the price of change.

The first glimpse of my dented fender was troubling. Underneath the pain of my three-ring wake-up call was a realization that though I had felt loved as a child, I had responded to certain family conditions by developing anxieties that were only compounded in adulthood.

In hindsight, marrying at nineteen was traumatic. In some ways, my wife and I grew up together, two small-town Indiana kids learning how to be parents and live on our own—before we were old enough to vote. We did the best we could with the little we knew. While my friends hit the beach to relax, I worked every hour I could to make ends meet. All of a sudden, summers were no longer luxuriant months of lifeguarding. I had to take the highest-paying job I came across, which turned out to be as a janitor on one of the Ford Motor Company's assembly lines, two hours away in Indianapolis. "Cleaner Number One, get to Section Number Four, immediately!" I can still hear the intercom commanding me to run with my mop, pail, and broom and clean up a spill. In hindsight, those cleanups were nothing compared to the emotional spills that were yet to come.

College loans hanging over me, a son in the cradle, and another five years later, scrambling to graduate and make a living—not exactly the kind of emotional testing ground that breeds security. At twenty-nine, I left a job at Shell Oil to start my own company, wholly naïve about what I was getting myself into. Until it was too late. The only way out was forward, with plenty of fear along the way. On my first day off Shell's payroll, I took my sons to Dairy Queen only to find myself wondering how I was going to have money for the next ice cream cone. Automatic checks on the first and fifteenth of the month, a company car, an expense account, profit sharing— instantly, all were relics.

An obsessive work ethic and an uncontrollable perfectionist streak pushed and pulled me through those years. I benefited in office politics from the peacemaker act I'd learned as a kid, negotiating detantes between people close to me. "I think what he's really saying..." I'd suggest smoothly. "Can you do this for her?" I'd recommend stealthily. "I think she'd be happier if you did." But this habit also revealed itself as a tendency to control both scenarios and the people in them.

As a father, I also couldn't resist playing the peacemaker. Once when my boys were young adults, they were arguing and I began, as I had a million times, to step in to "help." In tandem, they turned to me and said, "We can handle it, Dad!" It was a shocking recognition that they *could* handle it, that it was time I let go of that burdensome role—that, in fact, they'd never asked me to play it in the first place. Solving other people's problems had always seemed an admirable duty. In fact, I was erasing their opportunity to learn from their own challenges—and draining myself in the process. Control, it turns out, is a lot of work. Once I began refraining from playing Mr. Fix-it, I actually learned how to be genuinely helpful rather than offering assistance out of obligation. It can simply mean listening to someone brainstorm his own solutions. Other times it means offering a solution, pointing the way, and stepping back to let him get there on his own.

My long-standing personality paradox—the disconnection between my outer mask of confidence and inner world of fear—was painfully real. It was time to come out from behind my Cheshire grin. Yet I was firmly in denial; there was so much I was unwilling to admit to myself. It seemed obvious: the more honest I could be with myself, the more honest I could be with others. The only way was to replace suppression with genuine expression.

I reached the terminus of my fear-inspired bearing after several years and various types of counseling and education. I'd finally graduated from simply being the actor in my life to being the director, with my Higher Power as executive producer. I was the coach as well as the player. I did this by finding the perspective of a more detached observer looking upon my life, the way a coach watches a team. I saw the strengths and the weaknesses, with less of the emotional charge of defensiveness or denial. This coaching skill offered a clear path to productive habits, and shunted me away from some of the empty ones.

Searching back through my childhood, I could easily find incidents that had produced long-lasting emotional ripples. It was tempting to play the victim, to think, *Aha! That's why I am the way I am!* Understanding and changing behavior patterns can be aided by coming to terms with their origins; otherwise we can be hopelessly stuck in the past. Yet how and why I act the way I act, while important, is ultimately less important than asking what I am willing to do to change what doesn't serve me. You have the ability to change if you wish to, and you can act on it to the degree that you're ready to do so.

Imagine all the positive effects on our family and work lives if we all let go of poisonous patterns and replaced them with healthy dynamics. Breaking the cycle of behaviors that don't serve us—taking our genetic best and leaving the rest—is one of the greatest gifts we can give ourselves, our progeny, and our workplace families.

In case you think this talk is too distant or unconnected to daily reality, consider the epidemic of stress and stress-related illness in our nation. Many people think stress is all about what's "out there," but in fact stress is generally more about what's "in here." If we look for it, says my partner, Mary, "there's no scarcity of things we can find to create stress." Yet it seems a common theme among people who live long lives that they refuse to sweat the little stuff and have a great ability to roll with the punches.

To a large extent, how stress affects you depends on how you affect it. And how you affect it depends in part on your psychological wellness. If you grew up as a child who was always told to do whatever you could to please people, how are you going to say no to your boss when she doubles your already over-the-top workload? You may blame it on the boss, but to what extent are you just playing out the role you've always played?

Crossing the Line

The millions of Americans who suffer from compulsive and addictive behaviors bear witness to a potentially even more challenging face of dysfunction. Disconnected from an honest understanding of our internal motivations, we become ripe for abuse of romance, food, drugs, alcohol, nicotine, gambling, shopping, work, and sex (to name only the most common "substances" of choice).

Whether behavior falls into the realm of healthy moderation, compulsion, or addiction is a matter of internal degree. Many people, for example, have a lot of fun gambling, and do so responsibly. They're able to set reasonable limits on how much money they'll risk, and they're able to walk away with a sense of satisfaction. The difference, which can't always be observed from the outside, is the shift from enjoying an activity within reasonable limits into the relentless craving for more.

A person who has crossed the line into compulsive or addictive behavior becomes willing to risk reputation, career, relationships, and financial security in pursuit of the behavior. When the relationship with an activity or object (food, sex, gambling, work) gets in the way of our cherished relationships with people, it's a clear sign that our connection to ourselves and others has been compromised. Many people need outside help to break the cycle and to understand the specific dynamics that distinguish these behaviors.

Alcoholism is perhaps the most widely recognized of all addictions. Gambling addiction is becoming more of an issue as lotteries and gaming venues proliferate across the country. Workaholism, discussed in chapter 9, is an addiction many people don't recognize because being overly productive is usually a benefit for employers, and hard work is socially acceptable. Addictions to food and shopping used to hit primarily women, but with the shifts in social and gender roles, we're seeing firsthand that these and other addictions and compulsions are "equal opportunity."

While the recovery movement and pioneering twelve-step programs have helped bring addiction out of the closet, sex addiction in particular is still surrounded by misunderstanding. Often confused with deviant sex, but not at all the same thing, sex addiction is harder to detect than alcoholism or compulsive overeating. Linked with proof of appeal and virility rather than a lack of health, sex addiction can lead to situations that put both personal and public lives at great risk, a high price to pay for living with the disorder.

Recovery programs and centers offer a more structured way to address the psychological issues specific to high-risk, addictive, and self-destructive behaviors, and offer the support of professionals trained in these areas. For people who struggle with the intensity of these challenges, recovery centers and their ongoing community support programs can be the ticket back to a satisfying life. I have incredible admiration for those who acknowledge the issues they feel powerless over and willingly participate in these life-changing programs. While some people can actually become addicted to their recovery programs and not move on, most are real warriors, summoning up tremendous courage to face what may be the greatest battle of their lives.

I believe one of the most important things we can learn regarding compulsions and addictions is that they are not the result of a weak will or an undisciplined character. Self-control alone is rarely enough to overcome the powerful dynamics, both physiological and psychological, of compulsions and addictions, and shaming people who exhibit these tendencies or outright behaviors doesn't help them. Supporting them in seeking help, if they are willing, is the most compassionate approach for those struggling with these destructive behaviors. If you or a loved one feel you could benefit from the ever-increasing knowledge available, see the Resource section at the end of this book, and check with health professionals and the variety of support systems available.

Explorations: In Touch with Your Psyche

Whether it be compulsive or addictive behavior, or something less challenging, you may want to take a closer look to see what stands in the way of greater life success. If your behaviors are already in line with supporting your mission, self-awareness is already an ongoing part of your life. But if you sense that you could benefit from a stronger handshake between psyche and self, becoming more aware is the first step.

Some people find systems like the Myers-Briggs Type Indicator (MBTI) and the lesser known Enneagram useful. As tools of self-revelation, personality indicators can help a person understand where she falls in the spectrum of human behavior types.

Self-awareness doesn't always have to hang on outside evaluation. What follows are three quick explorations you can begin right here, right now, to take a peek at your and others' behaviors and its roots. If you are happy with your present level of self-knowledge, these explorations may help you understand others in a new way or provide a quick, confirming checkup for you. These are merely methods to heighten awareness, not yardsticks for judging yourself or others for good or ill.

Before embarking on these explorations, set judgment aside as much as you can. If you're using these explorations to look at your own life, kick into observer mode, looking at your life from the outside, simply observing what propels you toward your mission and what stands in your way. No shame or blame—only eye-opening, heartfelt potential to see the roadblocks clearly in preparation for taking them down. When you're ready, take a few deep breaths and ease into a calm, open state.

Exploration 1. The Birth of Behaviors

1. Review your mission statement from Chapter 1. If you haven't prepared your mission statement yet, think about your purpose in life.

2. Draw a line down the center of a sheet of blank paper.

3. On the left side, list attitudes, behaviors, and habits that propel you toward your mission or purpose. For example, I put "persistence" in this column for myself.

4. On the right side, list attitudes, behaviors, and habits that stand in your way. In some cases you'll feel you have little control over these things, things you do even though you know only too well that they're not in your best interest. That's fine, just list them. For example, I used to stick my head in the sand when it came to facing uncomfortable emotional issues, so "denial" was (and still is, though to a lesser degree) on this list for me.

5. Write beside each attitude or habit where you think you learned it, whether from mother, father, sibling, peer, or some other source. I learned persistence from my mother. I learned denial from a number of sources, including a peer.

Exploration 2. Issues Resolution Comparisons

1. Identify a behavior you'd like to change—something you feel isn't in your best interest, but that you continue acting on. If you've completed Exploration 1, choose something from your list. Think about changing the behavior and ask yourself:

+ How would my mother handle changing it?

+ How would my father handle changing it?

+ How would my sibling handle changing it?

+ How would my childhood best friend handle changing it? (If you can't answer all of the above, that's okay.)

+ How would a healthy, detached observer handle changing it? (If you're not sure, that's okay.)

2. How am I currently going about changing it?

3. What might I do in the future to change it?

Now look at all the answers. Whose strategy is most similar to yours? Mother? Father? Sibling? Childhood best friend? Observer? Some may be similar or overlap. Just notice the similarities and differences and how your method relates to others'.

Many of us make decisions based on the methods of people around us, following in the influential footsteps of family and peers. If your methods of change aren't working well for you, consider coaching yourself toward the attitude of a detached observer who has more clarity and objectivity.

An example: Jake tends to get mad at people he perceives have wronged him. Not only is he mad, but he also has a desire to pay them back for the hurt. In a similar situation, his mother and siblings would ignore their own anger, smiling and denying the hurt. His father and best childhood friend would get mad and get even. Now it's a little clearer whose footsteps Jake fills.

A healthy observer would talk to the people he felt hurt by, trying to understand their intentions before assuming the worst. If indeed they meant to be hurtful, the observer would let them know how he felt, directly and honestly. If that wasn't their intention, the anger and the misunderstanding can be let go without loss.

Now, Jake may want to discard modeling his father's and his childhood best friend's behavior and do his best to think of how the observer would act when faced with that situation again. Certainly easier said than done, but identifying the original model of a behavior that's not working well today can be a useful first step toward change, if that's your goal.

Exploration 3. Tracking Tendencies

Read through these scenarios and simply notice whether any of them resonate with you. If a situation sounds familiar, take note of it as a potential area for further exploration.

1. When a colleague or friend approaches you with a personal issue, do you feel you can't end the conversation until you solve the issue for them? (potential tendency to control)

2. When a co-worker offers constructive criticism, do you listen or do you immediately think he's wrong and justify why you're doing what you're doing, never really hearing him openly? (potential tendency to be defensive)

3. A colleague who's unprepared for a meeting asks you to cover for her. Though you yourself don't have time to prepare, do you agree to attend for her anyway? (potential caretaking tendency)

4. Your boss presents a real clunker of an idea, and you're asked to implement it without sufficient time and resources. Do you stifle your objections and wind up resentful? (potential people-pleasing tendency)

5. Your collaborator has a great idea, so great you wish it were yours. You, however, are a critical part of the plan's success. Would you give only partial effort, preserving energy for ideas you author? (potential sabotaging tendency)

6. There's an important family event. Despite having worked hard on a project for a week, you know it would turn out better if you stuck with it through the night and didn't attend the event. Would you continue the project? (potential workaholic tendency)

7. You've just completed a six-month project that won kudos from the entire company. Everyone tells you to kick back for a day and appreciate your accomplishment. Is your satisfaction significantly diminished by the feeling that you could have done even better? (potential perfectionist tendency)

8. You upbraid a colleague over a minor mistake. Later you realize your response was unfair and that most of your anger sprang from a breakfast disagreement with your spouse. (potential tendency to express indirect anger)

9. Generally speaking, do you feel you get the short end of the stick both personally and professionally, that while the spoils go to others and the work goes to you, this is your cross to bear? (potential martyr tendency)

10. Though you don't consider yourself an intimidating person, do you find satisfaction in the prospect of getting people to do what you want them to do, even if they don't want to do it? (potential tendency to bully)

11. Do you often know answers to questions, but decline to speak up for fear of being wrong or finding yourself in an uncomfortable situation? (potential tendency to be distant)

Behavior Summary

In any of the above explorations, an answer to any one question does not necessarily indicate that you have a specific behavior or habit. Explorations are just that—open doors through which you can understand your tendency for certain behaviors so you can see yourself in a clearer light that shows the way to a smoother mission road.

Who's in the Driver's Seat?

The behavior patterns you may have uncovered in Explorations 1 and 3 are all common in our culture. If you identify with any of them or know others who do, you're not alone. The point of self-awareness is to first become aware of issues and then note their origin, two important steps that will help uncover the powers arrayed against you (Explorations 1 and 2 can be helpful here). It's more difficult to deal with something you're not consciously aware of, in understanding either its dynamics or origins.

Almost all behavior is in one way or another an attempt to draw what we all crave: attention, love, approval. People who bully, sabotage others, or play the martyr all seek to fulfill these basic needs in their own way, perhaps not even realizing the healthy longings that are buried under layers of negative expression. Even someone who's distant can be using secrecy or mystery to hook curious people who are drawn to figuring out people or seeking information from those who are withdrawn. These psychological soap operas play themselves out every day and every hour, in ways both subtle and blatant.

One of the goals of psychological wellness is to reach a healthy state that erases the need for underhanded games to get attention or gain power. It's a state where we deal directly, kindly, and honestly with people, shedding the old behaviors that don't serve us so that we're emotionally available to plug into love and acceptance from our Higher Source. Our actions become driven not by cravings for attention and approval, but by desires to manifest our mission in the world. Acting out of love, we don't need to react out of fear. Free to be ourselves, we wind up exploring more of our inner and outer worlds. Our lives naturally fall in line with our personal mission, which, if we've gone within and listened to ourselves, is driven not by the magnet of nature, nurture, and peers, or an insatiable appetite for attention and approval, but by our innate higher wisdom.

Eight Key Plays for Coaching the Psychological Self

Now, with a glimpse at the origin of our behavior, we're ready to look at key plays that assist in fine-tuning what works and retooling what doesn't. My own self-examination called on a combination of resources to peel back the layers of defensiveness, denial, habitual behaviors and thoughts as well as rally my talents in a new game plan. Somehow, in 1989 I sensed that as a forty-two-year-old male my habits were so deeply and painfully ingrained that I'd need an all-out effort, not just a token jog, if I was to navigate the foreign territory of my own psyche.

There are many levels of education, from simple observation of self and others to intensive work with psychological professionals. Some methods are structured while others can happen in the normal course of a day. If you already have a winning game plan for psychological wellness, keep it cooking. If not, tap into some of the many psychological education methods that may make sense for you to pursue. For starters, here are eight options.

Play No. 1. Self Coaching: Just Say No

Bottom line: changing behavior comes down to the ability to make positive decisions on behalf of ourselves. Psychological education and support was and is ultimately a tool to prepare me to coach myself to "just say no" to behavior that is hurtful to others or holds me back. Some people have an inherent ability to create a winning game plan for themselves at an early age. If you're able to effectively identify behaviors that block your mission, become aware of how and why they happen, and learn to say no, you can stop at this step. This method is all you need. Whether this comes naturally for you or, like me, you pursue a more varied route to get your psychological wellness degree, it's all preparation for those empowering times that a "no" to behavior becomes a "yes" to your life.

Play No. 2. Psyche Power Tool: Affirmations

Affirmations express something we desire as if it already exists. It's not a "want." It's an "already have." An affirmation for someone who wants to be more loving, for example, could be "I am a loving person." Affirmations can actually help reprogram the faulty behavioral loops we've developed in our mental computers, patterns that result from the accumulation of millions of emotional and psychological messages we take in through our lives. My father, now approaching his eighth decade, uses the affirmation "I love myself" to offset the effects of his own father leaving the family when Dad was a young boy. Affirmations shorten the distance between who you are and who you wish to become, incantations that bring the future you want one step closer.

Affirmations have gotten a bad rap from some people, and it's true that if there are no teeth in the words, they become empty rallying cries. The underlying feelings and thoughts attached to the words give the words power, and visualization connects it all into a coherent program. The more intensely you feel the affirmation when you say the words, the more power it will have (this works whether the message you're giving yourself is positive or negative—an excellent reason to guard your thoughts and guide them toward positive ones).

Affirmations are a growth tool I used a lot in the initial years of psychological growth, and I continue to use them today in the form of sutras (more on that in chapter 6). One of my earliest affirmations was "I am authentic and real." To imprint it further, I visualized being very candid with a friend on a difficult issue—a situation I would not normally have had the courage to face directly. With this image firmly in my mind and an idea of how great I'd feel when I approached the friend successfully, I repeated the affirmation slowly ten times. This connection between words, image, and feelings is the key that restarts the engine of more positive behavior consistent with what you're affirming.

If you've identified a behavior or attitude you wish to change, think of words that capture a positive behavior that would offset the negative. For example, if you feel anxious about not having enough abundance in your life, words like, "I am blessed" may be appropriate. State it ten times, visualizing the ways that you are blessed and ways you do have enough of what's important in life. If this is a method you'd like to try, consider doing affirmations each morning or evening, or both.

Another great way to use affirmations is to keep an "affirmations file" containing uplifting notes from other people, pictures of loved ones, or reminders of inspiring ideas. Go through the file once in a while to remind yourself to bring the affirming thoughts of the past into the present.

Inherent in affirmations is the positive statement of being the way you want to be rather than not being a way you don't want to be. "I am authentic" draws you toward authenticity, whereas "I am not phony" makes phoniness the dominant thought—in spite of the intention to not be phony. This has become known as the Wallenda Effect, after the great high-wire artist Karl Wallenda. After decades of successfully walking the wire, at age seventy-four Wallenda fell to his death. Some close to him said that he had stopped focusing on walking the wire and instead thought about not falling.

Play No. 3. One-on-One

The most important and logical part of my psychological growth was studying under a psychologist. Home-run slugger Mark McGwire used therapy as a tool to help him out of a career slump that eventually turned into the record-breaking season of 1998. In fact, most people who seek the advice of psychological professionals are seeking education about a part of themselves that they don't yet understand or use as effectively as they'd like. Think of it as hiring a tour guide in a foreign country. Instead of "shrinks," think of these professionals as "expanders." After all, they can expand our consciousness, our effectiveness, and ultimately for many, the probability that we'll achieve our missions. While this method may not be right for many people, it was my most important.

Ever the practical businessman, I interviewed four psychologists before meeting Brenda Schaeffer, who possessed the right mix of sensitivity, intuition, and knowledge to inspire the trust I needed to explore my alien inscape. Over the course of four years, once a week I spilled my innermost thoughts to Brenda, telling her whatever came to mind. Sometimes she affirmed my growing awareness, while at other times she called attention to things I couldn't see. Her skill was in challenging me, in a nonthreatening and gentle way, to understand myself while simultaneously pushing me past my limits of understanding. At times it was uncomfortable. But the growth and the change I was experiencing was undeniable, and I knew it was in the right direction.

Brenda helped facilitate the discovery of my life mission. We set up yardsticks for gauging psychological growth goals. After four years, Brenda took an extended leave of absence, having helped me accomplish much of what I'd set out to do in my first phase of growth. The following year I spent studying under behaviorist Earnie Larsen, who helped me reinforce and practice what I had learned with Brenda.

During those years I made the pivotal transition from unconscious life player to conscious observer of my life. Learning the methods of self-examination—as well as living them—taught me how to carry those lessons into the future. In other words, Brenda and Earnie in effect handed me the tools to become my own therapist. It works, although the potential for challenging periods is always there, and I wouldn't hesitate to call on their expert counsel again when I need benefit of sage advice.

There are a tremendous variety of therapeutic approaches—Jungian, Freudian, Adlerian, Gestalt, Transactional Analysis, NLP (Neuro-Linguistic Programming), EMDR (Eye Movement Desensitization and Reprocessing), Experiential, and Humanistic (for just a start). They employ straight conversation, role-playing, dream interpretation, visualization, and many other methods of exploration. While important, the methods themselves are in the end less crucial than finding a competent therapist who inspires a sense of trust.

As Brenda explained to me later, most personal issues we encounter involve violations of trust, an emotional or behavioral betrayal somewhere in our history. If you can't feel complete trust with your therapist, you won't be able to share your thoughts and feelings candidly, or have the confidence to act on the counsel you receive.

As in any profession, there's a wide range of competency levels. If you choose to pursue this route, first think about what you want from a therapist and what you hope to gain or how you hope to change. Ask friends for referrals (an important part of the search), check references, and I suggest interviewing a variety of therapists as if you were interviewing someone for a job. In fact, that's what you're doing. You're hiring a consultant and educator for a valuable member of your Inner Team. Here are some sample questions you might consider after briefly sharing your general issues and goals:

+ What approach does the therapist plan to use? How would it translate into the practical reality of your time with this therapist?

+ What education, experience, success with others, and happiness in his or her own personal life does the therapist have in the areas you want to improve (for example, intimacy with a spouse, work satisfaction, parenting a blended family, anger management, addictions, or compulsive behavior)?

+ Is the therapist strong enough to point out your games if you're being less than candid or trying to control the process and outcome? If you choose a therapist you know you can buffalo, you may as well continue buffaloing yourself and save the time and money.

+ What does the therapist expect from you?

+ How does the therapist measure your progress?

+ What's the fee?

+ Is the fee covered by insurance? For how long? Plan your financial strategy to get care at the level you want. I began paying a share of this expense when I was at my lowest point of financial capability, yet without it I couldn't have progressed personally or professionally.

After hearing answers to these extensive questions, you will have a gut feeling for your compatibility, level of trust, and the therapist's potential for meeting your needs and desires.

Play No. 4. Group Dynamic

Initially, I was leery—more like paranoid—of group therapy. At first, the prospect of being emotionally honest with a roomful of strangers was beyond reason. With Brenda moderating the group, however, I had to surrender my usual defenses. I couldn't work the conversation by subtly shifting away from uncomfortable topics, or deflect the topic back to hit someone else's bull's-eye. Group therapy forced me to dump manipulation and interact with my peers as human beings. What I grew to realize was that everybody was in the same boat. We weren't there to prove how much more together one was than another. I began seeing group therapy's symbiotic magic: We learned from each other's candid feedback. I observed other people's behavior, healthy and not so healthy, and learned from their victories and defeats, just as they learned from mine.

It was the uncomfortable lessons that led to the greatest growth. In one session, one member of the group described a situation that scared her. To me, it seemed like nothing. Brushing her concern aside, I asked her, "What's the problem?" In a flash, the group was all over me. I was taken aback, but that lesson stuck.

The group also went on a one-week retreat, a "test lab" where we could practice new behaviors away from the usual distractions of daily life. I was up for the challenge, but by the end of the first day I was thinking about ways to distract myself. While others were settling in for quiet, reflective evenings, I was wondering what kind of excitement I might find in the nearest town. In some ways, going to the retreat made me feel like a racing car that had been jerked into neutral—all fired up and nowhere to go. Noticing my agitation, Brenda asked a simple question: Are you running from something?

What I had passed off to myself as an innocent excursion was, I had to admit, just another distraction. In spite of my belief in what we were there to do, it just wasn't comfortable being plopped into such close introspection with other people. This would be a bigger challenge than I had anticipated. Putting the car keys back down, I found myself shaking. The earthquake wasn't outside, however. It came from within.

That week marked a turning point. Forcibly putting away the distractions, I settled in to get to know myself and my fellows. Like rehearsals or scrimmages, we practiced our newly acquired skills to keep our emotions honest and compassion on tap.

I was in the group about two years. After that, I joined an informal gathering of friends who were on similar growth treks. We had a simple format for each meeting: each of us would start with a brief check-in, then move to a specific issue that was on the table that week. We would each decide whether we just needed our friends' compassionate ears to hear, or whether we wanted feedback to road-test what we were thinking and how we were planning to act. Their empathy and perspective kept me on track with my previous work. Both formal and informal group settings were great places to test ideas and check when my lens on reality was pulling out of focus.

Play No. 5. Meds

While I typically keep my medicine chest clear of any prescription medications, I do believe there can be a place for them. Prozac, the most popular, and a host of other prescription antidepressants have helped multitudes. On the herbal side of the fence, St. John's wort, in the form of pills or tea, has been an uplifting addition to many people's lives.

The triple shot of cancer, divorce, and financial challenges in 1989 prompted me to utilize an antidepressant and an anti-anxiety prescription for nine months to help me through the nearly overwhelming transitions I faced. Previously, I could always pull myself up on my own, but I discovered that prolonged or severe stress can knock basic body chemistry out of whack, making it nearly impossible to pull out without help. Medications helped restore the balance so I could find the energy and motivation to participate fully in my psychological education.

While the medication raised the baseline of my psychological state, it didn't dull my craving for personal growth. The pills were a helpful short-term fix, but I sensed that, for me, they were no cure for the cause that had provoked their use in the first place. With my shoulder to the wheel of my psychological wellness, new insights and new habits began to take hold over the months, enabling me to go medication-free.

Whether as a bridge through a rough time or a longer-term solution, many people's lives have been changed for the better because they were willing to consider the support of medication. Guidance from a qualified, trustworthy, credible professional is essential here to help make judicious decisions best suited to your own situation.

Play No. 6. Healing with Friends

I found that walking my newly learned talk was a lot more fun with company, so I sought out friendships with like-minded people who were on a path similar to my own. I met people through therapy groups, t'ai chi class, and A Course in Miracles classes, as well as other venues. Through discussions of the new territory we were exploring and the example of their own lives, my new-found perspective sank deeper. Friendships with people committed to psychological as well as spiritual growth continue to be an important circle of connection that keeps me moving on my path. You'll read more on relationships with friends in chapter 9.

Play No. 7. Soul Searching with Soulmates

One of my first romantic relationships after my divorce was with a woman who had been through extensive psychological education. She was extremely knowledgeable, knew the difference between healthy and unhealthy behavior, and had no qualms about calling me on my "stuff." The upside was I had benefit of a psychological coach for many of my nonworking hours. I'd sometimes get defensive, but on some level I listened and learned.

We were together for three years. After our relationship ended, she said, "I'm not taking on another project like you. It was a lot of work getting you to this stage!" I understood what she meant. Constantly challenging and evaluating my behavior did take a lot of her energy. Still, I'm grateful for her role in helping me break habits built over more than forty years. That "on-the-job training" nicely complemented individual and group therapy and supportive friends.

When someone close to you challenges you on your behavior, I encourage you to be open to the message. We can't always see our own actions, and in those moments when self-observation breaks down, we can learn from what others see.

Play No. 8. Tap into the World Around You

Over the years, I've tapped into numerous resources to delve deeper into an understanding of psychology and human behavior. Books, tapes, seminars, study groups, and retreats have been excellent complements to the other methods mentioned earlier. Considering the number of years it took me to develop my behavioral habits, I figured that a comprehensive approach with a well-stocked resource box was a given if I stood a chance of getting psyche into the game. Check the Resources section for more ideas on increasing the wellness of this vital Inner Team member.

Different Roads, One Goal

The changes in my own psychological development were a slow and sometimes painful road. Yet gradually, that uphill road leveled off as many of my new ways of thinking and being became new habits. I find that it takes about six months of practice to etch a new behavior into a groove. As the grooves stacked up, slowly but surely, my life became less stressful and more enjoyable.

It's important to note that in psychological wellness, one size does not fit all. We're all wired differently, so our choices, priorities, missions, and desires will also be very different. Some people come to psychological truths naturally, while others fare better using more structured methods to learn and grow behaviorally. Whatever your way, the bottom line is to become more aware of our actions today and do what we can to align them with our values, so that tomorrow we can look back with fewer regrets.

Certainly there are external factors that can create real challenges to tranquillity and wellness. Sickness, death of a loved one, divorce, or breakup of a relationship, loss of a job, or any other number of difficult times will come knocking. Better psychological skills don't exempt us from life's challenges. Healthy habits, however, can help us move through them with greater support, understanding and learning what we can, and returning to a state of balance sooner rather than later.

Emotions and behaviors are habitual, and they can be changed by the same process you would put in place to shift an exercise or work habit. Here are six steps that can help you unmask the motivation behind a habit and give you the upper hand when it comes to changing it:

1. Recognize the source—where did I learn this habit?

2. Recognize the feelings that go with the habit—how do I feel when I'm in the middle of acting on this habit? How do I feel afterward?

3. Recognize how the habit has served me—what do I get out of acting in this way? Is there a healthier way to get the same need met?

4. Recognize how the habit looks today—what triggers it? Has it changed through the years? Is it still appropriate?

5. Recognize the consequences—does the habit carry potential risk? Does it connect me or separate me from other people? Does it bring me closer or push me away from my mission?

6. Recognize the lesson—what hidden message or value is embedded in the habit? If I'm unhappy with the consequences of the habit, can I make an effort to discontinue it through understanding the source and recognizing its trigger and associated feelings?

Asking these questions connects the dots between the origin of the habit and the consequences it has in our lives. From its beginning as a mere thought, it moves through our psyche, and into actions. In other words, the way we think links to the way we feel. The way we feel links to the way we act. And the way we act links to the positive and negative consequences we put out and get back in the world. We might take more time for this kind of self-examination if we understood this equation and considered what we might hear if we recorded our thoughts and then listened to the replay.

Negotiating Negatives

Greater awareness and Self Coaching may lead you, as they did me, to shed some useless emotional habits like a down coat in spring. Nevertheless, some habits don't go quietly. Fear, anger, and guilt are three hot spots that bear special mention. Often thought of as purely useless, in fact these emotions have both positive and negative aspects. Their positives can prompt our protective instincts and charge us up to change our ways for the better. Their negatives can pull the shades on the future and rob us of the ability to be in the present moment. Engraved on the edge of that positive-negative coin is the question we can ask whenever we are faced with fear, anger, or guilt: "How is this emotion serving me?"

Cut off in traffic, anger and fear rise as a driver quickly brakes to avoid a collision. Emotions turbocharge the reaction, saving the driver from danger. That's positive. Now the driver, still angry at the offender (who's long gone down the highway), is running the incident through his mind, thinking of the things he'd say if that other driver were here.

This is the crossroads where the positives and negatives meet. The real danger is over, and the driver has expressed his anger in the only healthy way he can. That's positive. If he hangs on to it past this point, will it continue to help him? If he decides, for example, to pursue the other driver for an up-close-and-personal confrontation, will that help him or harm him? If he decides to let the other driver go, but arrives at the office still enraged, will that help make his 9:00 a.m. meeting more successful? Is his anger still serving him well, or has it flipped from positive to negative, turning self-protection into self-suffering?

Although the positive aspects of these difficult emotions tend to enter our lives, do their jobs, and move out, the negative aspects can cling to our mental walls, feeding on themselves and breeding only more negativity. That negative "plaque" leaves us living in fear of the future, feeling guilty about the past, or feeling imprisoned by ego needs. The burdensome weight of these negative remnants can make it nearly impossible to focus on the here and now.

The Russian philosopher P. D. Ouspensky expressed his unequivocal view on the negative aspects of emotion, saying they "don't help our orientation, they do not give us knowledge, they do not guide us in any sensible manner. On the contrary, they spoil all our pleasures...The only good thing about them is that being quite useless and artificially created by our imagination…they can be destroyed without any loss. Man must sacrifice his suffering." How to sacrifice our suffering? We can learn to recognize an emotion that no longer serves us positively, feel it, and then untie it from our inner harbors.

Even as I felt myself becoming more healthy, I would often get side-swiped by the negative aspects of the trouble triplet of fear, anger, and guilt. While managing these emotions in specific situations is an important skill, I had to move past managing the symptoms to get at the root of the challenges.

Sideswiped by Fear

Most of the fear we feel isn't connected to life-threatening situations. Most of us are not being chased by wild animals or being tested in combat. Many of our fears are on a symbolic level: feeling threatened or besieged by the demands of work and relationships, feeling emotionally attacked by people who don't understand us.

When faced with fear, we have three instinctual reactions: fight, flight, or freeze. In our modern age, "flight" is expressed as withdrawal or depression. "Fight" is expressed as anger, and "freeze" is experienced as emotional paralysis. You know the feeling: can't think, can't move, don't know what to do.

I've had times when I've felt paralyzed by fear, though (thank goodness) this happens more rarely now. When I'm in fear's grip, time shifts. Everything seems to speed up, but the solution that will soothe the fear seems to move toward me like molten lava. I feel an internal, unsettling quaking that tells me the world's turning upside down. Things seem out of focus. My view dims. Positives turn topsy-turvy negative, throwing additional weight into the fear cycle. My ability to think narrows. My ability to learn shuts down. The voice of any information that doesn't build the fear gets harder to hear. What could quiet and calm me is drowned out by the rumbling of ruminating negative thoughts.

The result is that love—for myself and for others—disappears during these times, because while love expands our possibilities, fear diminishes us. In these moments it becomes clear: a mind that lives in fear can't live in love.

FACE-OFF WITH FEAR + I developed an array of tools to use when fear and its close companion, anxiety, come knocking.

✦ **Draw on the wisdom of an inspiring saying.** "Fear knocked on the door. Faith answered and there was no one there."

✦ **Focus on breath.** Because patterns of anxiety show up in our bodies as well as our minds, noticing your breath can quiet fears. Breathing more regularly and deeply helps slow down the cycle of emotional shutdown and keeps the mind open to moving through the feelings. When a situation feels most dire, I remember what my college friend, Atlanta psychotherapist Bob Simmermon, says: "you can't die if you keep breathing."

✦ **Give thanks for your blessings.** Focusing on gratitude and moving through a list of blessings restores an important perspective of time and proportion. How big is the fear compared to the good things that have happened and will continue to happen in my life? Getting through my list can seriously deflate the object of my fear.

✦ **Visualize a worst-case scenario.** "Okay," I tell myself, "Things must be really bad if I'm this afraid. *So just how much worse can they get?*" Considering the worst possible outcome puts attention on the facts and sometimes confirms a real matter for concern. More often than not, much of the fear disappears in the light of the evidence. Bottom-lining fear opens the way to see that, yes, I'll still be fine, and then to strategize a solution rather than be paralyzed by phantoms. Either way the fear is diminished.

✦ **Call on higher inner wisdom** to help chart a course for a new direction. A mind open to inner wisdom will be open to finding solutions for the source of the fear. Developing an action plan, a schedule, and a to-do list minimizes fear's body-slamming impact and can flip the negative into positive. This step can offer a sense of comfort, assuring us that we've done all we can to manage the issue in the outside world.

✦ **Call on your Higher Power** and ask for assistance in manifesting an outcome that's in line with your mission.

✦ **Restore a feeling of love and openness.** I might do this by thinking of my family, a warm memory, or God. When we orient thoughts and feelings toward love, especially sending loving thoughts out to the source of our fear, there's very little room left for paralysis or anxiety.

✦ **Do your best and wait for the results in peace.** Knowing you've done all you can to meet the fear, take any actions you can to minimize the potential that it might become real, then let go. You've done your best.

MAKE LIKE A CAT ✦ Some people who have been consistently fearful throughout their lives develop a sense of hypervigilance, always antici-pating what might go wrong. Although preparation is generally a good quality, taken to the extreme it kills your ability to enjoy the moment. Hypervigilants are always waiting for the sky to fall or the other shoe to drop.

Instead, in the last ten years I've traded the shoe for a cat. Now I prefer to model feline vigilance—prepared, not scared; quietly aware yet not tensed for action. Alert and relaxed. This is the state I do my best to access today.

Sideswiped by Anger

Anger is also closely connected to fear. If you scratch anger's surface, fear is usually what you'll find underneath, because it's more culturally acceptable to get mad than to say we're afraid. Many in our culture were taught to suppress anger and regard it as some remnant of primitive life that civilized people don't engage in. But anger is natural and can be healthy when it acti-vates our instinct to protect ourselves and others from real threats. Anger can give us energy to confront what we may feel is too big for us otherwise. From the Civil Rights Movement to citizens angry over the dirtying of their local water supply, to a child who's willing to defend his buddy on the playground, anger can spark positive revolutions large and small.

Anger, however, is often expressed and used in ways that seek to control others rather than improve their lives. That's power *over* people, not power *to* people. Anger can come out as sarcasm, criticism, judgment. It can come out as personal slams that have nothing to do with the real source of the issue. The people we act out with end up confused and angry themselves, and why not? We're attacking them, and they don't even know why. *A Course in Miracles* states, "With thoughts of attack and counterattack pre-occupying us, what peace of mind is possible? It's a fantasy, created by our own mind. The good news is that it's not real."

While the drama is only in our minds, the consequences can be fatal, as I'm reminded every time I'm on the highway. Once I realized the stakes involved if I let anger control me, I made it a priority to minimize it. While direct anger beats suppression, there's another, even better option: not to get on the anger wheel to begin with. If I'm frustrated, there are better ways to clear the air. When I do feel anger, I ask myself if I'm overreacting to someone or misunderstanding something. I take a few deep breaths to reframe the situation, and then respectfully confront whoever is involved to resolve the conflict in a caring way. It's healthier for me, and it's healthier for them. Whether driving or in other situations, I don't feel the need to engage. There are other cases when I still do engage, but it's less often.

DEFUSE, DISENGAGE, WALK AWAY + Sometimes we're so shocked by a personal verbal attack that we're not sure what to do. In fact, doing nothing is often the best first step. Next, notice your reaction. Focus on your breath. Is this like situations you've had in the past? How do you usually react when you're in this kind of a situation? Do those usual reactions serve you well?

Third, consider your possible responses. Walk them through your mind to see what kind of reaction your response will beget. Remember, for every action, there's a reaction. See it. Envision what it would feel like and determine from the place of your higher self if it mediates or escalates the anger. Walking away can be the hardest thing you've ever done. We often want so badly to have the satisfaction of seeing the object of our anger suffer, or at least of having the last word. Ask yourself honestly if it will be worth the pain you'll cause yourself and others by entering the drama with your own angry arsenal.

It's essential to ask, in any dispute, What's more important? An optimum resolution, or my need to be right? If my anger is rooted in an attachment to winning, I do my best to take a deep breath and walk away until I can get a better focus on the real issue.

In confronting someone else's anger, it's important to acknowledge that person's feelings. "I can see you're really angry about this. Tell me what it's about. What would you like me to do to resolve it?" Many people's anger fizzles once you bring them into a real dialogue about their concerns. It's sometimes enough to change an unharmonious situation into a harmonious one. This doesn't mean you have to agree; it's the sense of respect and communication, of honoring the other person's feelings and needs, that removes the anger, clearing the way for discussion of the real issue. Without this sense of resolution, our minds tend to ruminate, hang on, and make issues worse than they really are.

Resolving the constant stream of challenges that we encounter is vital to keeping the anger tank near empty and the tolerance tank full. How we resolve things determines how we evolve. As Minneapolis health practitioner Dr. Viktoria Sears says, "Evolution through the highest resolution."

Sideswiped by Guilt

Guilt is last, but not at all least, of the trouble triplet. While fear keeps us anxious about the future and anger agitates us about the present, guilt keeps us stuck feeling shameful about events in the past. Guilt has incredible staying power, earning it a reputation as the gift that keeps on giving.

My dictionary includes two sides in its definition of guilt: "the fact of having committed a breach of conduct" and "feelings of culpability especially for imagined offenses or from a sense of inadequacy: self-reproach." As in the first definition, guilt may be rooted in things we've done that we regret. As in the second definition, however, it may not be linked to our actions but rather to our shameful perceptions of ourselves. As Brenda Schaeffer taught me, guilt can be a self-perpetuating feeling that often has its roots in others' blaming and shaming. If we buy into it, others blaming us becomes *us* blaming us. Feeling condemned by others, we end up condemning ourselves and act in ways that reinforce that low opinion.

Regret, on the other hand, is a healthy recognition that acknowledges we've done something out of line with our own sense of values. Willing to see where we've gone off track, regret can be used as a catalyst for positive change.

Recognizing this point of difference between guilt and regret helped me when I was locked down in feelings of failure over my performance as a parent, husband, and business owner. Letting go of the guilt and tuning in to regret from the depths of my heart and soul helped me turn a corner so I could get back in the game of life and make amends as best I could.

ANTIDOTE FOR GUILT +   Mourning the loss of an opportunity or feeling sadness about our actions gone wrong, as I discovered, are important parts of the healing process. We're human, and we learn most often through making mistakes, making amends, and moving on. Director Mike Nichols was once asked by interviewer Charlie Rose if he enjoyed the process of movie editing. "If only life had an editing process. That would really be great." We can't edit out our actions as if they hadn't happened, but we can disempower their effect on the movie of our lives.

The antidote to guilt? Making clear segues from mistakes through apologies, beginning with the painful sight of our own regret. Coaching ourselves with a plan not to repeat the error, and then forgiving ourselves and others, completes the process. For many, self-forgiveness is much more difficult than forgiving others, and may take more time. Because this is so central to my own emotional health, I include it as a step in my daily prayer.

Breakthroughs, Not Breakdowns

Deadpan, poker face, stiff upper lip—whatever you call it, hiding emotions can veil our emotional growth. In the mid-1990s, on an anniversary of the first volley in the Gulf War, I listened intently as former President George Bush spoke to a large group of CEOs in Orlando, Florida. Only five rows away, I had a clear view of every nuance of his expression. That day, Bush read from the diary he had kept during the war, and as he neared the end of his talk, he was visibly moved. As he continued reading, he began to cry. Poignantly honest, his tears said more about his memories of the war than a truckload of words. The moderator edged toward him uncomfortably, thanked him for sharing such a personal, intimate experience. Bush quickly pulled himself back behind his emotional armor, saying, "Well, you're not going to see it again. I'll tell you that!" The group, mostly men, laughed uneasily. Most of them could relate.

I wondered to myself what the election results would have been in 1992 if George Bush had allowed himself to show his emotions during televised debates and in other media. If charisma is the result of connecting effectively with all aspects of who we are (with emotions as well as body, intellect, and spirit), then tears are less a threat than a vital support.

One of the most difficult habits for me to break was my resistance to tears. Many adults, and particularly men, are trained not to show emotional vulnerability, much less a single tear. "Never let 'em see you cry" is a natural offshoot of the "never let 'em see you sweat" mentality.

In connecting my inner reality with my outer reaction, however, I had to admit that sadness was part of the human experience. Tears are a natural response to it, a part of being human that needs no explanation. The first time I remember crying deeply as an adult, at age forty-two, it actually felt life-threatening. I remember it vividly. I was alone, and after the tears ran themselves out, I checked to see if I was still in one piece. To my surprise, I found that I felt more alive than ever. The well of tears turned into a well of hope—a revelation.

I remember another occasion, a particularly stressful workday in 1991. On that day, two key people submitted their resignations. Also, the man who had accepted my offer for the position of chief financial officer suddenly recanted to stay in his current position. Trying to make light of it, he said he had been needled by his East Coast co-workers who would walk by his office pretending to shiver, a reference to the Minnesota winters. I was in no mood to laugh. Three strikes and I was out. I staggered home, where I found my son Chris. I told him I needed a hug, and I started to cry.

Through Chris's well-placed empathy and listening ear, I found the kernel of motivation again that was temporarily displaced by the stress. The tears helped move me to a better place.

"Choking up" is a revealing expression that puts a negative spin on what I have learned is ultimately a positive experience. There's a point at which you begin to feel the tears coming, and you can either choke them off or let them flow. Try letting them flow when you're in safe company. Sure, it feels vulnerable, but I end up feeling even closer to the people I'm able to trust in those times. It's also a great example to our children and others around us to let them know that expressing pain and sadness is part of life, too. When a teammate or friend cries in my presence, the tears are often accompanied by an apology for "breaking down." I say, "No need to apologize. What a *breakthrough,* not a breakdown."

Psyche at Work

It's natural that we would bring the same psychological and emotional habits we developed in early life into our adult families as well as the workplace. Co-workers become like siblings, managers become like parents. Back in the script of the patterns we learned growing up, we often repeat those patterns, both healthy and not-so-healthy. In fact, we tend to continue seeking out the same patterns in those around us. If our families operated smoothly, functioning in our workplace "families" will be similar. If our families operated with strategies that sputtered, we'll also sputter in our workplace dealings unless we face our history and make an effort to change. Tactics you used with your mother may now be present in your dealings with your manager. When you think about it, how could it be any other way? These are our learned baseline relationship patterns, until we choose consciously to become students of our own psychology and make any necessary adjustments.

I've seen this played out like clockwork in the workplace. Before my eyes were opened, I was a much more active participant in the dramas. Then, I wouldn't have recognized it in myself or others, let alone known how to deal with it when I saw it.

Are These Games Being Played in Your Neighborhood?

The biggest challenges in the workplace today aren't related to job skills, but to behavior. Controlling tendencies, defensiveness, people-pleasing, caretaking, workaholism, perfectionism, procrastination, sabotaging, displaced anger—do any of these sound familiar? I've seen and played many of them myself, and they're no doubt in progress at a business near you. The cost to organizations and employees is significant. Tremendous productivity and peace of mind is lost when energy is deflected from cooperation into emotional dramas. Work is compromised, stress levels flare, and employees' health, both emotional and physical, begins to fray.

My psychological education has been a trusted ally that helps me operate more effectively as a leader and teammate. At Tires Plus, we've been on the path to creating a healthier emotional environment through these approaches:

+ By my personal commitment to model psychological wellness as best I can in actions, feelings, and expression.

+ By sharing feedback about deeper behavior issues with teammates when and only when they're open to discussion.

+ By having psychologists give talks to our teammates.

+ By recommending and encouraging the use of resources, including the employee assistance program, that address psychological issues.

+ By candidly discussing the benefits I have seen from my emotional growth.

+ By encouraging an environment in which everyone is open and honest with feelings and able to confront other teammates in a respectful way about unhealthy behavior.

+ By conducting relaxation training within teams to encourage teammates to understand how their co-workers are affected by stress, giving them both permission and language to offer support.

I can't imagine being a worker, much less a leader, without making the study of psychology—my own as well as psychology in general—a priority. Most employees, especially those in leadership roles, can benefit from learning some of the basic skills psychologists use to observe, ask appropriate questions, and coach themselves and others on healthier communication, attitudes, and behavior.

I'm often asked by employees from other companies how they can help create an environment that's open to this type of thinking. I advise them to challenge their companies' leaders gently and persistently. What really needs to happen, I believe, is for a great many CEOs to first work through any of their own psychological and behavioral issues in whatever way works for them, and then bring these lessons into the workplace.

Get in the Game

Even the wisest among us encounters psychological and intellectual hurdles every day. To clear yours, think about the resources you already have at hand, and about ways you can add and fine-tune others. Fill your winning game plan with a good supply of

+ honest self-examination through exploration;
+ desire to make behavioral changes;
+ willingness to seek help outside yourself, unless Self Coaching alone will accomplish your changes;
+ methods necessary to support your change;
+ strategies you found effective in managing guilt, anger, and fear;
+ willingness to express feelings, sad and joyful, where appropriate;
+ desire to review and champion ideas to create a healthier workplace environment.

Clearing psyche's hurdles will help you become a healthier person in and out of the workplace—a gift to yourself and everyone around you.

6

Fit for Your Mission: Spiritual Wellness

IN CHAPTER 3 I talked about being spirit-filled as one of the traits essential to a winning life game plan. I discussed my views on the differences between "religious" and "spiritual" and how spirit-filled behavior can show up at home and in the workplace. In this section I'll go deeper into the reasons I believe spirit is the most valuable player of your Inner Team, and share with you my spiritual practice and the 'real game.' When spiritual wellness permeates one area of life, every other area is affected.

Of all the modes of wellness, spiritual practice is the most personal and open to interpretation. Talking about God is inherently difficult, because no thoughts can adequately define and no words fully describe this most essential force. Spiritual paths are as varied as those who walk them. Many people have found direction and peace, while others have had uninspiring or even damaging religious experiences, leaving them cynical and self-protective when they hear anything about "God" or "spirit."

As children we're not, for the most part, in control of our spiritual practices. As adults, however, we have the ability to redefine and rediscover spirit's meaning in our lives and reconnect with a divine source from which we may feel estranged. I believe a Higher Power wants clearer communication with each of us. Whether we've had good or bad experiences in the

Spiritual Wellness

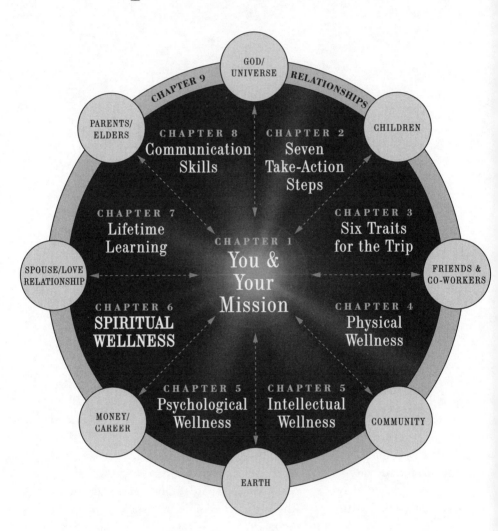

GOD/ UNIVERSE

CHAPTER 9   RELATIONSHIPS

PARENTS/ ELDERS

CHILDREN

CHAPTER 8
Communication Skills

CHAPTER 2
Seven Take-Action Steps

CHAPTER 7
Lifetime Learning

CHAPTER 1
You & Your Mission

CHAPTER 3
Six Traits for the Trip

SPOUSE/LOVE RELATIONSHIP

FRIENDS & CO-WORKERS

CHAPTER 6
SPIRITUAL WELLNESS

CHAPTER 4
Physical Wellness

CHAPTER 5
Psychological Wellness

CHAPTER 5
Intellectual Wellness

MONEY/ CAREER

COMMUNITY

EARTH

past, we can find the road that works today, given our particular blend of history and circumstance.

Just like physical, intellectual, and psychological wellness, spiritual wellness needs attention and practice to keeps its flame glowing. Some people are of the opinion that they'll wait for spirit to appear, and indeed, without even trying, many have sparks of spiritual inspiration or revelation. The danger of leaving spiritual connection in the hands of "inspiration," however, is that you can spend a lot of lonely moments waiting for a connection that you could be accessing in a more proactive and conscious way. For the same reason I don't leave my physical workout in the hands of whim, I no longer leave my spiritual fitness languishing until the mood strikes. If any of the following ideas interest you as a beginning or as a supplement to your current spiritual practice, consider them steps that may help keep your connection with spirit fit for life.

On Assignment

One of my favorite spiritual thoughts comes from *A Course in Miracles:* "My only function is the one God gave me—love and forgiveness." On assignment from God…that's a comfort. My part? Show up, open my mouth, put my pen to paper, keep the intention in line with my assignment (the root of which is love and forgiveness), and be ready to accept help from my Source, at every moment here to give me a boost. Talking to new Tires Plus teammates, teasing out numbers in a budget meeting, or playing on the basketball court, I'm reminded of this powerful relationship at what may seem to be unlikely times. I feel like a pilot getting instructions from the tower, receiving messages from God. When I'm not tuned in, I feel anxious, socked in by foggy thoughts. When I am tuned in, serenity transmits through my day.

Getting Past the Roadblocks

Being on a spiritual path is a process of forging a relationship with a divine source. Staying on the spiritual path that's right for you may not be easy. Embodying spiritual principles in daily life is a constant challenge. Sometimes it feels like oil and water. Spirit has no boundaries; we as human beings are reminded of ours with every muscle pang and bony creak. Spirit embraces infinity, human beings embrace the clock. Consider the intricate, ongoing effort it takes for two humans to know each other. Then consider the additional leap of complexity when a human reaches out to the divine.

It's complicated but not impossible. Reaching out is a start, a simple gesture that can be slapped down by our own ego-based needs and fears. Unduly focused on the world's favorite aria, "me, me, me," ego steals the stage from a more expansive life purpose.

Leggo My Ego

One of the central issues in discussing both spirituality and psychology is the role that ego plays in our behavior. American culture often focuses on lack of ego strength and self-esteem as a major roadblock to psychological and spiritual health. Low self-esteem and a wounded ego are held as major factors in people's feelings of guilt, fear, and unworthiness. Feeling unlovable, these people are not really able to love—conditions that are part and parcel of spiritual connection.

I heard a story recently of a small group of prisoners who, during a counseling session, were asked to tell things they liked about themselves. The silence was thick enough to cut with a knife. Struggling for something good to say, one finally blurted out, "I've been beat down, but I still give a crap about people."

The glimmers of compassion and hope we recognize in ourselves can open the way to a better future. If you find yourself bucking the basic premise that you are worth love and able to love, know that a wounded ego can heal, and consider the methods discussed in chapter 5 to find the support to begin the process. The flip side of this focus on low self-esteem is the overinflated ego. Too much ego strength raises the individual above others and turns relationships into bids for power rather than cooperative exchanges.

Eastern philosophies shine the spotlight on ego-related challenges from a different angle. Here, too much attention to ego is the basic concern. Even the question of whether ego is too strong or too weak puts energy into ego and takes it away from spirit. This attention to ego brings about a disconnection from spirit by causing us to feel separate from our Source and from others. Too much focus on ego puts oceans between the individual and the world until the individual feels like an island unto himself rather than a part of the continuum of all life.

Which is correct? East or West? For me, both viewpoints have a seed of truth. It seems to me that first we must develop a healthy base of self-esteem and ego, the self-assurance that gives us confidence to act in the world and be ourselves without fear. When a person has developed a healthy ego (which is harder than you may think), he comes to a fork in the road.

One way takes ego down a power road. Drunk on its ability to accomplish, arrange, structure, do, and create, ego forgets its divine source, loses its connection to an overarching purpose and to other people. *Things* gain more value than *people*. *What we have* becomes more important than *where we're going*. We all know these people. There's one inside each of us.

The other fork in the road leads to a place where ego is completely relinquished, recognizing that ultimately the dramas of the ego can only interfere with accessing spirit, love, and connectedness to the universe and all beings.

I try to walk a middle road that values ego strength insofar as I need to feel good about myself, feel deserving of God's love, and feel worthy of others' love and care. And I do my best not to venture on the other road, guarding daily against its two subtle signs—thoughts that tell me I'm better than someone else and thoughts that put material things above relationships. When I sense them, I pull myself back to the middle road, where my actions are not only for my own benefit but can resonate outward to benefit others.

The middle road sometimes feels like an eight-lane highway: easy to see, easy to navigate. At other times it's a razor's edge. We're all human, and we all struggle with the competing demands of ego desires and spiritual longings. A story from Jewish tradition counsels that each person should travel through life wearing a coat with two pockets. In each pocket is a piece of paper with a message. The message in one pocket says, "You are dust and ashes." The message in the other pocket says, "For you the world was created." We need to discern which message at which moment we should draw from to keep ourselves in balance.

As a kid, going to church, I remember the minister talking about "salvation." Being "saved" from "hell" wasn't something I completely understood, but I had some vivid images in my head. As an adult, however, I see one aspect of salvation as the divine grace that can "save" me from the pain of an unbalanced ego, which can create its own living hell. Left to its own devices, a strong ego can grow out of control and destroy everything. Nurtured unwisely, it can't support you when you need it to.

It seems to me that the antidote to unhealthy ego-based behaviors, simple as it may sound, is forgiveness and love. Hanging on to shame, guilt, and fear dramas only serves to separate us from our Source. Beginning with ourselves and then moving out to others, forgiveness opens the path toward healing and shifting focus away from self-protection to caring for others. The more forgiveness we experience, the more tolerant we become and the less fear we feel. Without this, we can't reach a place where we even feel deserving of God's love. As an ancient Buddhist philosopher once said, "There are many paths in life. All paths lead to nowhere. One is lined with heart and on the others your life is cursed." With a balanced ego on the path, there's plenty of room for heart.

Awesome, *Not* Fearsome

Fear is a spiritual roadblock that shows up in both subtle and overt ways. Many people find themselves living in fear of other people and their surroundings. While the instinct for self-protection is natural and healthy, many of these fears are unreasonable, and those beget spiritual disconnection. Living in a defensive stance to relationships and the environment, it's nearly impossible to act in spirit-filled ways.

Fear of change and uncertainty are other phantoms that disconnect many people's spiritual progress. Spiritual quests often raise questions that have no answers. In our achievement-oriented society, many people find it uncomfortable to live with these spiritual loose ends or shift their thinking to accommodate this lack of hard-and-fast solutions.

The need to fear God is spoken of by some religious doctrines, something I understood as a kid in the same way I understood fear of the big kid down the block. In 1995, I went to my Uncle Dick Alexander's funeral in a southern Indiana church. I listened as the minister said we needed to be God-fearing, and I was reminded how odd that had always sounded to me. Why should I fear God? Should I fear punishment? Should I fear terrorizing threats of judgment?

God, it seems to me, loves us unconditionally, even more completely than a parent loves a child, and forgives our inevitable mistakes. A loving concept of God can allow us to forgive and love ourselves. For if we don't believe this unconditional love and are living constantly in a knee-knocking fear of punishment, we can become guilt-ridden, shame-based, and unforgiving of ourselves and others, with love a distant reality.

Awe, related to fear, is a little different. While there's a piece of fear here, respect and wonder crowd out dread. Whereas fear can paralyze me, awe inspires me. Being in awe of God can be understood as a spiritual challenge to take understanding and practice to a new level. I reconnect with awe each time I really take note of creation. Listening to my heart beat, looking at the intricate structure of a tree, considering the breathtaking beauty of a piece of artwork or of the lake near my house on a fall day, the dream I had last night, the thought I had just now—all ultimately find their source in God, and that recognition breeds awe.

While fear motivates with the threat of punishment, awe motivates us to act out of deep respect, love, and a desire to be closer to the source of such wonder.

Pace is Grace

My biggest challenge in developing spirituality? That's easy: it's learning to s-l-o-o-o-o-w down. I once heard someone ask a group, "Any of us have a full schedule and an empty soul?" I always used to be in a rush and fifteen minutes late for most everything. I'm still used to moving briskly through the day when I'm "doing business," though I've found a much healthier pace, less hurried, more timely. And I still want to make more progress in this area. Actually, when I am able to move a little slower, I enjoy life more and experience it more fully. Although this can be seen as a challenge to high productivity, author Eknath Easwaran writes, "Don't confuse slowness with sloth which breeds carelessness, procrastination and general inefficiency. In slowing down, attend...to details." In some business settings I've found this difficult. When I choose to slow down (it's always an option, whether I like to admit it or not), it feels great, and I find that I don't get less done, but more.

Spirit Takes Control

There's no doubt about it: spirit is demanding. Spirit is the source of our conscience, which sometimes puts us in conflict with what our ego desires and what we know is the highest-level choice. Choosing what's best for me can be understood as a selfish act, but only when that decision is made from limited self-interest. When decisions are made from the level of mission consistency, the highest-level choice that's right or best for us also yields the highest-level benefit for others (and vice versa), even though from our limited human perspective we are often unable to see that common purpose and connectedness.

With a sense of spiritual connection, we have a better chance of finding the strength we need in moments when our good intentions aren't enough to pull us through. While we can be good people without a spiritual awareness, I think we more consistently practice loving, caring behavior when we're connected to a divine source than when we're not. Caring behavior is where spirit and humanness intersect. One of the usual purposes of spiritual practice is to turn awareness away from ego-based needs toward considerations of a higher good. The less I'm focused on my own ego-based power, the more beneficial, present, and serene I can be.

Warts and All

We all have desires and longings for things we think we shouldn't. We all have tendencies that we regret, things we're ashamed to share with others, things we keep in the dark. Our shadow side holds all these secrets. While this can be framed as a psychological issue, it also goes to the core of spirituality. Too many people equate being spiritual with being perfect, or at least with being very, very good. This is perhaps what you were taught as a kid, but that begs the question of the real *struggle* to forge a connection with your divine source, which is about anything but perfection.

An important part of feeling spirit-filled is embracing our own humanity, warts and all. How can we love God's creation—us—without loving the God within ourselves? Our lives are works in progress, and learning requires that we make mistakes. Learning from our mistakes ("atoning," "repenting," or "returning to a state of grace" in the language of some religious traditions) is a basic rhythm of life. Martin Luther used the phrase *simul iustus et peccator*—"at the same time a righteous man and a sinner." The Christian apostle Paul owned his own imperfection, calling himself "the chief of sinners." These men's words embody the paradox we all live with: at every moment we have lessons to learn, and at the same moment we are loved and valued just as we are. Accepting the idea that we're "on the road" to becoming more spiritual rather than at its end makes it easier to look at our darker parts.

A real danger lurks in suppressing the knowledge of our darker tendencies. It's much healthier—but often harder—to recognize and shake hands with that self-knowledge. If left to its own devices, a suppressed or denied shadow side can create a well of unworthiness that can completely outbid the good feelings you get from any job, loving family, or long-time friendships. All the blessings in the world mean nothing if you don't feel that you deserve them and can't accept them.

The shadow side holds as much worthwhile information for us as does any other part of us. If those messages are denied, they don't go away, but instead come out sideways, controlling our behavior in unexpected ways. Ever find yourself acting in ways that are completely at odds with your mission, but you just can't seem to stop yourself? You *know* better but can't seem to *do* better? That may be shadow's doing. Until we understand how and why shadow can put us on the wrong side of a behavior fence, our darker tendencies can continue to hold sway over our higher wisdom.

Reacting to our shadow side with secrecy and shame only ensures that we stay with our limitations, reinforcing the false idea that "I'm bad, and bad people do bad things." Unless we consciously own our imperfections and forgive ourselves, those shadows create a self-fulfilling prophecy, perpetuating the cycle of shame.

When we look at our shadow side honestly, openly, and nonjudgmentally, however—even when such honesty is uncomfortable—we can take back gradually increasing parts of us that have remained in the dark. This process may not be easy and is often more approachable with the help of a trusted guide, at least in the initial stages. However it's approached, it's worth the effort to begin moving out of the shadows.

Mirror, Mirror on the Wall

Seeing the good in others is a hallmark of a spiritual view. When we persistently see negative qualities in others, it can be a clue to our own unsuspected negative orientation. There's a story of a wise man on a road between two villages. A passing traveler asks him, "How are the people in the next village?" The wise man says, "How were they in the last village?" "Mean and greedy," replies the traveler, to which the wise man responds, "Then you wouldn't like the next village, for there they are all mean and greedy, too." Soon another traveler shows up, who also asks, "How are the people in the next village?" The wise man responds, "How were they in the last village?" "So kind and generous!" The wise man smiles and nods. "Then you will enjoy the next village, for there they are kind and generous, too."

Are you seeing the positive aspects in other people, or only their negatives? We can choose to see either, and that choice has more to do with how we feel about ourselves than it does with those other people.

People around us, in fact, can be a mirror for the traits that are too painful for us to face in ourselves; what irritates us most about other people is often the very thing we need to face in ourselves. But like the traveler on his way to the village, it's easier for us to see the problem as "out there" rather than "in here."

This feeling of not being okay with who we are is, I believe, at the heart of our obsession with following the media when it "gets" somebody for their behavior. When you feel less than others, you'll always enjoy seeing others brought down to your own level. Misery loves company. Our culture so highly elevates politicians, celebrities, and others that it's inevitable that as a culture we would want a self-correcting "fall" to balance out our unrealistic expectations of these people who are all too human. We want our heroes, but we also don't like feeling "less than" for too long. Wouldn't it be thrilling if our own self-esteem was so firmly in place that we were able to send people understanding and support when they needed it, instead of ridicule and anger. "Let him who is without sin cast the first stone," said Jesus.

Though we can hide our shadow from the world, we can't hide it from our higher, wiser self or from God. Those guiding forces already know, and have always known, about our darker sides, and they still love us, warts and all. If we can forgive ourselves, accept forgiveness from our Higher Power, and do our imperfect best to make our own repairs in the world, our spiritual connection is magnified.

An Observer on the Journey

The more we can observe ourselves and others without judgment, the better we serve our mission. Wrapped up in labeling life's events good or bad, we impose our own values on things that, in our limited perception, we have no way to understand fully. I love the story about the horse rancher who woke one morning to find that his horses had broken the fence and fled. A consoling neighbor lamented the loss. The rancher responded, "Not good, not bad, just is." A few days later the horses found their way back, bringing along a few wild mustangs with them. The same neighbor came by and said, "Not so bad after all!" The rancher responded, "Not good, not bad, just is." A short time later the rancher's twenty-year-old son fell off one of the horses and hurt himself. The neighbor said, "That's too bad," to which the rancher responded—you guessed it—"Not good, not bad, just is." A few weeks later the rancher's son got a military draft notice, but failed the physical because of the injury. "Good," said the neighbor, who knew how much the son's work was needed on the ranch, to which the rancher, of course, replied, "Not good, not bad, just is."

This rancher demonstrates an important aspect of being spiritual (even though if you asked him he might laugh loudly at that assessment). Only when we disentangle our emotional dramas from the world around us can we see events as they are, not as we'd like them to be. The ability to simply observe what *is* can be a huge step toward turning energy and intention where it can make a difference. People wrapped up in evaluating the rest of the world (and often other people) can find themselves pinned to a pendulum of enthusiasm and depression, depending on whether what's happening is "good" or "bad." But as the rancher demonstrates and history has shown, judging whether something is good or bad is entirely a human invention. Disengaged from judging events as well as ourselves and others, accepting both shadow and the prettier "good" sides, we begin experiencing and appreciating a new view of the world. Possibilities expand. Words that were too quiet to hear are now heard. Views that were too distant to see come into focus.

I've experienced this in both my business and personal life. At the time of my three-ring wake-up call, I couldn't imagine anything worse happening to me. But out of that upheaval I was pushed to grow in ways that I wouldn't have in that same way or time. Good or bad? Neither. It just is.

Eight Key Plays for Spiritual Practice

Like that endearing alien, E.T., I practically glow when I'm plugged into my spiritual source. Warm, loving, highly energized, caring, and tolerant feelings accompany me like friends. When the connection is weak, however, energy plummets into a sad, out-of-sorts wasteland. By observing myself with teammates, friends, and family, it's obvious when I'm not tapped into my Higher Source.

Before 1989, I didn't even know what it felt like to be spiritually tuned in. God was a distant and shadowy force in another area code, and I didn't have the number. Now I think of God as a most trusted companion who's right here all the time, if I'm willing to call. While I'm in awe of this presence, God also feels more available. While this may not be the way you see God, it seems to me that the form of our relationship with our Higher Power can fit us in whatever way necessary to support us, give us the freedom to love, and bring us closer to our earthly mission.

Play No. 1. Wise Words
My spiritual practice has included reading from a variety of sources including *A Course in Miracles,* the Bible, the *Tao Te Ching,* and Vedic texts, as well as other excellent books (see the Resources section). I also often use the daily lessons in *A Course in Miracles,* experiential exercises that combine study and practice. After reading a lesson in the morning, I sometimes practice it at various times through the rest of the day. Thinking, feeling, and doing allow the concepts to seep in deeply.

Plan No. 2. Good Morning, God
In addition to reading, every morning I engage in a four-step "Universal Talk." This process helps me to find my inspirational frequency, like tuning in a certain station on the radio. Feel free to plug into spirit using this method if it feels right to you.

1. **Ask for forgiveness** from God and yourself. I believe God forgives rapidly, generally faster than we forgive ourselves. Ask to be forgiven for

specific actions that hurt others, and keep asking until you feel forgiveness has arrived. Forgiving ourselves for specific actions allows us to release lingering guilt that interferes with an ability to be loving to ourselves and others.

2. **Congratulate yourself** for things you've done well and contributed to others. Putting a mental blue ribbon on those memories increases the chances that you'll be moved to a repeat performance. Taking a little pride in what we've done to help others helps us feel better in the here and now, a great spin-off that can fuel the rest of your day with an upbeat attitude. This is so important, and yet so difficult for many of us. I know people who are doing a lot of good in the world, including pinning plenty of ribbons of recognition on others, but they wouldn't be caught accepting one themselves. Still, we deserve to feel the satisfying effects of our work, especially because it stokes the fire of doing future good. If we don't stroke ourselves with Self Coaching compliments—or allow others to do so—we'll fizzle before long.

3. **Give thanks** for those things you've been blessed with (for example, personal health; the well-being of family, friends, and co-workers; the opportunity of another day to live your mission; the resources to play your game plan). This feeling of gratitude helps focus attention on what we have rather than what we lack. The "I don't have enough" scarcity mentality so common in our culture distracts us from accepting and enjoying where we are right now. "I need more" thoughts differ from our mission-connected wants and desires. Sure, we all have things we want, but their acquisition definitely isn't the driving force behind my day. My action plans and schedules reflect what I'd like to accomplish, but I think of them as building on what I already have. While I look at them at the start of a week or a particular day, I do my best not to keep what I *lack* at the top of my mind. What is at the top? Being in the here and now, connecting with others, enjoying and making the most of the day, moving slowly but surely along my mission way.

4. **Ask that certain things come into your life today.** Before asking, I first think briefly in a detached manner about my wants, and ask that my requests be granted only if they're in line with God's plan for me. My Higher Power and higher self are both aware of my wants, yet I also accept that this higher view is wiser than my own, and that's more than okay with me.

Play No. 3. Spirit in the Affirmative

The affirmations I use now are a bit different from those described earlier. At Deepak Chopra's "Seduction of the Spirit" workshop, I first learned twenty-eight spirit-focused affirmations called *sutras*. They've become a regular part of my spiritual practice ever since. In keeping with their ancient yogic tradition, sutras are only taught orally, so you won't find books on the subject. My practice, described here, is a brief view of how I use sutras, but it cannot adequately describe the real power of this practice.

Sutras connect such words as *holy* and *enlightenment* with specific bodily energy centers called *chakras*. Chakras form a network of seven physical or spiritual energy centers in the body. I learned four affirmations for each chakra, equaling a total of twenty-eight sutras.

The technique is simple; concentration and opening to the effect can be more difficult. Speak the affirmation, visualize and feel the meaning of the word, and focus attention on the energy center that corresponds to the affirmation. For example, "peace and harmony" is a sutra that corresponds to the fourth chakra, at the heart. Close your eyes, say "peace and harmony," and focus attention toward your heart. I also visualize people who embody peace and harmony or people I want to feel those emotions toward, letting the expansive feelings fill me up. I call them "super sutras," able to plumb depths and bring up riches I've never gotten from simply reading or thinking about these ideas.

Play No. 4. Spiritual Coaches
Spiritual coaches? Why not? If you've never thought of religious leaders or spiritual teachers in this way, you may want to consider them as specialty coaches in your game plan. Inspiring, challenging, and comforting, these people can create spiritual sparks at times when you may be temporarily out of internal fire. They can be especially helpful at transitional stages of spiritual development, when we may not know where to head next or may be too close to our own path to see the way clearly.

Play No. 5. Teammates in Spirit
When people who share similar beliefs gather to study, worship, or do good deeds, higher purpose emerges to help us stay a spiritual course and remind us that we're not alone in our beliefs or destinies. In sincere group worship, the community gains a strength that isn't available to the individual. Like the strength between two people who love each other, the love that emerges between a community and its Higher Source can become a power unto itself, fueling actions that ripple out into the world with greater effect.

Play No. 6. To Embrace Life, Embrace Death

I've come to believe that an awareness of death also plays an important role in spiritual health. Most of us shove knowledge of death to the dark corners, afraid it will cloud our enjoyment of life, but it's only by grasping an understanding of death that we can fully appreciate the present.

An awareness of death is so much a part of Buddhist philosophy that many Buddhists visualize their future death in graphic detail. I've done this and felt how powerfully it increases appreciation of my present life. We've all heard stories of those who wake up to life's wonder in the face of a terminal diagnosis. When death is imminent, the smallest detail can become a prism that refracts the whole of life. The Russian philosopher G. I. Gurdjieff wrote that humans would let go of their egotistical, hateful ways if there were in our midst a constant reminder of death, our own and that of everyone around us. Brought up short by that finality, emotional dramas pull into perspective and small stuff seems less worrisome. In our final hour, you can bet that many of the things we consider huge today will from that perspective seem inconsequential indeed.

An awareness of death heightens the importance of spiritual practice, which often takes a back seat to more mundane concerns in this hurry-up world. Aware of my eventual passing, I'm encouraged to focus on how I'll spend my time after this life, how I'll spend my life here on Earth, and how the two are related. The bridge between the two? Spiritual study and practice. His Holiness the Dalai Lama counsels us to consider how much time we have here on Earth compared to eternity. Then compare this with the time we devote to worldly concerns and the time we spend in spiritual study (preparation for our "life" in eternity). Most of us devote a small amount of time preparing for that endless span and a large amount focused on our relatively short lives on Earth—an inverse amount of effort for the amount of time we'll have to enjoy the benefits. Using an awareness of death to motivate us into practice and study can better prepare us for transcendence—in the final moment and in the present moment.

Play No. 7. SHHHHHhhhhhhhhhhhhh

Without a quiet mind, spiritual practice stands little chance of being more than a collection of techniques and texts. You've heard briefly about quieting the mind to benefit intellectual and psychological wellness. So, too, spiritual wellness benefits from its silent power.

Spiritual messages are available to all, but before we can hear, we first have to stop the chatter and clear the airwaves. This downtime from our do-do-do culture can be difficult and makes many feel guilty. Is it okay to just "be"? Do we constantly have to be doing, creating, producing, making? Remember, we're human be-ings first and foremost, and all the doing flows from that. The serenity of a quiet mind is unlike any feeling I get from my other doings. There's incredible satisfaction in a job well done. And the overarching tranquillity of a peaceful mind makes that satisfaction go even deeper.

QUIET ZONE ✦ Meditation is the primary method I use to quiet my mind. I use it on a frequent basis with great success. Since coming to the United States in a big way in the 1960s, meditation has inched its way toward the mainstream. At first, many Americans marginalized meditation. Perhaps they were puzzled by its proponents, people who didn't fit the mainstream mold of spiritual leaders—people with long hair and flowing robes who (worst of all) had transformed the Beatles into people we didn't quite recognize. Besides that, the stillness of meditation flew directly in the face of this "doing" culture. Placing value on sitting still and *not* thinking was something many mainstream Americans in the 1960s simply couldn't fathom.

Yet meditation has been a part of many religious, spiritual, and mystical traditions for millennia. Ancient Christianity had a history of meditation, and Eastern religions have long held meditation as a central spiritual practice.

In the past decade, meditation has gained more respect across America. The increased interest in the mind-body connection that doctor-philosophers such as Andrew Weil, Deepak Chopra, and Dean Ornish have championed has no doubt fueled the meteoric resurgence of this ancient practice. It is also a sign of our times, a natural outgrowth of the increased interest in spirituality and our growing need for a high-touch aspect in our high-tech world.

The most familiar form of meditation is done in a still, seated posture. Various types of sitting meditation include Transcendental Meditation (TM), zazen, Vipassana, Vajrayana, and Kabbalistic. TM is the most widely known, introduced in the United States in 1959 by the Maharishi Mahesh Yogi. Since then, more than 1.5 million Americans have taken TM classes.

Americans are attending meditation classes in ever-increasing numbers, and classes are now available most anywhere. Local health clubs and wellness centers offer classes. Tires Plus's health insurance company has provided meditation classes to our teammates at our workplace. Hospitals are getting into the act, including such respected institutions as the University of Massachusetts Medical Center.

Quieting the mind decreases anxiety and promotes a positive mental state. It also, therefore, reduces stress and induces just the opposite, relaxation. I get incredible glimpses of elevated joy when my mind doesn't default to its normal thinking mode. As the tide of thoughts is replaced by rhythmic breath, the glimpses of nothingness are surprisingly blissful. I'm reminded of a bumper sticker that advises, "Don't just do something. Sit there!"

The core benefit is that meditation expands our consciousness, gradually awakening us so that we are actually able to hear at all levels of communication—verbal and nonverbal, human and divine—a little more clearly. Generally, people become more aware of their surroundings and more peaceful after meditation. Whereas I sometimes used to drink alcohol to relax, I find that meditation can produce a state of calm that I never even got close to through alcohol. Alcohol numbed me; meditation wakes me up. And the meditation "hangover" is increased mental clarity, the polar opposite of an alcohol hangover.

As for the act of meditating, it is the one of the most interesting, fascinating, and misunderstood phenomena I've ever encountered.

Myth No. 1: It's complex. *Fact:* It is not. It is very simple.

Myth No. 2: There's only one right way to do it. *Fact:* There is not. As a matter of fact, there are many options to help you with the one simple goal—to be.

Rather than perpetuating the three activities we most often engage in— thinking, talking, and doing—how do we put ourselves into a state through which we live up to our name—human "be-ings"? Meditate.

A simple, basic method I use is as follows:

1. Go to a calming, private room.

2. Sit on the floor or in a straight-backed chair. Sit upright, with head, neck, and spine erect. If you sit in a chair, which is easier for most beginners, choose one that allows your feet to rest flat and your thighs to rest parallel to the floor.

3. Close your eyes.

4. Bring your attention to your breath. Don't try to control your breath; just notice it. This helps move you from a state of doing to a state of being.

5. Use any of the following methods to keep attention on your breath:

   a. Bring your attention to your chest and visualize it going out and in, rising and falling with each inhalation and exhalation.

b. Silently count your breaths.

c. Silently repeat a word or phrase, a mantra, that draws focus to the repetition and away from distracting thoughts. Mahatma Ghandi used *Rama-Rama*. Others use an easy-to-recite passage that has spiritual meaning to them, for example, *Om* or *Shalom*.

6. When distracting thoughts come, and they most certainly will, gently flit them away and return your attention to your breath and/or mantra. Don't worry about the frequency of the thoughts that will come in. In our scorekeeping society, this is a fine time to stop counting. Just do your best to be gently attentive and let go of expecting any specific result, and the rest will follow.

Although there are more advanced systems of meditation, this basic method can yield real results. I generally meditate in the morning after my workout, three-minute self-massage, shower, and sutras. If it doesn't happen then, it probably won't as the day gets rolling.

No matter what, I also watch for opportunities during the day when I can take five or ten minutes to quiet my mind. At first I would be self-conscious and embarrassed during meditation. Yet as I experienced the perspective-changing powers of meditation and was willing to let go of ego-based worries about how I'd be perceived, that self-consciousness faded away. Now, if I find myself having to wait for an appointment, either personal or business, I take the time to close my eyes and focus on my breath rather than tense up or pace as I often used to.

Arriving fifteen minutes early to a meeting with my book agent and a potential publisher in New York City in early 1998, I realized I could best use the time to ground my thoughts and focus my mind. I found an out-of-the-way place (though no place was completely out of sight) in the foyer of the publisher's building, sat down, closed my eyes, and began meditating. When my agent arrived, she said that a publishing executive (not the one we were visiting) had walked in ahead of her and stared in disbelief. I laughed, left my pre-meeting jitters in the lobby, and carried a greater sense of presence into our conference. Embarrassing? No. *Empowering.*

Meditation, like physical exercise, has become for me an acquired lifelong habit. Enhancements in psyche, diet, and spiritual practices helped prepare my mind for meditation. Without the other Inner Team members on board, letting intellect take a rest becomes much more difficult. Don't expect the benefits to come immediately. Hang in there. I've seen the "treasure," and one way to get it is to go within. Unlike monetary treasures, which pale in comparison to this one, you don't have to dress for success, and you don't have to get on a plane to go there. You don't have to do, say, or think anything. Only *be*.

MEDITATION ON THE MOVE ✦ Meditation can also be practiced in forms that combine movement with mindfulness. The slow, rhythmic pace of exercises like yoga, t'ai chi, and aikido calm the mind while encouraging the body toward greater strength, flexibility, and balance. Walking, when done attentively, can also be considered a moving meditation.

Instead of the pounding pace of an American-style workout, many moving-meditation routines are physically gentle and thus appropriate for most people of any age. Hatha yoga has become a regular part of my wellness regimen. Through its series of mindfully held postures and attention to breath, I've lost stiffness and gained flexibility and tone—benefits that show up in my basketball game and other exercise as well as in normal movements throughout the day.

Don't let the graceful pace of moving meditations fool you into thinking that these are not physically challenging disciplines, or that the benefits are not real. Results may seem elusive to the beginner, as Americans typically want to see and feel immediate change. The deeper benefits of moving meditations grow with the years.

Play No. 8. Spiritual Sojourns

I found that intensive retreats or workshops were a great way to jump-start new spiritual practices. In fact it was at a t'ai chi retreat in 1989 that I deepened my understanding of moving and sitting meditation. I learned other meditation variations at extended workshops with Deepak Chopra a few years later.

Getting away from the world has, through the ages, been one route to spiritual focus. Think of it as a way of clearing physical space to facilitate a clearing of spiritual space. Native American vision quests and sweat lodges create extended time focused on spirit. Buddha spent years meditating in a cave. Christian tradition holds that Jesus often retreated to find a "lonely place" to commune with God. In Mark 6:31, Jesus asks his disciples to "come with me by yourselves to a quiet place and get some rest." Phoenix Training professional Dr. Ron Fronk has, for the past twenty-one years, taken annual three-day silent retreats, an environment that he finds breeds introspection, reflection, and connection, as many fellow participants return year after year.

A weekly form of "retreat" is found in Jewish tradition. Shabbat lasts from sundown Friday to sundown Saturday every week, a day for those who observe it when no errands are run and no business is done. The day is instead spent focused on family, friends, community, prayer, and study. One person new to this practice described to me how tough it was at first to stop "doing" during a full day each week. In fact, she says it brought her face to face with how much of her self-worth was wrapped up in being productive. It also took months of adjustment in her thinking and scheduling until she learned how to get done in six days what she previously couldn't have accomplished in seven. Shifting priorities made time for what was necessary. She discovered what many Jews bear out: that withdrawing from the usual race for one day a week helps restore a vital perspective on what's really important in life. There's a famous phrase, in fact, that say Jews don't keep Shabbat as much as Shabbat keeps the Jews. No matter what your spiritual viewpoint, the lesson is clear: periods of renewal can reconnect us with our most essential foundations and fuel us for the work ahead.

This desire for an intense period of undisturbed renewal was at the heart of my deciding to take a two-week trip to the Greek islands in 1992. The primary plan for the entire second week was to do nothing but meditate. It may seem a little extreme to travel halfway around the world to go to a place to do nothing. But, still not fully recovered from my 1989 shake-up, I wanted to go to a place far from what I knew, far from business, far from a phone-and-fax-in-every-room, far from my everyday concerns. This would be the first vacation I had ever taken alone. When I told Brenda Schaeffer that I was taking my first vacation by myself, her advice buoyed me: "You mean *with* yourself. You're good company for you!"

That whole week, I meditated in my hotel room, sitting on the bed, with no sense of limitation on how much time I had. Having no pressing appointments, engagements, or schedule was extremely freeing. For one of the first times in my life up to that point, I was just being. Except when I ordered room service, I did very little, spoke very little, thought very little. After a week of virtually nonstop meditation, I was utterly amazed by the feeling that infused my whole being. I had always considered myself a very linear, prove-it-to-me kind of person, but I was feeling something completely unlike anything I had ever felt before. I could only liken it to the vision of the two people in the swimming-pool scene in the movie *Cocoon*. Despite not touching, they were completely at one, fully intimate in mind and body. I had never, ever felt more alive, more awakened, more connected with myself and my Higher Power.

In the latter part of that week, I was roused in the middle of the night to the strangest experience I've ever had. Wide awake, I saw on the pillow next to me a glowing treasure chest. Not an apparition, it looked very solid, detailed, and weighty. It was about three-quarters the size of the pillow. I gazed at it for about thirty seconds, then slowly reached out. As my hand approached it, the chest slowly dissolved. The clarity of what I had witnessed astounded me, and I promptly wrote down what had happened in case my linear, disbelieving businessman's mind might try to talk me out of it the next morning. The simple interpretation of this message sent from my Source: If I take time for self renewal, there are many treasures awaiting me.

In the remaining days and during my trip back, I continued to feel this incredible aliveness. Colors were much brighter, shapes more in focus. Internally I felt rapturous, a calm yet heightened level of excitement. Upon my return, I began meditating more regularly, though not for the same duration or with the same intensity. The degree of aliveness I had felt in Greece faded, and within three days only a portion of the feeling remained. But the portion that lingered was a beacon that the rest is waiting for me to access again.

Since that night, I experience life more fully than before. I notice that, as with exercise, the more I meditate, the more centered, grounded, and calm I feel. Meditation isn't always a high, though. When the negative aspects of emotions drift up and need to be released, meditation can feel temporarily unpleasant. I find that's very temporary, and I soon return to a more calm state. Annual retreats are now an invaluable part of my spiritual growth.

Time for Spirit

Some people think that spiritual practice takes too much time, while other people can't find enough time in the face of competing demands. While I average sixty minutes a day on some form of spiritual practice, some days I spend two hours with various methods. On other days I "take five to thrive" with a shorter version: Five Minute Prayer, Five Minute Reading, Five Minute Meditation, and Five Minute Sutras. When pressed for time, even these abbreviated versions and a four-step Universal Talk in the car on the way to work can enhance my day.

Consider that even thirty minutes a day is only 3 percent of the average American's waking hours, and what a difference that 3 percent can make. While more is better, less (even five minutes) is far better than no time at all. Unless we make an effort to keep spiritual matters in our line of vision, they tend to slip out of sight, crowded out by the rest of our already full lives. When I'm tempted to set my spiritual study aside, I remember the words of His Holiness the Dalai Lama: "Study is the weapon that eliminates the enemy of ignorance. It is also the best friend to guide us through all our difficult times."

But why study? Can't we be caring, loving, spiritual people without focused study? Certainly, but the rule of diminishing desire and our tendency to forget what isn't consistently reinforced demonstrates that the more we fortify positive habits with the structure of study, the more apt we are to be caring, loving, and spiritual, more deeply and more often. Daily study helps to focus on the important things and guard our thoughts against the useless melodramas that surround us at every turn. In the same way that a dietary program helps select what you put in your mouth, spiritual practice helps you select the thoughts that run through your head.

The form that a commitment to spiritual practice takes is as unique as each individual's relationship with his or her Higher Power. While some choose to devote significant time and energy to this, others may choose to give it only a few minutes a day. Some may seek a structured system, while others gravitate toward methods that are loose and spontaneous. Some prefer to study under a teacher or spiritual guide, while others choose self-study. Whatever your decisions, choose the spiritual regimen that is right for you. One size doesn't fit all.

Remembering Your Spiritual Being

I see life as a journey of spiritual development. Neale Donald Walsch writes about three distinct phases he sees: "When you live as a single-faceted creature, you become deeply mired in matters of the body: Money, Sex, Power, Possessions, Security, Fame, Financial Gain....When you live as a dual-faceted creature, you broaden your concerns to include matters of the mind. Companionship, creativity, new thoughts, new ideas, creation of new goals, personal growth....When you live as a three-part being, you come at last into balance with yourself. Your concerns include matters of the Soul, spiritual identity, life purpose, relationship to God, spiritual growth, ultimate destiny....As you evolve into higher and higher states of consciousness, you bring into full realization every aspect of your being. Yet evolution does not require dropping some aspects of self in favor of others. It simply means expanding focus...toward genuine love and appreciation for all aspects."

Forgetting the spiritual side of our being seems to be part of the human experience. Even the language of our farewell document, the will, speaks of foreboding doom and doesn't conjure up love in this world or the next. "Upon your demise…" my attorney Sid Kaplan said several years ago as we worked on my will. I stopped him and said, "Wait just a minute. You mean 'upon my transcendence'?" He said, "Sure. I've never had a request to change the 'demise' language, but I'll put it in," and he did. As I told that story over lunch to one of my mentors, Curt Carlson, founder and chairman of Carlson Companies, he said with a laugh, "Demise. Yeah. That sounds like you're going the wrong way!" Spiritual awareness, to me, is a big part of a correction in thinking that generates positive—not negative—thoughts, feelings, and actions.

The Real Game

While spiritual practice is important, it's truly *practice* for the real game: service to others. After all, is all this effort only for myself? Or is it also to help others when and where I can? If the only thing I give in this life is birth pangs to my mother and then spend my life using up natural resources, is that enough? What good is it if I do spiritual practice and then frown at the man sitting across from me in the subway? What good is it if I've built a great business for myself and not shared that success with others? What good is my own wellness and prosperity if I don't use it to become a beneficial presence on the planet? To study spiritual values and then fail to ground them in real-world action would be a terrible waste. Taking the lessons out of the textbook and putting them into the street puts life in the teachings.

Giving to others—whether time, attention, love, money, or our other unique resources—is a natural extension of feeling gratitude for being alive. As we harvest good, we're also obligated to plant the seeds that will help others yield their own harvest as well as replenish our own. If you want to keep it, you have to give it away. If we're fortunate enough to have resources to share, it doesn't make us better than anyone else; in fact it gives us an added obligation. It also can be a deterrent to spirituality if we focus more on the things we accumulate and consume than on nonmaterial, spiritual matters. Ultimately, the blessings we have spring from a divine source, and we are simply their stewards.

Jewish tradition has a term, *tzedakah,* which is sometimes understood to mean "charity," but a closer translation is actually "justice." When we recycle the good we receive back into the circle of caring, we become part of cosmic justice. Seeing others in need is a spiritual call to action. Typically, we're taught to think, then act. In fact, some traditions teach that if your spiritual intention isn't in line with your action, then it's better *not* to act. But when another's welfare is at risk, I believe that's no time to ponder the purity of our hearts. Whether my intentions are in line or not, a shivering person is still cold until I offer a coat. Give first; analyze later. As Stephen Grellet said, "I expect to pass through this world but once. Any good thing, therefore, that I can do, or any kindness that I can show my fellow creature, let me do it now. Let me not defer or neglect it, for I shall not pass this way again."

Compassion Under Fire

What about the times when it's difficult to feel caring, loving, or spiritual? When someone is upsetting or bothering you, angrily challenging or verbally attacking you, it's hard and sometimes even dangerous to remain open and caring. My natural reaction has been, like most people's, to armor up emotionally and prepare for battle. Caring feelings are quickly replaced by "get 'em" feelings.

In recent years, with spiritual practice, I've become more aware of this defensive reaction. I've learned to see it more clearly as a detached observer of my own behavior in many—but not all—situations. A graphic reminder of the need for continually alert observation came back to me in fall 1998 while I was playing in a basketball game. An opposing team player and I began mixing it up. He was, as we say on court, setting picks (also known as screens) on me. Setting picks, which means standing in my way so I can't get to the man I'm guarding, is perfectly within the rules. The trouble was that I perceived that he was moving and grabbing me so I couldn't get around him—*not* part of the rules. An elbow here, a bump there, and soon we were yelling at each other, each believing that one was trying to hurt the other. In the clear light of hindsight, there was no way to prove one's claims over the other, but fueled by righteous indignation, I was intent on letting him know I was in the right—down to the last word.

Yet, as Reverend Mark Holman of Minneapolis says, "There's no way to set a pick on your own humanness. Thankfully, it will always get through the screen." When the adrenaline subsided, it was replaced with a horrible queasiness. In spite of my best efforts to put that aggressive, ego-based behavior into the distant past, here it was again, like some long-forgotten mascot. After years of good relations on the court, I was shocked to see how easy it was to slip back into destructive ways. Self-protective ego was everywhere, and spirit had fled. As we lined up to shake hands as teams always do after a game, I stuck my hand out to shake his hand, a peace offering. He wouldn't shake mine. The damage was done, and the lesson was clear.

I resolved once again to do my best to withdraw the urge to get the other person back. Entering an emotionally neutral zone where I could look past the other person's defensive face into his heart, I remembered that anger masks fear. I could have better looked underneath this for the source of the anger, rather than getting hooked by its expression.

Aware that what I send out comes back to me, I'm aware that when I react to others' negativity with anger, I not only damage the other person, but also deny myself the peace and joy that God intends for me. When I can withdraw from my part in the anger dynamic, I can retain control of my state of spirituality and my ability to be a beneficial presence. Counselor Louise Hay speaks to the ideal: "No one has the power to irritate or annoy me. I focus my mind upon my highest good and let this inspire me." This is an ideal that isn't possible for me to embody always, but I take heart in doing better when I can. I relate to the philosophy that says evolving spiritually is measured when we try every day to be a little more humble, a little more generous, and a little more tolerant of things that are irritating.

Marianne Williamson writes, "Any situation which pushes our buttons is a situation where we don't have the capacity to be unconditionally loving. It's the Holy Spirit's job to draw our attention to that and help us move beyond that. Our comfort zones are the limited areas in which we find it easy to love. It's the Holy Spirit's job not to respect those comfort zones, but to bust 'em. We're not at the mountaintop until any zone is comfortable. Love isn't love until it's unconditional...and the Holy Spirit has a highly individualized curriculum for everyone. Every encounter, every circumstance can be used for these purposes." This ability to be tolerant and not to allow my buttons to be pushed is one of the primary measuring sticks for me in my spiritual growth.

The Last Real Frontier—Inner Space

An ancient Tibetan wrote, "We'll know we're in an age of confusion when iron birds fly, we eat standing up, and we replace meditation with sitting in front of the altar of false images and dreams." The way out of confusion? It's not in moving backwards, away from the advances of modern life. We need to be in the flow of life, one foot in this world while one foot is in the other. The antidote, it seems to me, lies in moving inward, balancing the aspects of body, intellect, psyche, and spirit, so that we can then move out into the world with clarity. Balanced and fully awake, we can use the tools the world offers to bring us closer to our missions and to each other, turning confusion into connection. With our Inner Team in the game, we can use the best of what the world has to offer—instead of letting it get the best of us.

Is my own life perfect because of personal growth and a higher level of wellness? Of course not. I have days and times when I feel incredible joy, affection, sympathy, and self-confidence. I also have those times when I'm mad, sad, or scared. Yet I live with much more authenticity and joy than ever before. And when I'm mad, sad, or scared, I feel it, express it, and move through it more quickly. I know there will be some dark days in the future, yet there's some comfort in knowing that those days can be blips on an otherwise bright field.

The last frontier isn't outer space but inner space. It's with you wherever you are, yet for most of us it may as well be millions of miles away. My former t'ai chi instructor, Robert Larsen, taught me this valuable lesson in 1990. I was taking lessons, but I wasn't practicing enough between sessions, and he wanted to know why. "I haven't been able to find the time," I said, "between my work and my working out." He responded, "Working out— as opposed to working in?" My defense was busted.

Once we let go of the need to constantly do, and tune into the spiritual frequencies, we begin to move inward, listening to messages from our Source that resides within and without. A story goes that a group of angels were entrusted with the secret of success, but they had a problem: where to hide it? They didn't want just anyone to get hold of it. One angel suggested putting it on a mountaintop. Another disagreed: "Humans are always reaching higher. They'd find it one day." Another angel suggested burying it in the deepest valley. "No," another replied. "Humans are always digging for answers. They'd come across it there, too." Another angel said, "Let's send it into outer space." Another replied, "No, humans are never satisfied with staying on the ground. They'll learn how to fly far out into space, and they'll find it there." Exhausted, a small angel spoke up: "Let's put it inside them. They'll never look there."

Time for Inner Team Wellness

I wouldn't trade the benefits of heightened Inner Team wellness—body, intellect, psyche, spirit—discussed in these last three chapters for anything in the world. Still, many people think it just takes too much time. If you're wondering if you can find time, take a look at how many hours the average person really has, compared to how much time a sample wellness program takes. Obviously, choose the practices that feel right for you:

168 hours per week (24 hours × 7 days per week)

— 49 hours work (some studies indicate this is
average, including a commute)

— 49 hours sleep (7 per night)

70 waking, non-work hours per week

Out of those seventy waking, non-work hours, a balanced wellness program may include the following:

5 hours education (reading, study, lectures, classes)

4 hours physical exercise

1 hour supportive bodywork (chiropractic, massage, etc.)

1 hour outside counseling

2 hours moving meditation (walking, yoga, t'ai chi, etc.)

5 hours sitting meditation/prayer/worship/affirmations

18 hours per week for wellness and self-care

If you devote eighteen hours per week to your wellness—26 percent of your waking, nonworking hours, that's still less time than the average American spends watching TV. That leaves 74 percent of your waking, nonworking hours available for all the other things in life besides work, sleep, and self-care. I submit that you'll be more available to others and live a more conscious life by valuing yourself and your Inner Team wellness in this way.

Because wellness is an ongoing process, keep yourself motivated with ongoing activities. Keep a book at your bedside and read a little each day. Have at least one weekly outside activity, a continuing-ed course or a study group, on your calendar. Find a mentor you can check in with on a regular basis to keep goals and progress on track.

The place you give self-care in your own life depends on your goals, priorities, and other commitments. Raising a young family, starting a new job, or caring for an aging parent may all challenge your ability to engage as fully in self-care. Whatever your situation, focus on what *is* possible. If you're in a phase in your personal and work life that doesn't leave you a lot of time, focus on things you can do that don't require a lot of time. Sitting at your desk for five minutes, noticing your breath, and focusing on opening your heart will yield greater benefits in the long run than spending that same time worrying about what you can't get done. Do what you can with what you have, wherever you are, and be at peace with that.

The Inner Team requires working both in and out. Just like a growing child who has to develop large-muscle coordination as well as the subtle touch required to pick up the smallest feather, so, too, we must develop all levels of our skills—physical, intellectual, psychological, and spiritual. The agility and flexibility of physical wellness give feet to the wings of intellect, whose creativity and logic span the breadth of the world. The intuition and insights of psychological wholeness give voice to the body and depth to intellect, reaching out to spirit. And spirit holds them all in the great chain of universal connection, guiding the team to a higher purpose.

Ten Lessons for
Lifetime Learning

LET YOUR WELL of learning never go dry. As you walk the now-familiar Seven Take-Action Steps that line the path to your mission, lifetime learning is essential company. As my Swiss-German great-grandmother Seifert would say to my father whenever he got too big for his britches, "Bill, it's what you learn *after* you know it all that really counts." That commonsense wisdom, popularized in recent years, holds as true today as it did when my father was just a boy.

American pop culture is saturated with the cynical "been there, done that" attitude. The concept "lifetime learning" defuses that cynicism by reminding us that no matter where we are in life, no matter how successful or how secure or insecure we are, there's always more to learn. "The beginner's mind," Deepak Chopra calls it. To me, a lifetime-learning lens is sensitive enough to recognize everyday lessons. Rather than fearing the challenges of learning something new ("that's not the way *I* do it"), it seeks the lesson each challenge offers.

Maintaining curiosity and an "I want to learn" mindset requires a conscientious effort. This chapter reviews ten potent areas to "juice" that learning mindset. The reward is more fuel that keeps you on track toward your mission.

Lifetime Learning

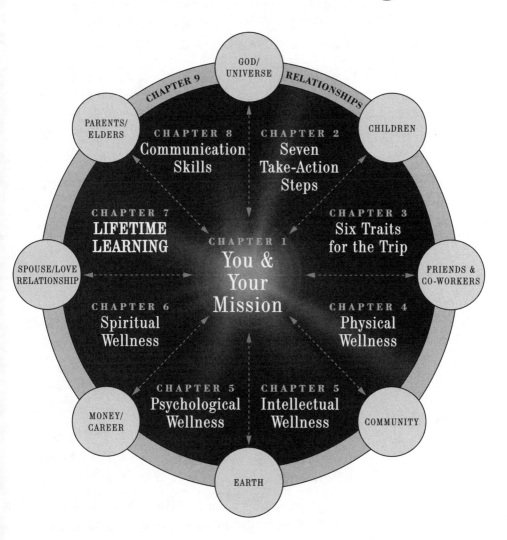

Why is lifetime learning important? Three reasons come to mind. First, because the world doesn't stand still, we can't afford to stand still, either. Change occurs faster and faster with each flip of the calendar. Consider, for instance, that what we call civilization has spanned millennia, yet we've only fiddled with electric motors and radios for two generations or so. Just in the last lifetime, we've been handed televisions, computers, plastic, penicillin, credit cards, and air conditioners—and put men on the moon. Unfortunately, all this technology doesn't mean that we're necessarily smarter. As the English historian G. M. Trevelyan wrote, "Education has produced a vast population able to read but unable to distinguish what's worth reading."

Relationships, both personal and business, are mercurial. Technology, competition, customers, the latest management fad—all daily visit change on the business world. A friend who attended a change management class related that one confused attendee blurted out, *"Change* management? Oh, I thought this was a class about *changing our management!"*

There's more. Evolving gender roles, shifting expectations of others, the manifold packages today's family comes in—all of it profoundly affects the way we live. If you don't keep up or at least gauge, now and then, where things are going, you will be left behind. In the game of hockey, embracing change is called "being ahead of the puck," anticipating where it will travel next. That way you conserve energy and get to where you need to be just ahead of when you need to be there, rather than constantly chasing our own tails. It's what made Wayne Gretzky "the Great One." Embrace learning, and you'll stay ahead of the puck. You can count on change because, as the adage goes, it's the only constant in life.

The second reason lifetime learning is important is that, regrettably, humans tend to forget some of what we learn. Unless you're alert, it's easy to slide into behavioral and mental ruts that sever your actions from your principles. Sometimes, when our knowledge slips quietly and mysteriously into obsolescence, forgetting is okay. When that happens, it's usually best to jettison useless cargo (redundant files consume valuable, finite human RAM). Still, there's a large swath of our forgotten knowledge that was and still could be useful. The good news is that lessons can always be relearned.

Finally, lifetime learning is important because many of us desire to evolve to higher planes. Learning is a road that can take us to varied and wonderful places: physical, intellectual, psychological, and spiritual wellness; career advancement, closer relationships; or a deeper understanding of our own potential.

The endless growth cycles my company lives through remind me constantly that I must overcome a natural habit to coast on routines that are outgrown, as the company doubles in size about every three years. Whatever your position, if your organization is growing, you'll need new skills to do the same job in a larger organization. Leadership is my role. But I wouldn't be able to lead a bathtub chorus without upping my skills to lead a larger and larger company as well as adapt to the business world's furious clock speed. At the same time, these and many other skills can help our personal lives. I ran headfirst into lifetime learning in 1989, an encounter that provided me with a firmer foundation on which to build relationships with family and friends. My only regret? It took forty-two years to discover the value of lifetime learning in all areas of my life.

Faces and Phases of Learning

We move through four phases learning and unlearning as we enter new relationships and face new challenges:

1. **Unskilled and aware.** Initially, we're perfectly aware of our lack of knowledge, and work hard to reach a respectable level of competence. We're beginners, and we know it.

2. **Skilled and unaware.** After a spell, we grasp the basics of the situation, hopeful of mastering all the necessary skills. We've become capable although we don't realize it, and thus endeavor more and more skill.

3. **Skilled and aware.** Suddenly we think we've grasped the Grail. Now we're reading our press clippings, reliving kudos over and over, resting on accomplishments and laurels. Learning takes the backseat. This is often the beginning of the end—a spiral into taking proficiency for granted. We're seduced by shortcuts. Tried-and-true principles and techniques are expediently pushed aside in the interest of convenience and the ease of routine. What was energetically learned is now lazily lost.

4. **Unskilled and unaware.** Having rounded off the corners of our tried-and-true track, we've worn down a new rut called obliviousness. No longer grooving on solid principle, we're ineffectual. But we don't realize it. Here, even the most successful personal or business relationship disintegrates.

In order to escape this fourth phase—or prevent ourselves from ever reaching it in the first place—we must go back to Phase 1 and admit that we need to learn and relearn the basics that got us to be aware and skilled in the first place.

Learning Employers Yearn For

Ironically, few skills that employers desire are found on school course lists. A 1995 study by the U.S. Department of Labor, for instance, reported that the perfect employee

1. innately hears the key points of a customer's concerns (listening)

2. thinks on her feet (problem-solving)

3. produces innovative solutions (creative thinking)

4. takes pride in himself and his potential for success (self-esteem)

5. knows how to get things done (goal-setting and motivation)

6. senses what skills are needed for maximal workplace performance (personal and career development)

7. gets along with customers, suppliers, and co-workers, and strives to achieve common goals (teamwork)

8. conveys appropriate responses (verbal andwritten communications)

9. senses where the organization is headed and what she can do to contribute (organizational effectiveness)

10. assumes responsibility (accountability)

11. motivates co-workers (leadership)

In addition to those skills, I place high value on a few others, in myself and in my Tires Plus teammates. All of us endeavor to

1. develop COPPSS traits: caring, optimism, passion, persistence, systems-discipline, and spirit-filled behavior

2. develop our intuition, a sixth sense of what is happening (this helps anticipate unpredictable change)

3. access our Inner Team energy and maintain peak wellness

Sure enough, many of us learn some of these skills when we're young, thanks to the guidance of teachers, parents, caregivers, siblings, and peers. Today, progressive schools offer courses on listening and goal-setting. For many of us, however, the nittiest of the grittiest of life's fundamentals have never been explained in a comprehensive way. We've picked up lessons here and there, succeeding there, failing here.

Aside from some of the skills mentioned above, think of all the other basics that we don't learn in school, such as how to understand ourselves; how to find and select healthy friends and love interests; how to nourish relationships; how to parent; how to manage our relationship to money;

how to plan and schedule; and how to multitask, or manage multiple demands.

Many of these are skills we employ every day, to varying degrees of effect. But we're oblivious to the ways we pick them up, like colds or like a little accidental afternoon sun. Life is the school where we learn these things. Class is in session. Are you attending?

While it's human to forget, it's also human to put the pieces of the puzzle back together, again and again. Respect and exercise the power of your mind, stay conscious of your learning processes, and reinforce principles that add value to your life and mission.

Ten lifetime learning exercises keep my personal and career skills agile. They've staved off the tendency to get rusty and assisted my evolution.

Lifetime Learning 1. Who, Me?

To paraphrase Yogi Berra, you can observe a lot about yourself just by watching. This seems obvious, but most people find it easier to watch (and analyze) other people than to watch themselves. They're missing the best show, themselves. Observing your own dynamics is a skill enhanced by the methods explained in chapter 5.

The point of observation? Think of it this way. A coach can't improve what he can't see. In order to turn a losing strategy into a winner, first you must observe the game of your life from all angles.

Once I was willing to study myself, it became more and more obvious what I needed to change. My wiser self now regularly sends in plays, as well as the kind of constructive feedback I used to get from my high-school basketball coach. "Tom, don't do that," I'll tell myself. "That's an old pattern. Avoid it." Or, "Tom, good job on that talk. You really provided something useful there." Or, "Tom, you need to apologize. Your comments weren't appropriate and served neither of us well." After all, who knows me better than, well, me? Who better knows the challenges I face, and their solutions? Who always witnesses them? I do my best, every day, to pay attention, to be fully conscious, and to coach myself honestly, based on what I see myself doing.

Three Roadblocks

Consider how well you observe and coach yourself. What stands in the way of doing a better job? How can you address it? P. D. Ouspensky identifies three roadblocks to studying yourself.

1. **Overestimating your knowledge and significance blocks your incentive to observe and learn.** Solution: Cultivate a dutiful attitude toward lifetime learning. Consider yourself a universal novice, and open yourself to living lessons.

2. **Detours into negative feelings—anger, fear, guilt, anxiety—distract you from the more productive course of self-study.** Instead of focusing inward on what we can improve, we too often focus outward on objects of negative emotion. Solution: Face these negative thoughts with the psychological and spiritual wellness techniques in chapters 5 and 6.

3. **Excessive talk, both inward and outward, makes it hard to observe and coach yourself.** The internal monologue loops that ruminate over every incident will not bring us to a more positive plane. Likewise, chewing over and over the same incident also prevents you from seeking the answers you already have the answers to inside. Solution: Guard your thoughts, breathe deeply, and see yourself in slow motion as you move through life, observing and coaching yourself. Take what's left of your day and practice self-observation and constructive Self Coaching.

Lifetime Learning 2. Experience: Your Best Teacher

Experience is a great teacher. A cliché, perhaps. But reflect on and use your storehouse of experience, what some call "trial and learning." Experience is the classroom for countless lifetime lessons. I look at my business and personal life as laboratories that yield results both painful and exhilarating. I try to learn from the snafus and fubars I encounter so I don't repeat them. I also learn from the good stuff.

As I encounter new situations daily, I ask myself, "Have I been here before?" and call on experience to inform my next move. I literally conjure up past scenarios and comb them for similarities. I recall how I handled things, what went right, what went wrong. Then I allow for changing circumstances—different teammates, different competitors, different factors.

Factoring in differences is critical. While the underlying dynamics may be the same, each situation is unique. On the personal side, most everyone's been hurt by a romantic relationship, though few would conclude that all relationships are destined for the same fate. Yet, if romance goes sour time after time, there's a clue to a potential pattern. There's probably something to glean from those relationships, some kind of change that's required to make your next relationship sweeter.

The Buck Stops Here

The lessons of experience begin with being able to look at your own role in past events, successes and failures. Relationships with others, personal or professional, are especially fertile ground for learning. By learning from mistakes in dealing with and leading others, I've profited from experience rather than simply living through it. I do my best to drop what fails me and repeat what succeeds. It's that simple.

After repeatedly finding myself going round and round with someone in a familiar negative loop, I admit that only one of two possibilities exist. Either I'm creating the negativity, or I've chosen a relationship with someone who brings negativity to the relationship. Either way, I'm responsible.

Lifetime Learning 3. Peers of a Feather

Look around. See all those people whose careers and relationships mirror your own? Peer power is what happens when you develop learning exchange relationships with these people. On one hand, we say that success is contagious, and on the other we say misery loves company. Either way, there's a lot to learn from people going through what you're going through. Not to be confused with mentors (people who have already faced your challenges), peers are friends and colleagues who travel in your sidecar down roughly the same personal and professional road. Both of you simultaneously experience similar thoughts and feelings, and the immediacy and intimacy you share can produce insights invisible to people removed from your situation by time and experience.

There's a comforting feeling of camaraderie with a peer who's in the same boat. Whether sharing triumphs or troubles, so much can be gained by eye-to-eye relationships of mutual respect. Thoughts are unencumbered by explanation. Feelings are confirmed and validated. Actions are planned and affirmed, honestly assessed, and open to alterations. So helpful is the information and counsel of some friends and colleagues that they begin to feel like family.

Mirrors and Road Signs

The biggest benefit of peer power is the sounding board they can provide. Peers are a mirror whose reflection of you is objective yet empathetic. They can reveal answers we already possess, yet can't see. Most answers lie within, and finding a peer who asks the right questions to help you access them is a true gift. Their feedback is reliable reality testing that reinforces or cautions against the direction you're taking. Their personal and professional life laboratories become open to you.

I feel that peers are signposts placed in our paths by a higher wisdom. But they require us to read the road signs. There are many ways our Higher Power informs us, and this is one of them.

Early Exchanges

I've been exchanging peer power from early on. Jim Calli, a close friend since first grade, was always a notch or two better than I was in schoolwork and sports. Yet from first grade through high school, his support and friendly competition in English classes and basketball was influential to my development. I use many of the lessons of those early years today, the most important being the value of people inspiring one another to greater and greater heights. The peer exchange we share today is enhanced by our chosen life paths and goes deeper with each year.

Four other elementary-school classmates, Davey Leach, Bobby Stoner, Donnie Miller, and Pat Kelley, also continue to influence me. Davey (a factory worker), Bobby (an insurance salesman), Donnie (a real estate investor), and Pat (a florist) stayed in our hometown, strengthening it with their unflagging optimism, strong character, and love for its people. Their natural spirituality and open natures have always provided valuable touchstones.

Peer Power Exchanges

Would-be business peers are everywhere. Look inside your own company. Elsewhere, service organizations and industry associations at the local, regional, or national level are ready-made pools of people whose circumstances likely mirror your own.

Personal peers also surround you. I've made lasting friends in t'ai chi classes, book groups, anywhere that peers congregate there's opportunity for a powerful exchange. Feedback from outside parochial career spheres hedges against the tempting shop-talk fallback position that can deflect focus from areas of personal growth. It's a vantage point that allows us to see the inner forest for the clutter of our business and personal trees.

I follow three criteria when choosing peers for power exchanges:

1. **Select peers you can trust.** The greatest exchanges come with people whom you can tell absolutely anything. This means, of course, that confidentiality is paramount. No matter how great the skills she offers, if you don't trust someone, the exchange will suffer.

2. **Select peers free of conflicts of interest.** A peer who's a direct competitor or who's vying for the same promotion may or may not offer the most objective counsel. Those conflicts of interest can potentially obstruct the flow of honest information that is so crucial to valuable peer exchanges. I guard against this by finding business peers who are retailers in the regions where my company operates, yet who aren't tire retailers. The same holds true for personal peers. If someone can benefit directly or indirectly from the decision you're facing, take his counsel with a rock of salt, and seek a second opinion. Nevertheless, there are peers who, despite glaring conflicts, can offer unbiased counsel. Just be advised of the inherent dangers.

3. **Select peers with attitudes and behaviors you admire.** Look for peers with traits that are energizing and motivating, like COPPSS.

Initiating a Win-Win

Peer exchanges are reciprocal experiences, unlike the mentor-student relationship, in which one person almost exclusively learns from the other. Because of their two-way nature, it's important to understand what the other person wants to learn from you and what you believe your peer can teach you. Deepak Chopra, for example, has shown me new paths to pursue in spiritual philosophy and practice, and I've been able to show him management principles that can help his organization. With any peer, the more you have to learn from each other, the better. If you sense a good fit, that's your cue to establish a fat pipeline for peer exchange.

Peer power exchanges can be scheduled or done on the fly. Grab opportunities as they arise. They needn't be formal. You can advice-swap without asking for, establishing, or even verbalizing that you're going to do it. It does work best with people you know well and see frequently. Alternatively, you can schedule these barter sessions if you need to explore issues that require an uninterrupted block of time.

A Memphis businesswoman I know joins seven peers for personal and career exchanges every month. At each meeting they reconfirm their mutual commitment to confidentiality. Their deep level of trust enables them to be more real with the details of their situations and thus get more meaningful feedback.

Takes One to *REALLY* Know One

Peer learning requires us to share what's really happening in our lives, both successes and defeats. When a peer asks, "How's it going?" the biggest roadblock we can put up is the pat answer, "Fine." Reflex responses like that say absolutely nothing. They don't engage. I'm not suggesting that every time someone asks how you are, you tick off a laundry list of woe, or that you share things you're not ready to reveal. Trust your intuition, yet don't be afraid to lean on the many trustworthy people who have your best interest in mind.

Say a peer, someone you trust, asks how you are. Offer up the one or two important issues weighing on you: "I'm doing okay, I guess, but I've got a challenge with my youngest daughter." That short comment could return a volley of immeasurable benefit. Remember, the simple act of unleashing feelings is cathartic. Add that emotional benefit to the learning you get from your peer's feedback and you have nothing to lose. "Ask, and ye shall receive," as Jesus counseled. Most people enjoy talking about what they've done, especially under these circumstances.

Peer power exchanges are vast caches of wisdom hiding in plain sight. Don't overlook them.

Lifetime Learning 4. Mining Mentor Gold

The shortest distance between ignorance and knowledge is a straight line to whoever has the knowledge. When looking for a mentor, find someone who's already pulled off whatever it is you want to do, someone who's willing to share with you what they've learned. Trusted mentors can coach and guide you down both personal and professional roads, pointing out the potholes that pock our mission's road. I lament that I didn't mine these veins of wisdom a lot earlier in life. Once I began, in the early 1990s, I realized how many personal and professional pitfalls I could have avoided with the guiding hands of mentors. If you choose well, you'll find people who have already gone through exactly what you're going through. They'll recite exactly where they were right and where they erred. Their guidance is pure gold.

The Magnificence of Mentoring

Suspicious of this mentor business? Feeling a wee bit too proud to seek advice from others? In days of yore, practically every trade was firmly grounded in the master-apprentice tradition, the skilled teaching the unskilled. But something tragic happened on the way to modern civilization—we've become a society that values formal schooling and knowledge-based enterprises over craftsmanship. In the process, the master-apprentice relationship has largely fallen by the wayside. Why not revive mentorship and match those who know with those who want to know?

Aristotle and Alexander, Sigmund Freud and Carl Jung, Louis Sullivan and Frank Lloyd Wright: knowledge transfer between the generations is a natural part of civilization, especially in close-knit societies. A return to the well of mentor wisdom is long overdue.

Professionally speaking, the mentoring shortage is more pronounced among women. Boomer businesswomen, many longtime members of the vanguard, are veeps and owners in unprecedented numbers. Yet, while their numbers are dwarfed by those of Gen-X women in the workforce, they're much less likely than men to either formally or informally share their valuable experiences with the generation to whom they'll cede power—all the more need to heed this call.

Choosing Mentors

How do you choose the right guides? For career mentors, I choose people who have been in a position similar to mine, in a field that's related to mine but is not the same, and who's farther along his or her path. That way, I benefit from their experience with the same organizational challenges I now face. I also look for people who have the principles, values, and ethics I strive for in my own business.

Six years ago, I sought out the leaders of two of the nation's most successful businesses in my area. I asked Richard M. Schulze, chairman and CEO of Best Buy Stores, the nation's largest chain of electronics stores, to be my first-line mentor, the one I visit and speak to most frequently. For my second-line mentor, I tapped Curt Carlson, chairman and CEO of the hospitality empire Carlson Companies (Radisson Hotels, T.G.I. Fridays). Both led incredibly successful businesses. Together, their guidance has given me the foresight to avoid many of the difficulties they experienced.

As you might imagine, asking busy people for their time isn't quite as simple as picking up the Yellow Pages and dialing. You have to find people appropriate for your needs, persuade them to invest time in you, and then optimize the experience. Here are the steps I recommend.

1. **Identify the personal and professional skills and information you prize most.** Who has the answers?

2. **Search your mind and research** mutual friends and associates for people who can facilitate a connection, or deepen one that already exists, between you and your potential mentor.

3. **Get active in organizations and events** where your potential mentors gather. Without stalking them, watch for opportunities to chat. Sincerely acknowledge their achievements and find common interests that help you to get acquainted. Never underestimate the value of sincere interest, heartfelt compliments, and a willingness to share some of yourself. I don't care who the people are or what their position in life, they enjoy this.

4. **Ask for a meeting.** Invite your possible mentor to breakfast or lunch. When she agrees, cement the commitment with something like, "Great, thanks so much. I really appreciate it. When's best for me to call to set it up?"

5. **Follow up** with a card that expresses your gratitude and confirms the appointment, such as, "It was great meeting you. I appreciate your working me into your busy schedule, and I look forward to seeing you next Monday at 8:00 A.M."

6. **Prepare focused, thought-out questions** for your mentor. List a short series of tactful, personal queries and key business issues. Find a middle ground between bashful and zealous. That way, your mentor will appreciate your focus and will be better able to offer good advice. In my first mentor meetings, I ask about challenges I've experienced:

"Did you experience that at one stage?"

"How did you handle it?"

"What would you do differently if you had it to do over?"

This is not only educational, but also a lot of fun for mentors, as they recall how they worked through things. As the old saying goes, "When you teach, you learn."

7. **Take notes.** You may think you'll remember everything, but you'll be glad you captured important thoughts so you can reflect on them later.

8. **Share information that could be beneficial to your mentor.** Most successful people are open to learning, from any source.

9. **Express your gratitude.** When you're done, thank your mentor for the value you've received and for taking time out for someone who isn't as far along the path as she is. Too often people don't do this because they fear coming off as apple-polishers. But if the feeling's real, platitudes become real gratitude.

10. **Ask for an ongoing relationship:** "Would you consider mentoring me for an hour or so three times a year?" Some will agree, while others may need time to think about it.

At our first meeting over breakfast, Dick Schulze said he would consider taking me under his wing. A few days after our meeting, I called his assistant and asked what Dick would most value as a token of my appreciation for what he'd already done. Best Buy had just moved into new headquarters, and his assistant said he needed a plant for his new office. I sent a plant with a thank-you note attached. The next time I called for a session, he agreed.

Some might call my gift to him as simply "giving to get." But it wasn't. I sent the plant because I was truly grateful. I wanted him to know that no matter what became of our relationship, my gratitude wasn't conditioned upon some future gain. Had he refused future meetings, I'd still be happy I sent the plant.

Does this seem like a lot of work? Finding a vein of gold isn't easy. You have to make a case that will enable your mentor to understand that your cause is worthwhile. Generally speaking, mentors don't methodically choose who they help. They choose from people who seek them out, who stand out from the crowd, people with whom they connect. Through this process, I've gained several ongoing relationships with business mentors who have passed on tips that helped me better lead and successfully grow Tires Plus.

Up Close and Personal

It goes without saying that our personal lives deserve the same scrutiny and care as our businesses and careers. It's a given, but it's not advice that's always taken. I have spiritual, behavioral, and self-care mentors. Just like my career mentor meetings, time with personal advisers offers live examples to model as I travel down my mission's path.

With an eye toward striking harmony between my yin and yang, I consciously balance the genders of my advisers. My female personal mentors have included psychologist Brenda Schaeffer, body and energy workers Leni Erickson and Carole Morning Smiley, and my mother, Elizabeth Cummins. Mentors among my Y-chromosome mates include behaviorist Earnie Larsen, author-philosophers John Robbins and Deepak Chopra, and my father, Bill Gegax.

Our primary role in life, it seems to me, is to learn and teach. Then—and only then—is the baton handed off to others and our knowledge and wisdom expanded beyond our own lifetimes. Look around. You may see many who would enjoy and benefit from your mentoring. When we give, we get. If we want to keep it, we have to give it away.

Lifetime Learning 5. Lessons from Our Youngers

Mentors turn up in the most unlikely places. Sometimes, for instance, it's hard to see what could be gleaned from children—either your own or other people's. Trust me, there's plenty. They know you better than almost anyone else does, and they're not afraid to tell it to you straight—often a lot straighter than many of our friends and colleagues who, for reasons politic or passive-aggressive, sometimes talk from both sides of their mouths. A single remark from the mouth of your babe, whatever his age, can press development. Discount and dismiss their advice at your own risk. Tapping the wisdom of your children and succeeding generations is the fifth method of lifetime learning.

Common wisdom holds that each succeeding generation is influenced by those that have gone before it. The elder affects the younger. True enough, but reverse generational influence can be no less profound. Young people adapt to technological and cultural change faster than their elders. Their habits aren't as deeply rooted, making them open to change. Whether it's computers, VCRs, or the Earth-friendly green movement, most teens and twentysomethings catch on quicker than boomers. Yet more often than not, the influence of the younger on the older is lost on people once they approach middle age.

Watch, listen, and learn…from kids? Sure enough, it's the exact opposite of the traditional image of wise-old-owl mentoring, which offers up the experience of elders walking the path before us. What they tell us is based on their reaction to sights, sounds, and circumstances that you've yet to face. Our children (indeed, anyone younger than us) can provide the inverse. They've just set out, fresh of eye, nimble of foot, at the beginning of the path you're treading. They're quicker to assimilate change, their ideas are less likely to be burdened by rules that no longer hold. In sum, they're more likely to be unconventional. "Out of the box" is the buzzword for the way their new brains react to old states of affair. "Shoulda," "coulda," and "oughta" less often enter their decisions or their vocabulary.

Respect Your Youngers

It's true that we should respect our elders. But we would be remiss if we did not also respect our "youngers." You can't benefit from their wisdom if you don't value their input. They'll give it to you straight if you don't try to kill the messenger. In the face of my sons' feedback, I sometimes get defensive before letting go and receiving their jewels of wisdom. From an early age, they've taught me invaluable lessons. Just for starters, Chris's ideas have improved Tires Plus, and his candid personal feedback has improved our relationship, while Trent has encouraged me (no, *prodded* me) to upgrade my abilities with new technologies and writing skills.

Younger wisdom, like all other learning, needs to pass your internal check to ensure that it directs you properly. Do their lessons coincide with your mission? Are there conflicts of interest that could cloud their counsel? Evaluate their lessons just as you would any other. Just the same, be wary of rejecting lessons out of hand in order to defend comfortable, entrenched habits. It's not a trusty enough barometer for their advice to simply "feel right." Feelings can be blurred by compulsions, addictions, and dysfunctional behaviors that, while comfortable, likely don't serve your best interest. Defending "the way it's always been done" only chains you to the past's pillory as time slashes by.

Learning from your children yields multiple benefits. You reap value from their unique perspectives. Your children learn the value of their ideas and opinions—a fringe benefit that encourages higher self-esteem, which is, in turn, a key determinant of high achievement in school, life, and one's mission.

Lifetime Learning 6. Modeling Success

In school, copying the exam of the guy next to you could land you in hot water. In life's informal classroom, however, copying others' behavior—if done carefully—can help you land a set of good habits rather than troublesome ones. There's a lot to gain from this subtler form of mentoring, called modeling.

When I was a kid, I'd spend hours watching Duke Snider swing a baseball bat, or local golfer Jack Miller swing a club. Then I'd model what I saw. That's also how I learned to dance, mimicking the moves of the fleet feet around me. In algebra or backgammon, it's easier to see and do rather than listen to somebody tell you how to do it. Watch, learn, and do.

Careful what you model. Take someone you admire. Again, it may sound obvious, but rather than adopting all her traits, learn her best ones and leave the rest. Remember what our parents asked: "Would you jump off a bridge just because everyone else did?" Anyone you choose to model will, like any of us, have imperfections that we unknowingly tend to ape. To avoid this, imagine making a best-of tape combining all the traits of successful people you've ever been exposed to. Naturally, you'd edit out what you don't like. Now imagine the higher power of synthesis combining the best traits of your parents, siblings, children, friends, peers, and mentors into one person—you.

Lifetime Learning 7. Columbo-Curious

The seventh method of lifetime learning is what I call the Columbo Principle, after Peter Falk's forever questioning TV character. To some, it seems artless, perhaps naïve, to ask ostensibly simple questions when you're in the dark. I disagree. Straight, frank questions are among my best ways to learn. "There's no dumb question" is part of our collective vocabulary, yet it's contradicted by the myth that we look dumb, if not simply nosy, if we ask questions. Questions, however, not only enhance your knowledge base but also strengthen your bonds with others. Whether confronted by a simple question or a complex issue, interviewing the people around you elicits their inner views. Most people love sharing their views on just about anything. Let them. Before you know it, a connection is forged.

Quelling your natural curiosity leads to endless lost learning. This is particularly true of impromptu questions that are responses to seeing or hearing something uncommon. This happens to me constantly, at work and at play. Whether it's an unfamiliar word or a report I don't understand, I ask in order to expand my knowledge. When it comes to asking questions, my curiosity overrules politics and ego.

Questions avoid misunderstandings. Each of us points his or her personal frame of reference at everything we hear. We make assumptions that are faulty and can interfere with learning. But the more you ask questions with a beginner's mind, setting aside preconceived notions, the better you'll hear the answer and consider applications of it. Rather than discounting new ideas outright, let the new information roll around and see where it lands.

Questions will never lead to learning unless you're open to answers that surprise, or even contradict, your comfortable assumptions. If you ask questions merely to confirm your point of view and cast aside answers that contradict it, or if you use the answers to prove others wrong, you'll learn little more than how to play clever games.

The way I count it, you have at least three strikes. Once you ask a question, be ready to follow up and lock in the answer. One foot in the water—just about to catch the information wave—is no time to break for the beach.

Commit yourself to developing a Columbo-curious nature by asking questions when it's appropriate. Unsure how to start? Watch a couple of four-year-olds in a toy store, then start modeling your youngers.

Lifetime Learning 8. Your Talk-Listen Ratio

When you talk, you can't listen. When you listen, you can't talk. Without the right talk-listen ratio, it's impossible to learn from others, to say nothing of yourself.

Think for a moment, what is your talk-listen ratio? What percentage of your conversations, from one-on-ones to group settings, do you spend talking? What percentage are you listening? Jot it down, then consider the following guidelines.

Aim for a fifty-fifty ratio for one-on-one chats. If you're talking, or listening, more than two-thirds of the time, notice whether it's a pattern. The math changes with additional people. Say you and three friends are talking. A proportionate balance here would have you talking 25 percent of the time, listening 75 percent. This of course isn't possible, or even desirable in every situation. But simply being aware of your talk time hastens movement toward a healthy range.

Why is it important to involve others? Actually, over-talking is a great source of lost opportunity. Any speaker benefits from the opportunity to reinforce concepts, make sense of challenges, and talk out the options. Valuable benefits, to be sure. But the benefit the speaker loses by not opening up the discussion is just valuable, if not more so—the chance to learn something new, those important messages and unique perspectives we can only get from others.

Think of the largest chatterbox you know. Consider what he's missing by trapping himself in the rapids of his own thoughts instead of easing into the refreshing stream of others' ideas. To offer a hand out of the rapids and into the stream, assist him (and you and everyone else he knows) by gently employing the "bottom line" technique discussed in chapter 2. One-on-one, a laser-sharp question that goes to the heart of the matter delivers a quick resolution. In a group, wait for the prattler to take a breath (inevitably he has to breathe), then jump in and shift the airtime to someone else with a simple question: "Andrew, what do you think?"

Tattletale Signs

Now for an honest interaction inventory: Do you find yourself constantly guiding conversation to issues you want to address? Do you prefer only to talk about things you know? Do you interrupt people to tie what they're saying to something you want to say? "I know exactly what you mean. I had this experience last week…" Then they grab the floor. These are things that make people say, "Ugh," not "Hmmm."

Another telltale sign of over-talking is traveling the long and rambling road. A bell goes off if I find myself talking in circles, not quite finding my point before trailing off in another direction. It's the surest way to lose someone. For many, this is a blind spot, especially deadly in business, where time is gold. People ramble when they are nervous, unsure of themselves, ill-prepared. Sometimes it betrays low self-esteem. At other times it indicates an overactive ego that needs to parade erudition and push its own views at the expense of others. Sometimes it's motivated by a need to control—control a conversation and you control others. Giving feedback on over-talking is about as easy as telling someone he has body odor. There is a gentle way to do this, which we'll get to in chapter 8.

The opposite of over-talking is just as frustrating. When we say little, the burden shifts to the conversation partner, who's deprived by our own silence of our unique message. If you don't have anything to add, ask clarifying questions and salt the issue. Suddenly, you're an active conversationalist, opening the door to further dialogue.

Lifetime Learning 9. Study Your Team's Playbook

Nearly every organization, from Boeing to Bill's Bicycle Delivery Service, maintains a variation of the "company manual"—a compendium of its philosophies, concepts, history, products and services, mission, vision, values, policies and procedures. I call these playbooks. A firm grasp of these playbooks will align your contributions with the mission of your organization. Knowing the plays is imperative for success, no matter the player or the team.

The thought of leafing through your company's playbook may elicit yawns more than dawning inspiration. Many workers consider it dry, boring companyspeak they can easily get along without. But how can we expect to successfully live the mission, vision, and values of our organizations, or champion their philosophies and concepts, if we don't intimately know them? How can we know where a company's going unless we know where it's been? If we don't understand the products and services the organization distributes, along with their benefits, how can we passionately serve customers and colleagues? Finally, if we don't know the policies and procedures, how can we play by the rules (or creatively break them, when living your mission is in the balance) and be systems-disciplined, thereby minimizing chaos and maximizing productivity?

Lifetime Learning 10. Tap Outside Resources

Seminars, books, tapes, magazines, television, zines, newspapers, the Internet—at no other point in history have we had more intellectual food on which to grow and learn, both personally and professionally, than during today's so-called Information Age. The breadth of subjects is breathtaking. Name it, from paleontology to polo, and you can feast on information about it.

A good place to start? Find out what educational opportunities your workplace offers or supports. At Tires Plus, we focus our educational resources through Tires Plus University, a state-of-the-art, nontraditional R&D "lab" that researches and teaches technical skills as well as improved ways to serve our guests, effectively coach ourselves and others, and work together. Encourage your organization to synthesize education into your corporate culture. The significant time, energy, and dollars we invest each year come back many times over in teammates' personal and professional development, and in their increased ability to offer the top service we strive for in the face of an ever-changing future.

Distance learning via the Internet is increasingly available. Convenient and flexible, classes can be formal or informal; you can earn credit and degrees, or simply blast your mind with a fresh breeze of learning. The University of Phoenix, for example, offered 120 courses in 1998 through its "On Line Campus" to some four thousand students.

With so many information options, the obvious challenge is separating the wheat from the chaff. Choose subjects in line with your personal mission, with your wants for the year. List seminars you want to attend and books to read. Books on tape, which turn your car into a rolling university, are increasingly popular. One of the many beauties of the printed word, however, is the option to highlight and review key language.

The challenge presented by this trove of resources is to enjoy intellectual spelunking, whether it moves you toward personal, family, or team missions, without aggravating information overload. Remember that despite the best of intentions, most people retain and employ little of what they read and hear. Here are a few ideas that can help you absorb valuable information:

+ Try to be childlike in the face of new ideas. Rather than thinking, "I've heard this before," I ask myself, "Have I tried that recently?"

+ Underline, highlight, or keep notes on points to implement.

+ Incorporate those points into personal or business action plans, schedules, and to-do lists.

+ Within a week of completing a book, article, or seminar, review your notes and what you have underlined.

Stay Ahead of the Learning Curve

It's necessary to enroll in the school of lifetime learning if we're serious about continuing on the road to our mission. Obstacles certainly exist. Today's speed-of-thought technological changes antiquate some of yesterday's learning, and it's only human nature to forget timeless wisdom and some of life's basics. To be sure, both can drain your tank. But you can refill it with these ten tenets of lifetime learning. To whatever degree you can, personally and professionally, keep your eyes and mind open to the lessons on the horizon. Like the long and winding road, learning never ends.

8

No Failure to
Communicate

"It's a communication problem."
—Everyone

NOTHING CAN DERAIL Mission Express like ineffective communication. The Seven Take-Action Steps get turned on their heads while two key mission pieces in particular, relationships and career, go south. We're left shaking our heads and wondering why with so many words there's so little communication.

Communication breakdown is the impediment of our age, despite the preponderance of meetings in every hallway and conference room, phones in every car and coat pocket—to say nothing of the e-mail, faxes, video conferencing, and pagers whose invisible digital paths crisscross the globe like a great ball of string. Nevertheless, this embarrassment of wordy, technological riches hasn't protected us against the game of Telephone we played as kids, in which one friend whispers a story in your ear, you pass it to another friend, he passes it to another, and so on, until the last kid triumphantly pronounces the message—inevitably a hilariously garbled version that bears scant resemblance to the initial thought. Regrettably, adulthood miscues like this are rarely funny; sometimes they're dire.

No one disputes the amazing progress in communications speed and accessibility. But few perceive that a crucial human skill—our ability to

Communication Skills

GOD/UNIVERSE

CHAPTER 9

RELATIONSHIPS

PARENTS/ELDERS

CHILDREN

CHAPTER 8
COMMUNICATION
SKILLS

CHAPTER 2
Seven
Take-Action
Steps

CHAPTER 7
Lifetime
Learning

CHAPTER 1
You &
Your
Mission

CHAPTER 3
Six Traits
for the Trip

SPOUSE/LOVE
RELATIONSHIP

FRIENDS &
CO-WORKERS

CHAPTER 6
Spiritual
Wellness

CHAPTER 4
Physical
Wellness

CHAPTER 5
Psychological
Wellness

CHAPTER 5
Intellectual
Wellness

MONEY/CAREER

COMMUNITY

EARTH

listen, process, and respond quickly to what we're hearing, thanks to all this gadgetry—isn't evolving at the same speed. No wonder we haven't kept up. It's much easier to improve the hard, objective science of chips and circuits than to upgrade the soft, subjective complex of the human brain. This chapter will take a look at some of the many ways we can enhance the human side of communication, whether speaking, listening, or writing.

Because communication ties us to the world and everyone in it, our skills (or lack of them) determine, by and large, the quality of our personal and business relationships. With stakes so high and clear, why is it so difficult to communicate?

Dams to Communication Freeflow

Four communication roadblocks come to mind. First of all, like so many challenges, it can be traced to questionable education. Formal schooling taught us random communication lessons that were often not interrelated. Speech classes may have taught us how to present to a group, but when were we supposed to learn how to listen and respond? Writing classes taught us how to write an essay, but where were we supposed to learn how to carry on the daily digital dialogue of the modern workplace? True enough, some students extrapolate lessons and form useful custom communications skills. The majority, I'm afraid, don't.

Second, to further destabilize our shaky grounding in the communication arts, the organizations for which we labor routinely hinder information flow. Too often, layer after layer of management promotes the downward flow of communication, only to stanch it before it can shoot back upstream. That restricts dialogue and discourages cooperation between these layers as well as among departments. Even in companies that embrace the latest "horizontal management" trend, openness can exist, yet without a structured flow, communication flies in all directions, and whether the pipeline is too open or too closed, communication chaos often results.

Third, as the globe shrinks and the office diversifies, language itself becomes a challenge. Imagine what can be lost or misinterpreted in a simple exchange between two people of different genders, age groups, and socioeconomic and cultural backgrounds. You begin to get a sense of the potential for info-chaos. We hear language through the filter of our own experience, and often we assume that everyone hears it the same way. Attention has been turned in recent years to the divergent communication styles of women and men. Awareness of those differences is fine, if not the source of some good-natured ribbing—as long as we reserve judgment.

Rather than drive us to further misunderstandings, gender intelligence can help us frame our words in order to bridge the gender gap. Healthy communication never means "my way or the highway." It's all about finding common ground.

Fourth, our ability to listen and speak honestly and openly is challenged by any number of physical and emotional factors. The result? We don't always hear or speak as clearly as we might assume. Stress and tension in particular inhibit meaningful conversation. As Dr. Albert Mehrabian showed in his respected studies on the nonverbal and verbal components of our communication about emotions and feelings, 93 percent of our message is body language and voice tone. That means only 7 percent of the message is transmitted with actual words. Now, imagine what we convey with a stressed-out face, tightly folded arms, or fists planted aggressively on hips. Even the most loving of words don't come off as sincere, when delivered from a body crackling with tension.

Whatever the cause, the consequences of bad communication are clear: at home, parents and children become strangers; mates miss each other's meaning; lifelong friendships sink into sad animosity. In the workplace, intra- and interdepartmental squabbles (especially the heralded staff-line conflict) can deep-six productivity, alienate customers, and stall careers.

Four Inside Moves for Mutually Fulfilling Relationships

The Honeymoon and the Morning After

Poor communication is the grounds for failure in a variety of relationships, love and work being two of the most common. Consider that 50 percent of all marriages end in divorce within seven years, and that most companies experience 50 percent employee turnover every four years, despite these new relationships starting off packed with promise. In the beginning, we hope to get and we hope to give, and we select mates and jobs that we hope will put us on a path to fulfillment. Giving and gaining may not always be equal, but we begin the relationship hopeful that we will help one another find a special balance. Sometimes, many times, it just doesn't work out. And when it doesn't, whether it's ending a relationship or leaving a job, we find ourselves facing some of life's biggest stressors.

Instead of leaping into thoughts of moving on after we fail to make mutual benefits a reality, we must ask ourselves, Where did I go wrong?

Was my choice bad? Did love blind me? Was I seduced by a company line? By money?

Perhaps, perhaps. But often the problem isn't so much our ability to select a relationship as it is our failed effort to realize the relationship's potential. The dark lining of a great beginning is that inevitably it runs smack into the trials of day-to-day relationship maintenance. That requires lots of honest, cogent communication.

High-Hurdling the Big "C" Relationship Ruts

When a relationship hits the wall, we frequently fear saying what's on our mind. (Or we do the extreme opposite and say a spiral notebook's worth of things we didn't mean.) But what's to fear in speaking our piece? Round up the usual suspects: rejection, judgment, anger.

As children, many of us were surrounded by people who weren't exactly open to our young views. For some, it takes little to revive the cacophony of those memories: "I pay the rent, and as long as you live here, this is the way it is!" "I'm the mother, I'll act any way I please." "On *this* team, you'll follow *my* orders." "In my classroom, you'll do exactly as I say!"

The message was as clear as the tears, shed or held back, that it provoked: your opinion doesn't count, and piping up may land you in hot water. That's dangerous territory for a child. People who grew up with this message often decide "it isn't safe to say what I think. I'd better be quiet. I can't trust other people." Quietly buried in the psyche, these beliefs unconsciously influence us throughout life. Even when people who grew up with these messages want to speak, a voice from inside says "stop."

Think back on some of your relationships—teachers, coaches, managers, romances, friendships. Did they give you freedom of expression? If not, it's likely that, to some degree, you didn't understand one another's needs. After all, it's not likely that one of you was a mind-reader. So you're left with unresolved misunderstandings, and they pile up like garbage, sometimes for years, until the accumulation rots the relationship. Then things get ugly: "Take this job and shove it!" "I don't need this marriage anymore!"

Unfortunately, we don't always know what we need. We only feel the pain, and hope someone will come to the rescue. How many of our past relationships could have been more fulfilling had we been more open and honest? "A lot," is my answer. In myself and in others, I've seen the idyllic beginnings, the troubled middles, and the heart-wrenching endings, followed by those dazed days when the pain is shaken off and the whole thing starts all over again. A new employer. A new boyfriend. A new wife. Ah, wherever you go, there you are.

To jump this rut and land in a groove of healthy communication, I use four steps that apply to both business and personal relationships. They help me take greater part in and responsibility for the communication process and help create gratifying, mutually beneficial relationships.

Big "C" Step 1. Ask What's Expected of Me

Do you know what your boss or mate expects from you? How about your children? Even if you think you know, it's worth the effort to find out if everyone's on the same page. Sometimes those expectations, when fully verbalized, paint a picture far different from what we previously believed. At other times we sort of know the other person's expectations, but even that doesn't eliminate the potential for rifts. Even if your goals are the same as your mate's, your priorities and the relative weight you give them can differ and work at cross-purposes. That is when you've got to keep in mind that your connections with others are symbiotic; your lifelines are tied together. Each party gives to the relationship, and each gets something back. To fulfill your part of this symbiosis, it's paramount that you negotiate an exchange by defining what both parties want and need.

We're not always in touch with our hopes and expectations, because many of us have gotten used to adapting to others' and setting aside our own. It may take some time, effort, encouragement, and permission for those around you to get in touch with their own hopes and feel comfortable expressing them to you.

In a business relationship, it's generally a manager's responsibility to make sure employees know what's expected, yet many don't. When they don't, you need not abdicate your responsibility to understand how you can make things easier. You, your manager, your company, and your customers all profit from clarity, no matter who initiates it. Look at it this way: If you walk into a dark room and no one flicks on the light for you, would you wait for someone to hit the switch or would you find it yourself? Unless you can tick off with crystal clarity your manager's expectations, hit the switch. You probably learned a lot during your initial interview and during the normal course of your day, but like life, jobs can be mercurial. Keep up with the company you keep. Do you know your priorities and, for instance, the performance expected of you?

Some managers avoid being direct or try to generalize, either because they're pressed for time or because they lack the skill to be direct. Don't accept this. It's not the guidance you seek, and it will come back to haunt you when your manager himself gets clarity (likely forced upon him by his own manager). Unless you hit the switch, you'll suffer for lack of understanding about issues that were "surely obvious to you." If your manager says, "Just do your best," counter with something like, "I always do. But in order to do my best, what, in your mind, are the top six things I could contribute to the department in the next six months? And, by the way, how will you measure my success?"

Most of what applies in a business relationship applies in a personal relationship—except, of course, the tone. Sample something like, "Honey, I'd like you to help me be clear about what you need and want from our relationship. That way I can do my best to do my part." Expectations are quite different in a personal relationship. But whether personally or professionally speaking, it can be valuable to write down what's expected of you. Sound too structured? Look at the upside. It takes the guesswork out of expectations that can come back to haunt us if we're incorrect and creates a benchmark from which to review and refocus, when necessary.

Big "C" Step 2. Share Your Hopes, Dreams, Expectations

After seeking to understand their expectations, it's time to complete this exchange by sharing yours. Too often, managers make assumptions about their employees' wants and needs, and too often employees assume that their managers can intuit, without being told, what they want and need. The same danger exists on the personal front.

Get this on the table during the same meeting at which you inquire about your manager's expectations of you. With those expectations in hand, follow up with something like, "Terrific. I'm going to do everything I can to do these things for the team. By the way, are you open to hearing my hopes and expectations?"

This same type of follow-up is important in a romantic relationship. You might say, for example, "I'll do my best to give you what you need and want, and I'd like to tell you what I hope for our future. Are you open to listening?" Who's going to say no to that? If, by some chance, he refuses, ask why. If he still won't address the issue, consider enlisting the help of an objective third party, perhaps a counselor or therapist. If there's still no progress on getting a hearing for your hopes and dreams, ask yourself whether the relationship has a future.

If the sharing is done tenderly, with your heart and spirit present, you'll come away with an understanding of the energy that each party is willing to devote to the exchange of giving and getting. If, on the other hand, the discussion is scripted, rote, and methodical (especially the personal one), its power will be diminished. Even if it's uncomfortable, give it a whirl. Don't be concerned about doing it flawlessly. Even doing it clumsily will get you further than not doing it at all. Think for a moment about your most important relationship. Do you have an up-front agreement about the contributions and benefits you're both making and receiving? If you do, you're one step closer to having a mutually satisfying union on your hands.

Big "C" Step 3. Don't Forget to Ask How You're Doing

Agreement is consummated. Now ask for feedback on a regular basis. "How am I doing?" Whether we're dealing with a mate, a daughter or a manager, oftentimes the expectation is that they'll give us feedback—positive and negative—without prompting. But it's not always quite so simple. Consciously ask them, "How am I doing?" It's a much more reliable way to get feedback.

Many managers find it difficult to appraise their employees genuinely and directly, except within the safe confines of an official performance review. Expressing feedback directly yet gently is no walk in the park. Absent skill, it's often easier for them to forgo feedback than to take a leap that could wind up a stumble.

A perfect example: During a review, your manager brings up an incident that happened months earlier. In a similar vein, say your mate brings up something irritating you did, weeks after the fact. They may feel safer speaking from a distance, but correcting the course is much more difficult once the tracks are cold. The vitality of feedback is proportionate to its proximity to the action being appraised.

One way we overcome feedback obstacles at Tires Plus begins with titles. Everyone on our management team is formally "Coach" of one department, area, or store. "Managing" conjures up images of control, criticism, and manipulation, while "coaching" suggests enthusiasm, instruction, and encouragement. And just as coaches give players feedback while the game is in progress, we need to hear feedback at the moment our learning window is open widest.

So if a manager or spouse doesn't give enough feedback, why don't we ask for it more often? We're not all able to approach feedback casually. For those with a history of negative self-talk—"I'm not good enough," "I'll never make it," "you can't trust anyone"—constructive feedback can be easily heard as destructive reinforcement of those messages. When feedback intended to help instead feels like harm, we tend to arm ourselves against it.

Before 1989, I thought I was genuinely open to constructive suggestions. At least I told everyone I was, though I discovered that my tone and body language said something entirely different. While I listened with my ears, my face was tense and strained, my tone of voice frequently defensive. This weakened my ability to absorb what people were saying, and it sent them a clear message: I don't like hearing what you're saying. Until I better learned to align my verbal and nonverbal messages, I was contradicting my own request for people to be honest with me.

Some managers or loved ones will waltz around the question "How am I doing?" with a perfunctory "Pretty good" or "Fine, I guess." Be ready to follow up. Try saying, "That's great. By the way, what are the three things you like best about what I'm doing?" Then follow with, "What are the three things I could do better?" Most people will 'fess up if you first ask, directly and specifically, for positives followed by areas in which you could improve. Drinking in a balanced mix of positives and corrections infuses the exercise with a sense of fairness. Instead of feeling like criticism, it becomes an objective assessment whose obvious goal is improvement.

Still, some people can dance for a long time. "Oh, I don't know," they'll say. "Sorry, but I can't think of anything off the top of my head." Out of your hearing, however, they could most likely run down a whole laundry list. If we're afraid to press on, and they're afraid to answer, we end up in a stalemate—and our growth just gets stale.

Check yourself out. If you're not getting frequent, balanced feedback, get in the habit of asking, "How am I doing?" Do it sincerely, open your body language, be genuinely willing to hear whatever answer you get. Here, ignorance is not bliss. A rocky relationship road is paved with denial over our relationship agreements, whether implicit or overt, and how we are, or aren't, living up to them. Smoothing away the rocks with improved communication may require courage and discipline today, but it's better than the pain of failed relationships tomorrow.

Big "C" Step 4. Gently Tell Them How They're Doing

Hearing feedback about yourself can be difficult. But giving others feedback is often harder. Whether difficult or simple, though, it's necessary. When someone—your girlfriend, your manager, a cousin—does something irritating, notice how you react. Do you tell them how they're doing?

Most people behave in one of four ways. Only one response supports mutually fulfilling relationships. The other three can only deepen a rift.

The first way is criticism without compassion—yelling, sarcastic remarks, slights. This escalates the battle, setting up a round of attacks and counterattacks that completely overarch the behavior under discussion. Protecting personalities, not changing the behavior, becomes the prime target. The second way forgoes communication entirely ("the cold shoulder"). It may seem like the noble route, but silence is destructive. The third way is giving foggy feedback that's not really honest about how you feel and is too vague to learn from.

Any of these leaves the other person in the dark about what you really think (even when it seems obvious to you). Sure, they may have a clue, but they can't mind-read the whole how and why of your feelings. Letting issues fester drains energy and blurs focus. The anger they breed can pop up unexpectedly in various arenas. Most important, they handicap the person with whom you're having a problem. Not knowing what's wrong, they have no opportunity to make it right.

The constructive response, the fourth, is the gently honest approach. You want to convey what you need from others. Easier said than done, right? Before I offer a technique for presenting diplomatic feedback, first consider a few questions and what you want to say to the other person:

+ Why do you want to say it?

+ Will it help the other person improve—even if it's tough for her to hear, or for you to say?

+ Are you trying to clarify an issue, or set the record straight?

Now, move to the next stage: Ask yourself how you feel about the person at issue.

+ Do you want to speak up because you care about him or her?

+ Could your desire to speak up actually be a case of muscle-flexing?

+ Are you sitting in judgment of the other person?

Be mindful of your motives, and make an effort to think about the process and the bigger picture, rather than about the personalities involved. Even in the midst of giving someone feedback, it's just as important to remember what people do right as it is to tell them how they can improve. Because we take people for granted, especially those we see every day, it's easy to forget the value of this sensitivity.

In giving feedback to others, I learned firsthand how important a soft touch is to smoothing troubled waters when I was twenty-two and working in the Employee Relations department (called Human Relations today) of Shell Oil Company's Midwest regional headquarters in Chicago. One of my office's duties was to ensure that the various department heads issued salary increases commensurate with corporate policy. It was my job to evaluate the proposed raises and tell the department leaders which were within guidelines and which were not. After I'd spent a miserable week butting heads with department heads, my manager, Neal Pettit, was deluged with complaints about me. But Neal was a patient fella. He asked me to tag along as he approached a few of these heads. What followed was a clinic in diplomacy, what I've heard described as the art of jumping into troubled waters without making a splash.

After a few minutes of small talk, he lightly inquired about the logic of the raises they proposed. Overall, he praised their reasoning, then he'd scratch his head over a few cases that didn't track. They walked together down the path of cooperation rather than running headlong down two separate paths smack into each other. Together they explored options and found solutions. This southern Indiana boy's first lesson in "down home diplomacy" had bailed him out of troubled, big-city waters.

The underlying principles of the lessons learned that day have evolved over the years into the Sandwich Technique, an effective method for giving feedback designed to short-circuit defensiveness and reach win-win resolutions.

The Sandwich Technique

The Sandwich Technique squeezes the critical issue between two positive appraisals. The language is gentle, and addresses the matter with words that reflect *your* feelings and perceptions rather than words that assess or judge *the other person's* attitudes and behavior. This defuses defensiveness because, while it's easy to disagree with your assessment of their actions, it's difficult for someone to dispute your feelings.

Why, you might ask, all this gentleness—what in my home state we refer to as Minnesota Nice? Most of us have fragile egos, whether or not we'll admit it. If you attack, others will defend. If you approach with an extended hand, others will extend theirs in kind. I, for one, am more open to critique if I sense someone's speaking to me out of compassion and not from a desire to slice-and-dice me.

We treat receipt of news that we've done something wrong as if we've been handed a scarlet letter. Feedback is not an official notification that, yep, we're bad people, failures. Yet, give feedback in a less-than-caring way and you'll surely create this perception. You'll face a wince, hastily assembled walls of defense, if not flat refusal to listen.

The Sandwich Technique works for any issue, personal and business. The exact language in the following examples is less important than the feeling and intent behind them.

1. **Start by saying something positive—and true**—about the person you're talking to. Look him in the eye. Smile. Look for the good. It's there.

2. **Broach the issue:**

   a. Ask if he's open to hearing a concern you have.

   b. Explain it, with care, focusing more on how you feel and what you sense, and less on what he's doing. If possible, mention your perception of the effect his actions have on you.

   c. Hit the ball into his court: "Give me your take on this." "Your thoughts?"

   d. When he answers, notice whether he's being specific. If he keeps the discussion general, or delays, ask for details or reach an agreement on when he'll get back to you. Often the issue can be resolved on the spot, but if not, suss out his initial thoughts: "Do I have your support?"

3. **End on a positive note:**

   a. Thank him for listening: "It feels good to have a manager (or mate, colleague, friend) that I can talk to about issues like this."

   b. "I enjoy working with you. Have a great day." Or "I love the relationship we have."

Here's an example: Say an issue arises between you and your manager, Claudia. The crux of the matter is that you feel as if you're the only one staying late and working weekends. Here's how you sandwich Claudia.

FIRST, POSITIVE +

You: "How's it going, Claudia?"

Claudia: "Busy."

"Well, the good news is that business is good."

"You can say that again."

"I enjoy it when it's busy, and I enjoy working here for you."

"Thanks."

NEXT, ISSUE +

You: "Claudia, something's concerning me. Are you open to hearing about it?" (Ask for permission.)

Claudia: "Sure, of course."

You: "It feels like I'm working a lot more evenings and weekends these days. Don't get me wrong, I'm a team player, and I like contributing. But the extra work is causing me to miss my daughter's soccer games, and it's straining my marriage. Any thoughts?" (Toss the ball into her court.)

Claudia: "Now that you mention it, you have been working some long hours. I guess you've shouldered more than your share. I'll look at doing something about it and get back to you."

You: "That'd be great, Claudia. Thanks for understanding. When do you think you might get back to me?" (Clarify the timing.)

Claudia: "I'll shoot for this afternoon."

END POSITIVE +

You: "Fantastic, Claudia. I really appreciate your support. I feel great having a manager I can talk to about this kind of thing. Thanks for listening, and have a great day."

It's Up to You

Make no mistake, everyone has a stake in resolving differences, especially when employee turnover and divorce rates are painfully high. These four communications steps work because they place the responsibility where it should be, squarely on our shoulders. When one of the four steps is omitted, our intentions and actions can spill out of control, running fast away from a win-win. Think about your romance, or your office relationships. Do you take these steps with relation to them? Do you skip some? Could others be improved?

There's an empowering effect in seizing responsibility for good communication. It rejects the notion that a select few hold keys to fulfilling relationships and accepts that doors aren't locked, they simply need to be opened. If we don't clearly know what's expected of us, we ask. If our boss doesn't inquire about our hopes and expectations, we tell him. If someone isn't telling us how we're doing, we inquire. If we feel slighted by someone else, or feel our relationship isn't being served, we say so, carefully, genuinely, and directly. Reject thinking that someone else is responsible.

The upshot is a life of more fulfilling relationships, with more serenity and greater longevity. It doesn't preclude relationships from ending, but if and when they do end, the primary reason won't be lack of communication. You'll wind up better appreciating the relationship's meaning and the mutual benefits that sprang from it, regardless of its life span.

Eight Magical Phrases

Step back for a moment and consider eight phrases that, time and again, can prove to be most powerful when communicating with others. Regardless the language or country, most of us learn these words as children, and their value is timeless. Hearing them is magic; saying them works the magic.

Remember, however, some people wield these words by force of habit rather than sincerity. Don't join that crowd. Without passion behind them, even these mighty words are impotent. Any ear knows the difference.

Please
Kids know that "please" is the number-one magic word. When Disney first lured Michael Ovitz away from the agency he'd founded, he agreed, he said, because "they said 'please.'" That simple word says that we both need and appreciate someone's help or cooperation.

Regardless of whether a request is simple or huge, "please" always applies. Rather than barking orders—"Do this!"—you could request, "Would you do this?" But even that isn't as effective as the polite entreaty, "Would you do this *please?*" Whether you're asking a favor of someone to whom you report, or of someone who reports to you, "please" signals basic respect. I smile when I hear one of my store coaches ask a tire technician, "Can you please get the inventory done by 9:00 P.M.?" The simple addition of that one word cultivates cooperation and, most important, honor.

Thank You
You hold a door for someone. You stay late at work. You do a few extra chores around the house. Whatever it is, hearing "thank you" somehow makes you feel better about the task. When thanks aren't expressed, your kindness effectively feels taken for granted. Again, tone and body language is important. A curt acknowledgment is worlds apart from a heartfelt thanks.

Thank people every time you catch them helping you in even the smallest of ways. "Thanks," to the bus driver as you exit. "Thanks," to the traffic cop who's creating order out of chaos. "Thanks," to the busboy who fills your water glass. Sure, they all get a paycheck, but the quality of their work helps you and others every day. These two encouraging words are the non-material paychecks of human appreciation. I can see it in the eyes of anyone I genuinely thank. That's worth far more than the cost of uttering two small words.

You're Welcome

Excess baggage? Not really. Omitting this expression diminishes the thanks. "You're welcome" tells someone that you heard and accepted their gratitude. To protest, "Oh, it wasn't anything," may seem humble, but in a way it discounts the value the other person places on what you did. In other words, saying "you're welcome" is a way of accepting recognition of your self-worth.

You Betcha!

In my Minneapolis hometown, you can't ask for anything without someone responding jauntily, "You betcha!" For all the *Fargo* kidding, its enthusiasm is delicious compared to nothing at all. Asked to do something, the simple reply "sure" can sound ambivalent. Besides "you betcha," you can affirm that you're on board with substitutes like "my pleasure," "no problem," or "sure thing!" Lack of a response leaves one wondering whether they've been heard, whereas an active response imbues any relationship with a sense of cooperation that makes the day pass just a little easier for everyone.

Exactly!

When someone says something completely aligned with your thinking, "Exactly!" is extremely affirming. Silence, a quiet nod, or "uh-huh" can be misunderstood, but an enthusiastic "Exactly!" drives home your agreement without doubt.

I'm Sorry

A thorough apology must include the essential phrase "I'm sorry." Tap-dancing around forthright acceptance of responsibility only prolongs the guilty party's atonement. An apology without those two words isn't likely to be fully accepted. Nor does it work to hedge the emotional impact—on themselves and on the listener—by omitting "I am." A simple "Sorry" disconnects the apology from the personal. *Who* is sorry? Sincere apologies take full ownership: "I'm sorry." Making heartfelt amends has helped heal many wounds in my life.

I Love You

What sweeter words are there? Honestly declared, these three words change worlds. But use them wisely. Just as you treasure those you love, treasure your expression of that love. And, like all good things, enjoy it and express it when it's appropriate. If you feel it, don't let it go unsaid.

Names

Most people consider their name the most delicious word in the language. Using their name, when appropriate, deepens your connection to them. Many cultures acknowledge this power, identifying a person's name with their essence. Handle this power carefully.

"Adam, I'm sorry," for instance, is a more effective apology than "I'm sorry." "Thanks, Mrs. Westin," rings more sincere than just "Thanks." In service situations, it's prudent to use someone's surname until rapport is established or they've given permission to use their first name. Simply remembering someone's name can be a challenge all its own, especially upon an initial encounter. If this is a challenge for you, there are numerous books on improving your memory.

Why the Eight Phrases Are Magical

I began to sense the value of these words on my first job out of college, at Shell Oil. Within months I was selling to dealers in the field, which made me wholly dependent on office support. It didn't take long to see that honoring the staff at HQ with the vocabulary of respect and kindness encouraged them to go that extra mile on the occasions when I needed it. Don't do it simply for that reason. Rather, remember that the most important reason to respect one's support staff is that that they deserve it.

These words will enhance your communication skills and ultimately strengthen your personal and professional relationships. They'll bind you to manners that honor others. I was fortunate. My mother taught me subtlety by using the magic words in notes, in her exchanges with others, and in gentle suggestions to me as a child. If these words are already fixtures of your vocabulary, congrats. If not, the opportunity to start is right before you.

Reach Out and Touch Someone

A great way to use some of the Eight Magical Phrases is by seizing occasions, whether happy or sad, when recognition and support can make a difference. Look for those spontaneous, illuminated moments for recognizing associates, acquaintances, friends, and family. The list of occasions is longer than an aisle at the Hallmark store—birthdays, Father's Day, Mother's Day, graduations, weddings, job promotions, special accomplishments, bereavement, illnesses, appreciation of kind deeds.

A heartfelt message is water that can cleanse a foul day. It lifts my spirits every time. These compassionate communiqués—notes, e-mail, voice mail—enhance connections with others and remind us and them of the unique qualities they bring to the world.

It doesn't take that much time. I always have stationery and greeting cards for various occasions on hand so that moments of inspiration don't die on the vine. And there's always a phone nearby. A potent bond is forged when you let others know you're with them, during occasions sorrowful and joyful.

Keep special events like birthdays and anniversaries on your calendar. Being on time is half the surprise, although better late than not at all.

Listen Up

Listening effectively is a key component of having a good talk-listen ratio, discussed earlier. Our high-volume, message-saturated world dissuades us from taking time out to listen, let alone learning to listen. There's a mistaken impression that because we all have ears, we all listen. But while hearing is involuntary, listening is a learned skill. Prior to my mid-thirties, my listening skills were like the skills of a gun duellist; I talked more than I listened, and as far as I could tell, whoever got their point across first won. In reality, a finely tuned ear does just the opposite. Around that time, in the early 1980s, I happened onto an "active listening" seminar by the well-known consultant and author C. J. Hegarty. I never listened or talked the same way again. The basics:

+ **Seek to understand before seeking to be understood.** Simple, yet I had been doing just the opposite, often feeling the familiar pang of regret over weighing in with an opinion before I'd heard the full story.

+ **Mirror the person you're speaking with.** People like people who are like them. If he talks slowly and you're zipping along at the speed of sound, he's not likely to hear much. The same goes for decibel level. Communication is limited if you're blustering loudly while she's speaking softly.

+ **Whatever you hear, evaluate it with an open mind.** Is your mind open to opinions and ideas unlike your own? Or are your beliefs so strong that you listen only for the kinks in the speaker's armor and then pounce? Remember the Native American proverb, "Listen, or your tongue will keep you deaf."

It's a mistake to keep a discussion going when you don't feel like listening. Heck, it doesn't even rate a conversation if you're not open to what you're hearing. Nor is it easy to hide. Ever notice someone listening *against* you? You can see it in their face—pursed, tense, blank. What does your face say? Does it wear a sign that reads "Closed for Business"? Are your arms folded across your chest, or relaxed at your sides? Are you sunk into your chair, or canted toward the speaker?

It hurts when an audience, even an audience of one, doesn't listen. Conversely, a certain satisfied, affirming feeling washes over you when you've been heard. Listening, actually following beat for beat what's said, tells the speaker that not only is there value in what he's saying, but he himself is valuable.

+ **Read the unspoken part of the message.** Remember, words are only a small part of the message, and they merely reflect its intellectual value. To gauge a speaker's psychological and emotional state, watch her eyebrows, pay attention to what she does with her hands, whether she sits squarely before you. When visiting our stores, I'll ask Tires Plus guests waiting for their cars how they're being treated. "Okay," they may respond, although sometimes the concern in their eyes and their wound-up posture tell another story. That prompts me to press them, "Are you sure? What's happening to your car, right now?" "Well," they'll respond, "it was supposed to have been done by now." At that point I have enough information to seek a follow-up resolution.

+ **Repeat back what you heard.** Without parroting the speaker, tell him your interpretation of his message. Now he knows he's being heard, and you both have a chance to sort out any miscommunication. You'll know you're on track when he responds to your paraphrase, "Exactly. You've got it."

Active listening, authentically employed, crumbles resistance to new ideas. It requires attentive watering, but it bears a bumper crop of trust and understanding. Ultimately, you're blessed with a confederacy of cooperation. But don't use it to trick anyone. Employ it only because you want to listen and respond in a manner that's respectful of you both.

Speak Up

All the right words and communication skills in the world mean little if you're not willing to put them to use. Before we can communicate better, we first have to believe that what we have to say is worth saying. How often do you speak up about something that concerns you? Whether as a dissatisfied customer or frustrated co-worker or a friend who wants more from a friendship, learn to see and seize the time to air your thoughts.

I remember one instance a few years ago, when passion stepped up to the plate. Nervous about having a low-grade cancerous mole removed from my stomach, a relatively minor procedure, I had resolved to stay calm through it by breathing rhythmically. As Dr. Jansen (not his real name) injected a local anesthetic into my belly and began cutting out the mole, I began my focused breathing. "What are you doing?" he asked angrily. I told him it was a stress-reduction breathing technique. "How does that help?" he asked. I said that deep breathing reduces stress, to which he blurted, "That's the stupidest thing I've ever heard." My serenity vanished. "You mean that's your *perception*," I shot back, "not fact!" A verbal donnybrook broke out as he continued to cut and then stitch me up.

Later, as his assistant looked on in amazement, the doc said, "I've never had a patient talk to me like that while I was cutting on him." True enough, given my vulnerable position, it probably wasn't the best time to argue a point. Under attack for something I knew was helpful, however, I felt that caving in to intimidation would have created even more turmoil and stress inside me. The more enlightened response, needless to say, would have been to continue my breathing technique and gently reason with the doctor later.

Ultimately, however, I may have scored one for both teams. When the doctor was finished, he marched for the door before hesitating. He turned around, came back, and shook my hand. And when I came back, a few weeks later to have my stitches removed, the receptionist looked puzzled. "This is weird," she said. "The doctor is taking your stitches out. He never does that." This time around, our encounter was wonderful. Out of the blue, he said, "We all make mistakes." "I understand entirely," I said. We connected because in the end we were willing to stay engaged, albeit imperfectly, with something until it was resolved. By speaking up, we both learned.

Speaking up sometimes means pointing out people's blind spots, the things we sometimes do unconsciously. When we have a loving attitude and we call people on that kind of behavior, we're actually being caring to ourselves *and* to them. I encourage this in my teammates by telling them, "Challenge authority, challenge reality." Authority isn't always right, and reality isn't always what it seems.

...Unless You Ask

A nugget my father used to advise me when I was a boy came from the Bible: "Ask, and ye shall receive." Throughout the day, we all get by with a little help from our friends, whether at home or at work. But asking takes skill. Tact is the lubricant that gives your friends permission to say no without fear of angering you—not an unreasonable desire. To honor that silent pact, ask for what you need and simultaneously cultivate a healthy distance from the outcome. Ask, and ye shall resolve to accept the answer with grace.

Sometimes the shoe's on the other foot, and we find ourselves on the receiving end of these requests. Similarly, you shouldn't shy away from your own right to accept or decline requests for help. Our internal reply mechanisms tend to default to "yes," a credit to our humanist impulses and the power of empathy. But sometimes a "yes" is a deceptively easy choice of appetizer that's quickly followed by a bitter, silent stew—angry regret over an ill-considered commitment. Saying no from the get-go may seem difficult, but if you find yourself brewing batch after batch of commitment resentment, step back and examine where your needs and boundaries meet. Indeed, identify them, embrace them, and wear them on your sleeve.

Some of us were raised to believe that it's inappropriate to ask for what we need. That can injure our self-esteem, which in turn prevents us from identifying what we need for our mission. It's a spiral catch-22. It's as if you drove up to a filling station, only to deny that your empty gas tank needed filling. At the end of the day, we can't move along the road to our mission unless we get our tank filled with regularity.

Pump Up Your Passion

Authentic, accurate communication doesn't happen spontaneously when two people open their mouths in front of one another. Good discourse lives on passion, one of the COPPSS traits explored in chapter 3.

Some of the most effective comments pour from my gut. "That's not fair," I'll say reflexively. Or, "Ouch, that certainly doesn't feel good." It's a candid response, no games, no manipulation. Whether with a close friend or in multimillion-dollar negotiations, genuine expression strips away the layers of rhetoric that conceal basic understanding. Passion binds your Inner Team players—body, intellect, psyche, spirit—and puts them in the communication game. It also has a way of steeping your words in truth and drawing support and attention from listeners.

STRUT YOUR STUFF, BUT STUFF YOUR STRUT ✦ As a reflection of healthy self-esteem, communicating with confidence—not cockiness—can speak volumes. A new era of personal confidence is the most obvious and immediate payoff to finding passion and connection to your mission. Your expressions, your gait, your willingness to talk, all of these reflect this new strength, which serves to hold off competitors—whether of the personal, business, or sports variety—who may use any weakness against you the moment they detect it. Your response: trust yourself, cultivate confidence. It's amazing how much confidence others place in you, once you place it in yourself.

Anything and anyone, alas, can be prone to excess. Cockiness, arrogance, audacity—all of these spring from excessive confidence. Unless we balance confidence with humility, we naturally become cocksure, our healthy egos spiraling into egotism. Whereas confidence is a strength that binds you to others, arrogance simply alienates. There are few bigger communication turnoffs, and people sense it a mile away. The Bible refers to conceit as the pride that "goes before a fall." Since, without fail, there is always a faster gun coming around the next corner, it's only a matter of time before the cocky find themselves before the metaphoric cocked trigger.

Many paths lead to confidence *sans* cockiness. To steer clear of cockiness, I do my best to practice various forms of wellness, maintain action plans, stay connected to my Higher Power, and remind myself how much I have to learn. Humility is never far off when I reflect on how much God has blessed me. It serves to remind me that I'm not here to celebrate my own ego, but to use my talents to build communication bridges, not barriers, between myself and others.

HEY, SMARTYPANTS! ✦ Communicating with sarcasm can puncture the lofty goals of even the best message. It's often said that we live in the Irony Age. It's a time when smug ignorance too often passes for smart humor. To be sure, the end of the twentieth century has produced a fair share of official and unofficial vice and folly that satire exposes and expunges best, whether on screen, online, or on the printed page. But too often satire slides into a celebration of sarcasm. While razor-sharp wit entertains on the big screen, it can shred relationships in real life. Sarcasm is rarely helpful; it's an angry, indirect way of expressing criticism. It alienates people by putting them on notice: they're fair game, especially the moment you're vulnerable. If you want conflict, sarcasm is a sure-fire way to fuel it.

If you find people aren't as open with you as you'd like, scan your comments for sarcasm. It may seem like harmless joking, but there are healthier ways to get a laugh.

Clarity Conquers Calamity

Everyone gets burned now and then by wrong assumptions. To avoid the scorch, I spend as much time as I need on insurance against misunderstanding—clarifying, rephrasing, confirming, double-checking. This keeps my active-listening skills nimble and helps clear up misunderstandings. I never assume that one explanation is enough.

A double-checking technique is asking the other person to repeat what they understood you to have said. You might preface the request by telling them that it's less a challenge to whether they're listening than it is communication quality control. Once in a while, I'll ask, "What is it you heard me say?" If they get it exactly right, we've established a clear line. If they didn't get it right, or have understood only part of it, I repeat myself more clearly, and ask often, "Just to make sure I'm making sense, tell me, briefly, what I just said." By then it's generally clear, but if it's not, I repeat the process until it is. Sounds like a lot of trouble, but it's great insurance against mistakes that can cause pain and cost multiples of time and energy.

Another way to ensure clarity is to keep people in the information loop. People's minds go strange places when we don't communicate adequately. They may feel discounted, believing that their concerns aren't being heard. Running late for an appointment? Call ahead and let them know. Concerned that someone may be thinking something that isn't true? Let them know what's really going on so they don't sit and stew. If plans have changed, inform everyone involved. Most people love surprises, but not the kind that make them feel you've been keeping them in the dark.

The Sweet Sound

Given the trillions of words spoken and written silence sometimes feels uncomfortable. How often have you been with someone and felt awkward at a pregnant pause? It may only be five seconds, but it's not long before discomfort sets in.

Indeed, silence is powerful. It's often more potent than the words that surround it. The next time silence spreads, bathe in it like a hot spring. Unless there's something important you need to get out, use that extended pause. Contemplate, or notice your breathing. You'll automatically take a deep breath. As you do, notice the scents lofting through the air. Notice the sounds around you. Notice the quality of light. Take a moment to establish better eye contact. Check in with your feelings and see if the external you is reflecting the internal you. All this awareness can happen in a flash. From zero to sixty in an instant. There's a lot there between words—greater presence, deeper connection, and fuller senses. So much can be experienced, learned, and communicated in these precious moments.

No-Sweat Public Speaking

Of all the forms of expressing yourself, public speaking leverages the power of words ten, fifty, a hundred, even a thousand times over one-to-one communication. Many Americans fear public speaking more than death itself. And indeed, an inability to speak in public can be death to a budding career. So for future business and community leaders, it's a fear worth facing. By and large, it's a matter of preparation and practice. Books, tapes, seminars, and simple observation are good places to start. But there's nothing like practice, practice, practice. Dale Carnegie courses and organizations like Toastmasters support theory with real-life experience. A few other thoughts to keep in mind:

1. **Prepare your material with your listeners in mind (know your room).**

> a. Determine the purpose of your presentation. What results do you want to achieve with your message?
>
> b. Focus on communicating with your listeners. What information do they need to know, and what would be the most engaging way to present it to this group?
>
> c. Use examples to illustrate your points. People remember interesting stories and real-life experiences more than they remember facts and figures.
>
> d. Use note cards and visuals to stay on track. Use key words to trigger important points. Never write your speech out unless you're required to for legal reasons or you need the security as you're getting your speaker's legs.
>
> e. Memorize judiciously—it will build your confidence to know your first sentence and your last and be familiar with the rest of your speech.

2. **Mentally prepare yourself.**

   a. Ask for help from your spouse, mate, or best friend. Practice by conversing rather than by giving your speech. There are limits to preparation, after which you must trust that the words will be there once you open your mouth.

   b. If fear hampers you, put it into perspective: it's a speech, not a life-threatening illness. I control butterflies with a few deep breaths, positive talk, mind-quieting techniques, and physical exercise prior to the talk.

   c. Check your appearance, microphone, and visual aids prior to the presentation. Many speakers like to have a glass of water nearby.

   d. I always ask for help from my Higher Power just before going on. Then I can open up and let the words flow.

3. **Settle into your presentation.**

   a. Move with energy and enthusiasm.

   b. Build rapport with your listeners. If you are honored to be there, say so. Smile and use people's names when appropriate.

   c. Reference your cards as little as possible so that you can maintain eye contact with your audience. Remember, you need to communicate the essence, not the exact words, of the notes you've prepared. *You're better off missing some of your intended words and being more spontaneous than to hit every word and come off as canned.*

   d. Don't sweat the pauses. This gives your audience time to digest what you've said. Use the time to take a deep breath.

   e. Loosen up. If you are excited about your message, let it show. Vary your tone, relax your body, and your enthusiasm will flow.

   f. Whenever possible, have fun. If you're having fun, your listeners will, too.

The Ethical Sell (No, It's Not an Oxymoron)

One of the most prevalent forms of communication is something called *selling*. About 15 million Americans sell for a living. Trading and bargaining happen in myriad forms every day. We persuade bankers to grant us loans.

We tell someone what our business does well. We persuade a potential employer that we're right for the job. We sell our kids on the importance of good values. Every time we ask someone to do something, in fact, it could be considered selling. Selling is a vital form of communication, a conduit that binds society by ensuring that our mutual needs and wants are frequently met.

None of this prevents "selling" from getting a bad rap. It conjures up tricks, not treats. If the word was a person, many would see a chattering, jargon-spewing salesmen in a plaid sportcoat, preying on people during their weakest moments. It's practically an institutionally reinforced notion. Incredibly, even the dictionary connects the word *sell* with manipulation and deception. Definitions include "to deliver or give up in violation of duty, trust, or loyalty: betray;" "to give up in return for something else especially foolishly or dishonorably;" "to give into the power of another;" "to dispose of or manage for profit instead of in accordance with conscience, justice, or duty;" and "to impose on: cheat."

For Sale: A New Definition of Selling

The word needs a good libel lawyer. It's no wonder people are dubious about learning the techniques of the trade. There's a grain of truth to some of these stereotypes, of course. That said, sales is generally an honorable relationship that time and again gives way to the sort of mutual benefits that barter offered in the grain-for-gunpowder days. Without selling, it's impossible for wonderful ideas, products, and services to reach the people they're intended to help. Consider selling not as a vehicle for preying on people's vulnerabilities but as a magic carpet that enhances their lives by providing options they otherwise wouldn't be aware of. As a methodology for facilitating win-win scenarios, there's nothing but upside in learning to sell ethically.

In fact, I propose a new definition of selling, one that focuses on the symbiotic exchange between buyer and seller:

> **sell** (sel) *v.* **1.a.** To connect and communicate (with another person) in order to determine wants or needs. **b.** To propose beneficial solutions that fulfill wants and needs in exchange for a price, reward, or agreement.

The solution can be a product, service, or idea. The point is that value is received and benefit is given. The benefit the buyer receives is equal to or exceeds the payment, monetary or otherwise. Selling, in this positive context, is both an art and a science. Whether you are selling products or services to customers or selling your boss on an idea, the principles of good selling are the same. The whole process is healthy as long as information is shared honestly and value is received. That means orienting your energy toward service and value rather than give and take.

Selling Success Factors

As long as he's been alive, my father has been the very model of a great salesman. He has sold everything from homes to mausoleums, men's clothing to—yes—used cars. The finest exemplar of ethical, win-win selling, Dad has inspired me as well as my brothers Gary (a clothier) and Tim (an ink salesman), both models for mutual-benefit, ethical selling. Dad's wisdom and my own experience have helped me develop six gentle, collaborative methods for selling that benefit both the receiver and seller:

SELLING SUCCESS FACTORS

1. **Knowledge** of your product, service, or idea
2. A clear selling **method**
3. **Passion** for your product, service, or idea
4. **Self-acceptance** that prevents rejection from killing passion
5. A desire to repeatedly **get up to bat**
6. **Inner Team wellness** to give you the energy to just do it

Selling Success 1. Gain Knowledge

You're a seafood lover, and it's summer. Your grill is heating up, and your neighbor comes over to ask how he should prepare his tuna. Unless he's trying to trick you into cooking it for him, you're likely going to wind up telling him to buy fresh basil, extra-virgin olive oil, and a basket of fresh vegetables. When you know your subject, you're confident, passionate, and eager to help. People sense your expertise and listen closely. You're not surprised if they take notes. The same goes for selling.

Study whatever it is you're telling people about. Study it backward and forward. Pore over product and marketing literature, the better to understand its every attribute and benefit. If possible, give the product, service, or idea a test spin. Tinkering in the laboratory of your own life translates into the kind of firsthand expertise that turns a recommendation into *the last word*.

Selling Success 2. A Selling Method

Let's dispel a myth. Selling techniques, systems, methodologies—whatever you prefer to call them—are not clever, codified ways to outwit helplessly confused customers. They're systems, and systems channel energy and communication into every corner of your life. Whether we're playing tennis or repairing a computer, methodology guides the process. How we use these methodologies (to help or to hinder) is entirely up to us. I use a five-step process to structure and enhance communications when selling. This process works for any exchange of value, regardless of whether it involves a "customer." Most apply equally to exchanges between activist and donor, between civic leader and constituent, or even between friends.

1. CONNECT WITH THE "CUSTOMER" + Make a personal connection. Whether you're dealing with strangers, with people you haven't seen in a while, or even with good friends, rapport breaks down the barriers people constantly build around themselves. Those walls wind up concealing two things: understanding of what they need and of what they stand to gain. There's also a reason to connect with people that has nothing to do with buying or selling: because they're fellow travelers on our life's road.

A handshake, a smile, warm eye contact, use of their name, a question—these are easy ways to plug into one another. Doing this without crossing wires—which, of course, causes sparks—depends entirely on your intent and empathy. If you're motivated by respect for your "customer" as a human being, it's unlikely you'll violate her space and trust. If you intend to manipulate her, she'll sense that, too. Empathy is a wonderful emotion that allows us to pick up on obscure human emotions—via subtle things like tone of voice, body language, and words—and gauge what someone feels comfortable with. This first step, connection, is often neglected. If you're shy or in a rush, step back, take a deep breath, and remind yourself of the whole point in the first place—benefiting your customer. That cannot happen without first connecting on a human level.

2. DISCOVER YOUR CUSTOMER'S NEEDS AND WANTS + This is pretty obvious, yet it's often forgotten. Does your customer really want and need what you're selling? How will you know unless you ask? Many salespeople shortcut this step so they can show their stuff. Say you visit a cardiologist, and before asking you any questions, or even examining you, he recommends heart surgery and flies headlong into explaining why. (I'd report the guy to the American Medical Association.) In the same manner, salespeople often assume that after posing none, or just a few, token questions, they know what's best for their customer. But doctors don't prescribe before diagnosing.

Assumptions aren't accurate. First of all, customers themselves often aren't even sure of their wants or needs. A salesperson isn't going to know any better. He may have a vague idea, but until it's fleshed out with a sincere process of discovery, real answers are scarce. This is where a salesperson who's willing to take time to ask the necessary questions is worth his weight in "Sold" signs. Traditionally, this step is called "qualifying the customer," with the inference that the salesperson is deciding what the customer needs. But that misses the point. The benefit of asking questions is the "Eureka!" moment when the customer discovers her own wants and needs. That allows her to make an informed, comfortable decision.

Let's say you were representing the American Cancer Society and meeting with a potential donor. Here's an example of how to "sell opportunities" to support ACS. After rapport is built, questions like these could help gauge a potential donor's level of interest.

+ Do you believe in giving a percentage of your income to worthy causes?

+ Which causes do you support?

+ Has cancer ever affected you, a friend, or family member?

+ If you supported an organization that fights this disease, what would make you feel good about your contribution?

+ If what I shared with you about the American Cancer Society met your terms, would you be interested in supporting us with a portion of your charitable contribution budget?

After hearing your customer's answers, you may decide it's not worth her time (or yours) to explain something that doesn't interest her. Mindfulness of mutual interest and benefit loosens tension between customer and salesperson. It registers that you're not on opposing teams. You're on the same side, willing to end the conversation if it's clear there's nothing of mutual interest to talk about. Approach your customer as a friend, inquiring thoroughly, openly, without presumption, and the process will be cooperative and beneficial for you both.

Draw up a list of questions, more than you've ever asked or been asked, about what someone may need related to your offering. Think of yourself as a detective. Your case: How to help your customer? Far down the list is how you stand to benefit yourself. Mind you, it's perfectly fine to make a buck. The selling process is about mutual exchange. Yet you create a conflict of interest if you consume yourself with that pot at the end of the rainbow. Rest assured that if you have a beneficial product or service, if you get the message out to enough people who have a desire or need for it, and sell in the way laid out here, you'll naturally find rewards, both material and emotional.

3. PROPOSE A SOLUTION ✛   Once you and your customer determine there's a need or want that you can fill, it's time to propose a solution. Now, the likelihood of agreement increases significantly here because you've taken the time to make sure that the product your customer needs fits her hand-in-glove.

Start by checking off your product's attributes. Tie each of them to the needs you discovered while you were building rapport and asking questions. Try something like, "You said you wanted to contribute to an organization that emphasizes preventative measures and channels most of its revenues into non-administrative costs. Well, only about x percent of our budget goes to administration, while y percent funds preventative measures." Tying benefits to specific needs shows that you were listening; too often, people feel that salespeople don't hear them. Here, product knowledge is essential, and sensitivity to your customer's interest in that information is important. If you sense that she's more quantitative than emotional, give her more statistics and detailed service descriptions than you would someone who's more instinctual.

4. SEEK AGREEMENT ✛   When and if you sense that your customer is warm to your solution, seek agreement. There are three ways to do this. First, try relating back to a question you asked during step 1. "You said earlier that you were open to supporting the American Cancer Society with one thousand dollars if the organization operated in a way that made good sense to you. Do you feel that's the case?" If she agrees, answer, "Wonderful, then we can count on you." (This is what some call the presumed agreement.) If you're a little less sure, try the multiple-choice option: "What level of contribution would you feel comfortable with, five hundred, one thousand, or fifteen hundred dollars?" Finally there's the yes/no offer: "Terrific. Then can we count on you?"

If the opportunity still doesn't fit her well, ask if she's open to more discussion. If not, thank her for her time. But if she is up for more information, keep building that bridge between your benefits and her needs. Ask what would make her feel comfortable. Give her straightforward answers, and once again seek agreement. If agreement is still out of reach, ask her where she'd like to see the discussion go from there. Wherever that may be, make it happen if it's possible.

Be careful not to jump the gun. If you seek agreement too early, you may forget to address your earlier discoveries. It's important to seek agreement only after your customer believes that the benefits meet or exceed his desires. If he's leaning forward in his chair, nodding at everything you say and talking excitedly, go for agreement. But back off if you sense that he's confused or stressed. Allow him space to recall that this is his decision. Never, ever apply pressure. There's a clear difference between pressure and gentle persistence. The former involves mental games to manipulate him into wanting something that doesn't mesh with his needs, while the latter is borne on our genuine interest in our customer and a desire to fill his needs. Ask him whether he has questions or concerns. If he has none, again, ask what he'd like to see happen next. If he simply needs more time to think, ask if and when he'd feel comfortable with a follow-up call. Make note of it and, without coming off as a stalker, let him know that you'll call again.

5. THANK THEM GENUINELY ✦ Whether or not you strike an agreement, be grateful for the time and energy a customer invests in you. If a "sale" doesn't transpire, and there's no reason to follow up later, thank the customer for her time by pointing her in a helpful direction and sending her off with a nice wish, such as, "Hope you find what you're looking for." If you sense that you may be able to offer a solution down the road, communicate that, too.

If you do wind up striking an agreement, thank your customer for her time and attention, and for trusting your solution. Tell her you believe your solution will meet or exceed her expectations—if you really believe that's true (if you don't, you should have stopped at step 2).

When your heart's in the right place, and you care about your customer, your MO is inseparable from your conscience. Mutual-benefit selling respects both parties, a process very different from the coldblooded, Serengeti-like image of customer and salesperson stalking each other until finally one succumbs. Selling is showing, not hiding. Instead of deceiving, do your best to enlighten. Instead of overpowering your customers' will, empower them to make informed decisions and solutions with new information.

Selling Success 3. Access Your Passion

If you can't see the value of your offering, your customers certainly won't, either. Keeping in mind the animating effect that voice tone and body language have in communication, what does your customer hear and see when you sell? If you don't have passion for what you're selling, ask yourself why. Does it help people? If the answer is no, seriously consider not selling it anymore. If it's beneficial, study its features so you can draw a clear line between what you're providing and how you're helping people. If you still can't communicate the benefits with enthusiasm, get your heart, gut, tone, and body language in the game (see chapter 3, on how to increase your passion). "Passionate selling" isn't a nice way of saying "loud, pushy braggadocio." Passion's power is authenticity, not volume. It comes from the heart and spirit. Our bodies only reflect our inner energy.

Selling Success 4. Accept Yourself

Most successful salespeople are all but unaffected by rejection. Self-acceptance protects them from this, selling's most powerful enemy. They stroll from one client to the next, rejection rolling off their backs. Their passion for their offerings never falters.

At times, it's a challenge to access your passion after strenuous sales interplay. When your customer can't seem to shape with his mouth anything other the rounded frown of "No," some feel diminished of everything—confidence, energy, enthusiasm. But it's a catch-22. Without those emotions, you can't maintain your passion. The result? Your next customer immediately senses you're on passionless autopilot. She doesn't hear the words you're saying. It's obvious you feel rejected, because your body language and tone read like a sour creed, regardless of whether your words communicate positive attributes.

How do we feel genuine self-acceptance after someone says no? First, as the previous selling method demonstrates, sales rejection needn't be personal. Done right, the decision is firmly rooted in the customer's needs and the benefits of your offering. You're merely a consultant, counselor, and investigator all wrapped into one professional. Second, counselors and consultants are detached from the outcome because their chief concern is what's right for their customer, not what's right for a personal victory.

Before your next client or customer meeting, imagine a positive outcome by recalling successful past encounters. Visualize that the next outcome will be positive instead of projecting forward previous unsuccessful exchanges. And the time will come when you don't even need the supportive imagery of past successes. You'll understand that all interaction, if handled as we discuss here, is positive, that in the end every interaction achieves an agreement of one kind or another. Collaboration with customers never really need result in rejection, "sale" or no sale.

Selling Success 5. Batter Up!

Sales is associated with many metaphors. Here, I like baseball. When you have something to offer others and you receive rewards for matching it with what people need, then it only makes sense to get up there as often as you can (while still observing your work-life boundaries). Call it the McGwire-Sosa Syndrome. The St. Louis Cardinals' Mark McGwire and the Chicago Cubs' Sammy Sosa enjoyed giving fans something to cheer about in the home-run race of 1998. They couldn't step up to the plate enough. The more they got up to bat, the more opportunities they had to punch home runs.

How can you increase your own at-bats? Increase marketing or advertising, for one. Could you prospect more in your target markets? Go for it. There's no downside when you're passionate and respectful and have a tangible benefit to offer. Take the bat off your shoulders and start swinging.

Selling Success 6. Inner Team Wellness

Finally, Inner Team wellness is your essential source of energy and clarity of mind, critical for communicating with potential customers. Intellectual wellness keeps you on top of product knowledge. Bodily health allows you to relax while remaining alert, and fuels your physical stamina to get up to bat repeatedly. Psychological health enables you to meet the public with ease, sharpens your sensitivity to your customer, and helps you cultivate acceptance rather than rejection. And a healthy spirit keeps life in perspective. It grounds you to the point that you become detached from the material outcome of the customer-salesman relationship and focus instead on an outcome consistent with higher wisdom.

Coming Through Loud and Clear

Make no mistake. Your ability to communicate cogently, convincingly, and effectively is a vital part of manifesting your mission. They're my trusted allies.

Ask people how a phone or e-mail works, and few can tell you. But they can certainly tell you when they're *not* working. If you can't evaluate when your own communications tools are functioning well, it's doubtful you'll know when it's time to upgrade. And you may wind up missing out on major benefits.

In many ways, we are ourselves the most important piece of communications technology. Look upon your Inner Team and your communications skills as a complex network that creates the messages you send and receive (call it the World Wide We, or we-mail). Is there static on your internal transmission lines? Is your server down? Are others getting busy signals when they try to get through? Do you take advantage of free upgrades for your "inner technology"? Communicate poorly, and you'll be locked into endless loops of misunderstanding. Communicate clearly, and plug into the World Wide We.

Ten Communication Methods to Smooth the Way to Your Mission

1. Understand the dams to communication flow.

2. Use the four inside moves for communication to high-hurdle relationship ruts.

3. Use the Sandwich Technique for sticky wickets.

4. Go forth with the Eight Magical Phrases.

5. Reach out and touch someone in their joy and sorrow.

6. Speak up! Challenge reality on issues and causes you believe in.

7. Communicate with confidence. Get rid of cockiness.

8. Prioritize education and practice no-sweat public speaking for career rejuvenation, not sudden death.

9. Communicate by selling ideas or products and services with the Six Success Factors and the five step method for ethical, effective selling.

10. Know when silence speaks louder than words.

Relationship Circles

Happiness, success, and the ability to stay "on mission" all stem from how well we relate to ourselves, to other people, and to the worlds we move in and through. Built on a sound ground, these relationships create and sustain us. Built on faltering foundations, they trip us down one painful step after the next.

Examine your web of relationships, beginning with your Inner Team and radiating out to your mate, parents, children, friends, community, and—of course—your Higher Power. Into that equation, factor your relationship to money, career, and the other areas that demand your time and energy. Taken together, you begin to see that this web is dynamic, a turning kaleidoscope that constantly shapes and reshapes your life.

Seen another way, our web of relationships forms a mandala, a word whose Sanskrit origins mean "sacred circle." The mandala's circular symmetry shows up in ancient and modern religion, art, and architecture (Washington, D.C.'s city plan can be seen as a mandala) as well as in everyday objects (like the tires on a car). Carl Jung considered the mandala an image of the soul, and the circle a symbol of the totality of self and life. Projected out into the world, images of circles can reflect our natural urge

Relationship Circles

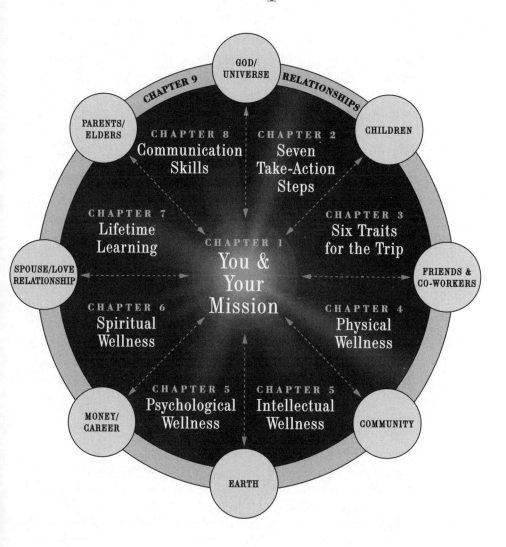

GOD/
UNIVERSE

RELATIONSHIPS

CHAPTER 9

PARENTS/
ELDERS

CHILDREN

CHAPTER 8
Communication
Skills

CHAPTER 2
Seven
Take-Action
Steps

CHAPTER 7
Lifetime
Learning

CHAPTER 1
You &
Your
Mission

CHAPTER 3
Six Traits
for the Trip

SPOUSE/LOVE
RELATIONSHIP

FRIENDS &
CO-WORKERS

CHAPTER 6
Spiritual
Wellness

CHAPTER 4
Physical
Wellness

CHAPTER 5
Psychological
Wellness

CHAPTER 5
Intellectual
Wellness

MONEY/
CAREER

COMMUNITY

EARTH

to live out the symmetry of our whole personality, through the events of our lives and the circles of our relationships.

The elements of a winning life game plan—determining your mission, manifesting it with Seven Take-Action Steps, and supporting it with your Six Traits for the Trip, whole-person self-care, lifetime learning, and effective communication—combine to immeasurably strengthen these circles of relationship with others. While the vague idea of "success" is often defined in terms of dollars and titles, successful Self Coaching shapes a game plan that begets something much more expansive. At the end of the day, the cloth of success tends to be rather humdrum unless it's woven with an awareness that we're all linked—that no one moves without moving others, that, ultimately, success and mission achievement is defined by the strength of this web of relationships.

Self: Knowing Someone in There Cares

We can't give what we don't have. Before we can truly love and care about others, we first have to love what's right here under our nose: our self. With our eyes and minds perpetually geared outward, looking inward can be a challenge, a challenge we'll begin with right here. Okay. Stop reading for a moment. Get up and spend a few minutes looking in a mirror. Stare deeply into your eyes. Ask yourself, Whom do I see? Whom do I really see? The first time I tried looking—*really* looking—I must confess it was uncomfortable. I think I had been so accustomed to moving, to achieving, to executing, that it was unsettling to contemplate the Sphinxlike face staring back at me. It simultaneously contained my entire history, yet revealed little of who I am or who I will be tomorrow.

I no longer feel that way. The habits of Inner Team wellness, mapped out in this book, permit me to see myself with greater insight and acceptance. I see the future with more clarity and accept the past for its lessons and goodness. I keep some childhood pictures of myself among the more recent family pictures hanging on my walls. They're constant reminders of my youthful optimism. To me they whisper, every day, that my life is a continuum running from that little boy of wonder and enthusiasm to the man of experience and spirit that I am today—the man who carries that little boy's mission like a plastic play torch into tomorrow.

Dig up a childhood picture of yourself. Study it. Admire its simplicity. What dreams gleam in that child's eyes? Unstained by years of stress and fears, that child's face is the purest reflection of your essential being. Contemplate who you have become in the intervening years of conflicting priorities and expectations. Does that child's face hold hopes that were dashed or abandoned? It's an important consideration. Those long-buried dreams reveal a deeper connection with your earthly purpose. There's no reason why you can't dig them up and rediscover your true identity.

"I'm a student."

"I'm a salesperson."

"I'm a teacher."

"I'm a preacher."

"I'm a doctor."

When asked who we are, many of us offer up our occupation, often before saying our name. An occupation doesn't really tell anyone who we are; it says what we do—an obvious yet important distinction about two very different aspects of our being. An intimate relationship with our self takes our sense of personal identity to a deeper, more complex level than the title on our business card, the name plate on our office door, or the name on our mailbox. Again, who are we? Again, who would we like to become?

Your Career: A Diamond in the Rough?

When your mission, values, and vision are in harmony with those of your employer, work is naturally inspiring. In a mission-centered world, your career is a natural outgrowth of your values and desires. Rather than simply looking at what you're good at, ask what you *like* to do. Given that, what work role enables you to use what you're good at (your natural gift) and what you enjoy (your passion) to support your mission?

Be aware of your options. Beyond the familiar one-track career or go-for-the-gusto models, alternatives are emerging out of the spreading notion that careers, convictions, and missions are not now (and never really have been) mutually exclusive. The idea of "right livelihood" has steadily gained ground since the spend-it-all 1980s gave way to the it's-all-spent 1990s.

Some professionals tired of selling out their ideals began "selling in"— creating conscious change in their workplaces to raise the bar on office ethics. These people may not be willing to completely exit the rat race, but they are trying to transform it back into the human race.

Sell-ins feel a need to work hand-in-hand with their desire to follow their bliss. Case in point: Porter Gale, who in 1996 bagged her account director position at the hip Manhattan ad shop Kirshenbaum Bond & Partners in order to join fellow bliss-seeking ex-exec Donna Murphy on a five-thousand-mile cross-country bike trip to raise awareness of breast cancer in young women. Along the way, thirtysomethings Gale and Murphy raised $100,000 to support awareness programs, and filmed the documentary *2Chicks, 2Bikes, 1Cause,* which aired on the Lifetime Channel. Gale said the "risk" of doing what she loved also opened new doors in her career as well as providing her insights that she values daily.

Another Sell-In is Bill Haber, co-founder, along with Michael Ovitz, of Creative Artists Agency (CAA). A few years ago, Haber quit CAA to run "Save the Children Fund," where he put his talents to work supervising four thousand employees in forty-one countries to feed starving kids. Whether mainstream or against the stream, more people are considering their career choices as opportunities for life as well as livelihood.

How Much Is Too Much?

Time is tight. One of the most important factors in a career decision revolves around how much time you're willing to spend on the job. You can spend too much time, too little, or just enough.

Workaholism, a first cousin of perfectionism, is a particular danger to people who have unreasonably high expectations for their careers. Often these people are not prepared to balance their work and personal lives. There can be many reasons. Some people avoid poor relationships with their spouses by spending more time at work. Hard-driving overachievers can be spurred by troubled childhoods and a need to prove they're worthy. Moreover, from our earliest days, we're indoctrinated in the Great American Work Ethic and its slogans: "No pain, no gain." "The harder you work, the luckier you get." "There's less traffic on the extra mile." We rarely question this ethic's assumptions, accepting their grains of truth as the whole truth, until things get so out of hand that our career crowds into every corner of life. That's not to say professional discipline is bad. On the contrary. The point is, work is not an end in itself. Your career is a bridge to accomplishing your mission, which comprises manifold priorities.

The symptoms are predictable. Workaholics miss important family, social, and recreational activities. They routinely overshoot their compensation goals and go far beyond their position's call of duty. Even when they're not on the job, workaholics think about work and find themselves a bag of twitches and half-completed sentences. To be sure, it's not uncommon for them to recognize the excessiveness of their work commitment.

But because they're caught up in an emotional rut, recognition doesn't make it any easier to change. Their sense of self-worth is tied to their productivity: "I do, therefore I am." Other workaholics are perfectionists whose distrust prompts them to assume other people's responsibilities rather than risk those people's potential mistakes. Still another type of workaholic is the achievement-oriented person who has little need for outside activities or emotional commitments, and instead finds ultimate joy in her job.

Indeed, workaholics can be happy and satisfied people. Only the individual can determine how healthy his balancing act is. If thriving on work makes you happy, then by all means enjoy the long hours and their rewards. If, however, you have a gnawing feeling you've lost touch with your family and friends, or you find that your identity has become so inseparable from your job that you don't know who you are once you leave work, it's time to stand in front of the mirror and search your self for your deeper mission. See the Resources section for books that can help with this challenge.

Your Career Here

Does your job give you enough time for all parts of your mission? Is your job a livelihood in more than financial terms? Does it take advantage of the range of your talents and interests? Whether you're at the beginning of the road or well on the way into your working years, take a few minutes to evaluate your relationship with work. It can help turn what may be a grind into new ground.

If you're at the beginning of your career, you've got an open field for this discovery exercise. If you're already established, set aside your work identity for the moment. Imagine you have the option to go back to the beginning of your career, and choose any position in any field you want. You're completely free to choose a job that best fits your mission. Before you answer, read over your mission statement, then ask yourself these questions:

+ What do I like to do? This seems an obvious question, but many people spend their entire careers in jobs they are good at but don't particularly enjoy. This is when work is *work,* but when we work at what we like, the lines between work and play begin to blur.

+ What am I good at? Don't limit your answer to the work-related skills you're trained to do. Look at your answers to the preceding question and think about skills related to those activities. Usually what we're good at and what we like to do mesh. A person whose favorite skills don't line up with her position ends up having to work twice as hard as someone whose skills match her position better.

+ Do I want to work for myself or do I prefer working for others? Each has its upsides and downsides.

+ What services, products, businesses, or industries attract me?

+ Where do I want to live, and what options are available in those areas?

+ Considering the answers to the above questions, who can best put my talents to use and best support my mission?

As in your mission discovery exploration, let your imagination go with this exercise. Your answers could reaffirm that you're already on the best track for mission accomplishment, or they could begin a career shift, small or large.

While exploring your options, be careful not to rule out the unglamorous. Take the tire biz. Twenty-three years ago, I researched the tire and automotive industry and found a vast sector of commerce that was considered somewhat unprofessional, dirty, and mundane. That didn't throw me off the trail. To me, those qualities signaled that this was an underserved, little-explored retail niche. Maybe, I thought, just maybe we could affect it positively; give people an experience they weren't getting but certainly deserved. Then, as we got into it, I thought perhaps we could even influence an entire industry. It wouldn't be the first time. After all, think back to what the theme-park industry was prior to its Disney-fication: traveling carnivals. Rough diamonds are everywhere, hiding in plain sight.

Career Decisions, Decisions, Decisions

At the crossroads of a decision for a particular job or career, try either of the following strategies for weighing your options. The first option is good for a quick analysis. The second option is better for in-depth, complex decisions.

OPTION 1. THE BEN FRANKLIN BALANCE SHEET + An oft-used analysis tool, what's commonly known as a Ben Franklin balance sheet is very simple. Draw a line down the center of a sheet of paper. Call this sheet Option A. In the left column, write the pluses you'll gain from a decision for a particular position or company. Down the right column, jot the minuses. Take another sheet of paper for your Option B and repeat the process. Then do the math.

OPTION 2. WEIGHT AND RATE ✦ This is a decision-making model I've found to be very effective for weighing two or more complex decisions against one another. Its beauty is that it considers both the relative value of the factors you're looking for as well as the likelihood that any particular option will be able to deliver it. In the example below, we're assuming you've got two job offers. One has an unbeatable schedule while the other offers much better money. Instead of being caught on the horns of this dazzling dilemma, let's look a little closer at each offer.

Things I want from a job	Job Option 1			Job Option 2		
	A Importance of this factor to me	**B** Likelihood this job will give this	SUBTOTAL	**A** Importance of this factor to me	**B** Likelihood this job will give this	SUBTOTAL
Flexible working hours	10 x	10 =	100	10 x	5 =	50
Sufficient money	9 x	4 =	32	9 x	10 =	90
Good benefits package	8 x	6 =	48	8 x	7 =	56
Chance to further my education	6 x	8 =	48	6 x	5 =	30
Supportive corporate culture	6 x	9 =	54	6 x	3 =	18
TOTAL POINTS			282			244

1. Write in the leftmost column the factors weighing in your decision. Make this list as long or short as you like.

2. Weight each factor's importance to you (column A in the example), 1 through 10, with 10 being the most important. You can use numbers twice. In the example, a chance for further education and a supportive corporate culture feel about the same in importance, so they're both rated a 6.

3. Now take your best guess at rating the likelihood that each job option will offer what you want (column B in the example). Again, use 1 through 10, with 10 being the most likely. If you don't have enough information to take a guess, do more research. You'll need to know it anyway.

4. Now multiply column A by column B to get subtotal ratings for each factor, then add up the subtotals for your final result.

Whether you're using the Ben Franklin balance sheet or a Weight and Rate analysis, remember that these are only part of the decision-making process. Complement advice and analysis with your intuition. After all the advice and analysis fades, you're left with your intuition. That gut feeling, the one that tells you that a decision falls in line with your mission, is an undeniable voice in the wilderness. Listen to it. Trust yourself. Go with whatever balance of logic and intuition makes you comfortable and turns your decisions, career or otherwise, into a vehicle for reaching the greatest good.

Conscientious career choices are the product of many considerations. Carefully note the aspirations that guide you. Balance your pressure to earn with your financial outflow. Partner with loved ones on your career decisions. And interlace your life with the applicable concepts you read about in this book. Formulate your own breakthrough personal and career game plan; it will help you to be fully present in your salad days and reap even greater rewards in your gravy years.

On the Job

Most companies' mission statements are gathering dust somewhere, but they are important documents. Dust off your company's statement, look it over carefully, and consider how it aligns with your own personal mission. Then, at every turn, champion your organization's mission—or those parts of it that are meaningful to you. Factor it into your day-to-day decision-making. Naturally, every move you make that supports a like-minded organizational mission is going to support your personal mission.

Whatever your position, make it more important than you've ever thought it was. Champion your professional goals and let others know how they will help the team as a whole. Ask for their help to promote a positive agenda. The more pride you feel and show in your position, the more others will appreciate your job. Your bonuses will include more self-respect and maybe even a promotion.

An unlikely and inspiring example is Minneapolis icon Wally the Beer Man. Wally has sold beer at sporting events in the Twin Cities for nearly a quarter-century. His wide smile and quick-witted pitches endear him to fans and have earned him regional celebrity. His personality and commitment to what some would consider a modest occupation have landed him on TV commercials and "Wally the Beer Man" T-shirts. A lot can be learned from a guy like Wally.

Consider your own job. Whether you're the company president or a receptionist, ask yourself how you can be as passionate as Wally the Beer Man. To
say it another way, how can you provide more value to the people you work
with and for? Take the initiative to expand your position. Consider it a
higher calling than you do now. Remember, if your organization's mission is
on some level congruent with your own, then it really is a higher calling.

Money Matters

Jing, coin, greenbacks, bucks, cash. Whatever you call it, money represents
one of the most mysterious, misunderstood relationships in which we find
ourselves. The dynamic defines us more than we may want to admit—
from the energy we give to get it, to the things we're willing to do for it, to
the feelings we nurse over having too little of it, to how we define "riches."
Our relationship to money has the power to affect other relationships. It
determines whether we feel we have too little, hoard it, employ it for negative purposes, or put it to work to positively affect others. Some people
stockpile their riches for their progeny, while others, in the growing "die
broke" movement, spend their money in worthy, measured ways that
spread satisfaction while they're alive to see the benefits.

Just as it can tend to possess a rank smell, money can have an especially
ugly side. A callous regard for it can produce excessive consumption and
neglect for the Earth, its resources, and its people. Whether it's new piles of
stock market riches, the waves of bankruptcies among people in their thirties and forties, or the ever-rising debt shouldered by twentysomethings, all
fuel the confusion Americans feel in their relationship to money.

I know what it's like to have experienced money pressures. In my twenties and thirties, satiating the monetary appetite of a young family and a
young business was no easy feat. Ready Reserve was an ever-present friend,
and the treacherous credit card lines a seemingly necessary enemy, as I
struggled furiously each month. Monetary pressures can be, as you may
well know, extremely stressful and all-consuming. Yet in the midst of this,
the three-ring wake-up call reminded me unequivocally that my Inner
Team development was a vital part of the solution.

Then, in the mid-1990s, with the children grown up and the company
grown profitable, I was surprised to realize that I felt increasingly guilty
about my attendant prosperity. Struggling for so many years had become
the norm, and the sudden absence of the pressure to pay made me feel that

money was somehow bad, or that I at least didn't deserve it. Then it dawned on me: I had to reassess money's role in my life and redefine what "deserving" meant. I realized that the word assumes responsibility for putting prosperity to work for the good of others, in addition to giving myself permission to enjoy the fruits of my labor.

Hokey or not, I see money as a form of energy—a ray of gratitude, perhaps—that we point at people who give us things; it's not something that has value in and of itself. After all, we receive money when we expend energy. That money becomes a medium of exchange for acquiring some of the energy of a person who's willing to work for something they need or want. If you hire a mechanic to tune your bicycle, you're really exchanging the energy she spends on the tune-up for the energy you burn at your workplace. Call it metaphysical bartering.

The Real Cost of Making Money

Generally speaking, the greater our material wants and needs, the more energy we must devote to making money. Bona fide get-rich-quick scenarios are few and far between, and winning the lottery has rarely proven to be a sound financial strategy. Most people "buy" dollars by expending real time, real energy, and real attention.

Meanwhile, advertisers are more than willing to feed our visions of the ever higher piles we need to be happy—tonier homes, tinier phones, humongous TVs, anything with the right logo. To the legions heeding the advertisers' call, it doesn't take long to realize that keeping a wardrobe current with the latest fashions or a house stocked with the trendiest goods is a never-ending race.

On the flip side, some are reacting to this with such movements as Voluntary Simplicity and co-housing, which represent millions of people, sometimes entire communities, downshifting their needs, simplifying their lifestyles, and breaking the vicious cycle of working harder and longer for the ability to spend more and more. Slow down that cycle and there's less outgo, which requires less income. The upshot is more time for family, friends, yourself, and the wider world.

A great many more people live between these two ends of the spectrum, striving to balance their comfort, security, and quality of life. It's no easy task to fund a house in a desirable neighborhood, pay for education, plan for retirement, and provide for memorable family trips, as well as the other sundries of life. At times, even reasonable wants and needs can keep us running harder than we may like.

The hard question is, how much of yourself are you willing to sacrifice to the altar of material needs and desires? This decision, of course, will affect your choice of work and directly impact everyone around you, particularly your family and mate.

I decided to become an entrepreneur when I was twenty-nine-years old, a move that cheated my young family of considerable time with me, and vice versa. Had I been wiser, I would have more closely involved them in the decision to make that profound career shift. Together, we would've examined the pluses and minuses and made a final call rather than discussing it in generic terms that sidestepped the full impact. The perspective of hindsight reveals that building a corporation from scratch, with all its associated anxiety and fierce focus, stunted my ability to be as present mentally, emotionally, and spiritually as I would've liked during my thirties and early forties. That was a large price to pay.

What rewards have all that blood, sweat, and fear bought me thus far? In part, sacrifice in the name of career in my earlier years has turned the last decade into pools of time I can bask in with my children, parents, and mate, vacationing and developing interests like writing and public speaking. I also have been blessed with the ability to share materially with my loved ones.

Still, when I think about how easily money can grab the spotlight in our lives, I cringe. Whether out of necessity ("I owe, I owe, so off to work I go") or from a need to make more of what one already has, money can easily overshadow more valuable relationships if we're not vigilant.

How Much Do You Need or Want

So now where to begin? Before you pull out your calculator or sharpen a pencil, let's first consider a more basic factor in your financial life. No math skills are needed to answer this: How much money do you need or want? Everyone will draw the line between their wants (the icing) and their needs (the cake) in a different place. Until you draw that line, purchasing decisions motivated by outside pressure rather than mission-driven desires will have a greater chance of throwing you off course.

When faced with an unreasonable itch to hear the *ch-ching* of the cash register, I conjure up the image of a man I once met in rural India. Through an interpreter, he asked me why Americans had so much "stuff." Stunned by his question, I asked him what he thought about it. Puzzlement passed over his otherwise serene face, then he said, "I don't understand it. I've got my family, food, and a roof over my head. What else do I need?"

Indeed, a lot of the "stuff" that we want is icing on the cake of the basics we're already blessed with.

How much money do you need to accomplish your mission? How much do you want beyond that? Scan the list of needs and wants you developed while determining your mission, and ask yourself whether it's in line with the way you spend your money now.

Money in Motion

Many of us tend to spend off-road, out of line with our missions and even our commitment to a particular spending plan. If you're caught short, or you're not sure where your money goes each month, a glance over your credit card statements or through your checkbook register can be a revealing tell-all shocker.

For an animated look at your relationship to money, observe your spending habits. Ask yourself these questions:

+ What motivates me to peel out the credit card?
+ Do I shop to reward myself?
+ Do I carefully plan my purchases, or do I buy on whim?

Try monitoring your emotional and psychological states while you're exercising your wallet. If being thrifty reflects a conscientious decision to simplify your life, more power to you. It's a different story, however, if your frugality is rooted in insecurity and an unfounded fear of scarcity and hardship, all related to stinginess and hoarding. On the other end of the spending spectrum, profligacy can be healthy or unhealthy. It can support your mission if you spend freely to spread the benefits of abundance among other people. Being a spendthrift, however, can be a way some people prop up their fallen self-esteem, buying to impress the gal next door or the guy in the next cubicle. These are all forms of financial self-sabotage that can compromise your most valuable priorities. Like anything else, discovering the underlying motivation and triggers, which only you can do (by yourself or with the methods described in chapter 5), is central to understanding this mysterious relationship.

Run Your Money

Does money run your life? As I did for some time, you may be scurrying from one bill to the next through the years, without ever slowing down long enough to get hold of the fact that money serves us, not the other way around. How to turn the tide?

Take personal responsibility for your finances. Take the time to clearly review the reality of your financial situation. Either alone or with a financial adviser, know where you stand.

Define your goals and write them down. Sound familiar? Just as with the rest of life, you'll get where you want to go faster with a plan in hand. Review your plan annually, and reassess your strategies. Along the way, develop your plan with those who will be affected by it, so that everyone's on the same financial page.

Educate yourself about key financial planning concepts. It may seem like mumbo-jumbo, but understanding the effects of those high credit card balances, how a dollar invested today can equal more than three dollars invested down the road, and how your money is deflated by inflation, can help you make wiser choices. Read up, get online, or talk to a money pro to find out about money-management concepts that apply to your situation.

Provide for the unexpected. We all know that life can turn on a dime, and when it does, it often costs much more than a dime. Protect yourself from financial thin ice by managing risk at levels appropriate to your situation. Consider whether you're adequately covered with

+ health insurance

+ disability income insurance

+ life insurance

+ professional liability/malpractice insurance

+ wills, trusts, power-of-attorney documents

Partner with financial mentors, paid or unpaid, to get the support and information you need to play out your game plan.

Hold On Tight . . . Future Ahead

Certainly the future isn't cheap, so budgeting in tomorrow's needs today would seem to be a given. Yet many Americans reach their twilight years with more golf balls than financial plans. In our *carpe diem* culture, we rarely feel a sense of urgency about planning for the future. For many of us, it's easier to imagine ourselves running away with the circus than to imagine ourselves retired.

Years and years ago, a lifelong friend, Skip Thaler, taught me a powerful lesson about putting pennies away for a retirement day. One night over a beer, when we were in our mid-twenties, Skip whipped out a compounding table that charted out how he was going to retire at age fifty. A quarter-century later, Skip made it. In 1994, he launched his new career as a sailor. Meanwhile, I'm still working.

COMPOUNDING MAGIC ✦ Compounding is a key financial concept worth wrapping your mind around. What Skip says is sometimes referred to as the Eighth Wonder of the World, compounding starts with the simple premise that a dollar invested earns interest, which builds on itself through the years. As the years pass, not only does the dollar earn interest, but the interest earns interest. Basically, the longer your money is invested, the more it grows, and the effect is astonishing.

Put another way, the earlier you start saving for retirement, the less you'll have to save in order to reach the same goal. Quick quiz: Which earns more—$12,000 invested over forty years or $36,000 invested over thirty years? If each investment earned 8 percent interest compounded annually, the smaller amount over the longer period would net you some $50,000 more than the larger amount over a shorter time. By investing early, you can begin with less and end up with more. And while earlier is better than later, today is earlier than tomorrow.

RETIREMENT ON THE HORIZON ✦ Have you thought about when you want to retire? Many, many mental miles lie between *choosing* to work longer and *having* to work longer. Pinpointing an age provides you a time-line along which you can clearly plot financial goals. Look out on the horizon. Once you've set your sights on the ideal age at which you'd like to start your next chapter, work will likely take on new significance and satisfaction. Moreover, you'll be less tempted to sell out your mission, the quickest way we can turn ourselves into the walking dead.

Going with the Pros

If this broad brushstroke has gotten you thinking about financial life current and future, it may be worth delving into the particulars of your situation with a financial professional. It may seem a little nonsensical—spending money to get advice on spending money. The services that a financial planner offers, however, go much further than that, and, given how complex finances can be, their expertise can help stretch and grow dollars in ways you may not realize. Consider financial planners paid money mentors. Nor should you believe that financial planners are just for the well-off. It's never too early—or too late—to tap them.

If you go the professional route, ask friends and colleagues for recommendations, and then interview several before selecting someone who will do right by you and your game plan. Don't let their titles intimidate you or their jargon mystify you. Ask clarifying questions so that you can make an informed decision. Take notes during your conversations so that you can compare and review later. Here are a few important questions to consider asking a prospective financial adviser:

1. What's your training and background?

2. What resources do you and your firm have available (legal services, tax advisers, up-to-date technology)?

3. How does your fee structure work?

4. Do you sell any financial products yourself?

5. What process do you follow with your clients? How would we begin? How often would we talk about my financial progress?

6. How will we measure whether our course of action is successful?

7. Do you have a list of clients you've worked with who would be willing to talk to me about their experience?

After you've spoken to the potential adviser, ask yourself:

1. Am I comfortable with this person? Do I sense that we share similar financial values?

2. Does this person seem genuinely interested in my needs and the particulars of my situation?

3. Does this person have expertise in the area I'm concerned with (e.g., retirement planning, bill consolidation, insurance, stocks), and offer access to a full range of products?

4. Do I prefer to work with a financial planner who is a consultant and is compensated with a flat fee or with one who sells products? If I prefer the latter, does the planner sell a wide range of products and have knowledge in each area? Does the person I'm considering fit my preference?

5. Can I trust this person with my money? Do I believe he/she is objective in his/her recommendations? Would I be willing to follow this person's advice?

As with any determination, combine your logical fact-finding with from-the-gut feelings. With a shared understanding of your financial goals and values, a good financial adviser can be a key player in putting a winning financial game plan in place.

Your Money Mission

Writing a financial mission statement is a great way to put your relationship to money in perspective. From a financial mission statement, you can then create action plans and strategize your spending decisions to support your goals. Each step of this process can be simple or complex, depending on your particular circumstances. A financial adviser can be helpful here, especially if you're unsure about estimating your needs for retirement (an area of financial planning many Americans avoid like a winter vacation in Siberia). Here are the basic considerations in determining your financial mission statement:

1. Look at your personal mission statement and family mission statement (discussed later in this chapter) and decide how much money you need or want to give and get what you want for your current phase of life. Think out one, three, five years. If you have a spouse, mate, or children, ask for their help in co-crafting it and their thoughts on what they want to give and get in the coming years.

2. Assess your current income.

3. Assess your current outflow. Categorize the major areas of expense each month. Note which expenses, such as house payments, are fixed and which, such as entertainment, can be adjusted to better fit your mission-inspired goals. Think not only about *where* you spend your money but *how* and *why* you spend.

4. Compare your current income and assets with your outflow. How do they stack up?

5. Estimate how much you need and want for the future. How many years do you have before you'd like to retire? How much will you need to save each month or year to get there? How do your current assets—savings, retirement plans, investments—affect your ability to meet those future retirement goals? Check financial services worksheets online, in books, or with a financial adviser to fully understand this crucial aspect.

6. Write your mission statement in points that address how you'd like to divvy up your income over the next year, the financial commitments that are nonnegotiable, and the financial commitments that are more flexible. Include behavioral goals as well as financial goals if you realize that the way you spend money affects your wallet as much as the amount you spend.

7. Discuss the priorities, values, and strategies with those who are affected. Building consensus for any decision is important so that everyone

is part of the plan and no one feels left in the dark when it comes to the reasons behind daily spending decisions.

8. Review the plan and re-strategize annually.

Whatever your goals and strategies to achieve them, be vigilant about ensuring that money and what it can buy doesn't sabotage your life. Your final determinations about the place money has in your mission will affect your lifestyle, your ability to enjoy that lifestyle, and the amount of time and energy you'll have for those you love. In the web of relationships, there are no one-way streets.

That Wonderful Thing Called Love

Some say money makes the world go around; I'd say it's love. A love relationship with a spouse, mate, or partner can be a guiding force that helps us discover our mission and stay on its road through times bumpy and smooth. Ideally, a love relationship helps us to see and become the person we were meant to be. In this way, the embrace of a love's arms can be at the same time the most intimate circle of human relationship as well as the most expansive.

Love is a great healer—great for our health, and great for our souls. Study after study confirms that, on average, people in loving relationships live longer and enjoy greater happiness than those in chilly non-relationships. While it's certainly possible to be fulfilled *sans* spouse, partner, mate, significant other (whichever term you prefer), this type of particularly loving relationships engenders unique opportunities for growth and support.

A loving relationship is the commingling of two personalities, the co-creation of a distinctly separate, third reality. It's a mini-miracle unto itself. A relationship requires communication, compromise, and understanding to link divergent backgrounds, upbringings, emotional orientations, and communication skills. When two people collide in a synergistic symphony of needs and desires, some sort of evolution (mutual and individual) is inevitable. Each partner's speed and direction of change, in both personal and professional growth, will vary. But if your growth gap becomes large, you may need to fortify your connections with dedicated time set aside for activities and shared interests. An example of this is provided by a dear friend of mine, Bill Jorgensen. He tells me that he and his wife, Joan, of thirty-two years, have a relationship that thrives on the belief that "an hour a day keeps the doctor away." Their devotion to listening time every day has kept their relationship strong through (and beyond) their child-raising years.

Some point to the mistaken notion that it takes children to make a family or hold a marriage together. In fact, "family" exists between any two people in a loving relationship, as my brother, Gary, and his wife, Pam, have shown for twenty-five years, in one of the strongest relationships I've witnessed.

Looking for Love?

Why are we attracted to some people and not to others? Part of the answer to this esoteric question is chemistry, a mysterious magnetic pull that defies explanation. Beyond pure chemistry, however, are other factors of attraction. One of the most powerful? Two people finding themselves at similar junctures in life, whether in personal growth or career arch. By learning to love ourselves, for instance, we attract people who know how to love themselves—and thus love others.

When we're absolutely clear about our wants and needs we're more likely to find a mate whose mission meshes with ours. Consider constructing a profile of your perfect mate—behaviors, traits, characteristics, and interests. Then ask for that person to come into your life, if it's according to the Universal Plan. A successful fortysomething publicist I know wrote such a profile, and shortly thereafter her soulmate appeared. They're now happily married.

Beware of type-casting. People often screen out healthy partners because they're fixed on the notion that they need to be loved by a certain type before they can feel good about themselves. This limits your options and unjustly discounts others. It turns a blind eye to people who may suit you, even though they're not exactly the person you expect to meet. By way of example, here is a handful of qualities I value in a romantic relationship:

+ **Flexibility.** As John Lennon said, life is what happens to you when you're busy making other plans. In other words, our time on Earth is packed with surprises. I appreciate a partner who approaches life with a positive outlook and embraces change.

+ **Honest and gentle caring.** A nurturing partner helps me grow. She supports what I do well and offers honest feedback on what I need to improve. This ability hinges on whether a partner possesses an unconscious craving for control, which can breed a need to criticize.

+ **Healthy conflict resolution.** Conflict can bring out the worst or the best in a partner. For me, she needs to be able to listen openly to my thoughts as well as sincerely and calmly share her own. Closing gaps of misunderstanding brings you close together. Everything that remains unresolved only serves to clutter the growing space between.

+ **Desire for growth and learning.** Life never stops, so why should we? I enjoy transmitting and receiving a continuous flow of new ideas and experiences. That kind of two-way transfer creates a dynamic, endlessly exhilarating team.

+ **Common values and interests.** While no two people share every interest, it's nice if, at the end of the day, you have more than geography and two eyes in common. Are there enough spiritual and intellectual tendrils there to keep the relationship connected and growing higher and higher? I enjoy a balance of individual and shared interests with my mate, Mary.

Eight Principles for Enhancing Love Relationships

A state of intimacy in a healthy love relationship produces infinite joy and learning. By intimacy I mean more than physical love. I mean full intimacy, which touches every layer and every level of our being—physical, psychological, intellectual, emotional, spiritual. Rooted in the Latin word for "innermost," *intimus,* the state of intimacy compels us to shed our masks and dare to share our deepest thoughts and feelings. Pronounce "intimacy" slowly, listen closely and you might hear...into-me-I-see.

You can create a safe harbor for two. Just reveal yourself and allow your partner to open up without fear of judgment. That kind of trust supercharges the sensual side of a relationship. It merges body and spirit and impregnates intimacy with its mystical power.

What can you do to enhance the joy of intimacy? Following a divorce—and not just a little soul-searching and analysis—I've come up with eight principles to help keep me on track.

1. **Focus on your own personal growth rather than on how your partner should grow.** I used to hear personal growth tips in light of what my partner needed to do rather than what *I* needed to do to improve. Commitment to lifelong psychological and spiritual growth lifts perspectives and priorities to healthier ground, not only in yourself but in those around you, including the love of your life.

2. **Resolve differences as they happen.** It's impossible *not* to find mistakes in other people, especially in someone we live with. But mistakes in the big picture of life are nothing more than irrelevant little smudges. What's really important is the ability to accept those mistakes, or differ-

ences, resolve them and return to that artful state of love and acceptance. Finger-pointing and critical attacks have never created lasting, positive change, and a pointed finger punctures any apology.

3. **Give love.** Getting love is an automatic by-product of giving love. Following those blissful early days of a relationship, when giving showers down like spring rain, it helps if we take the conscious steps of transitioning into a life sprinkled with daily gifts of love.

4. **Confront relationship challenges as vigorously as a career challenge.** Say you happen to be a natural at your profession. You may have noticed, habits flow like rivers in that they avoid obstacles. Likewise, people prefer their strong suit over trying a move they're not so good at. If we put the kind of effort into relationships that we put into jobs or hobbies we love, the divorce rate would drop precipitously. Accept that growing pains are inherent to relationships and deal with them. After all, those pains pale next to the anguish of a breakup.

5. **Seek input.** Include your partner in deliberations that cover the time you spend apart. They'll be and feel valued, involved, and connected.

6. **Confront negative emotions.** Anger, jealousy, stubbornness, and self-righteous pride all can stand in the way of resolving differences. A healthy self-esteem will listen to critics and minimize negative emotional reactions, without expecting that they'll be eliminated altogether.

7. **Act rather than react.** The laws of physics aren't restricted to atoms. Every action causes an emotional reaction. Sometimes it's wisest not to react at all. Righteous anger is overrated. I learned this in a group therapy session some years ago while observing a guy I'll call Gabriel, who could absorb another person's anger, see it for the fear it represented, and turn around and clearly articulate the meaning of the exchange. It was amazing. Had that anger been directed at me, I would have come unglued. But Gabriel was able to *act* where many of us can only *react*. He wasn't suppressing his emotions, however. Gabriel just had no need or desire to jump on the cycle of anger. It wasn't a ride he wanted to take.

8. **Depersonalize confrontations.** Ever notice that people often tend to push each other's emotional buttons like a video game—right at a moment that demands careful diplomacy? The irony is that the closer two people become, the more buttons they learn to operate. Intimately revealing yourself to someone is a double-edged sword. Deeper intimacy is the joyful side. The other side is if that knowledge is used against you after you've entrusted it, you're naturally going to feel alienated from the trustee.

I recommend the Sandwich Technique in addition to the three following methods to stay focused on the issue, and not the person.

+ *The dynamic process of give and take is more important than a dispute's actual outcome.* It's embarrassing to think of the tiny issues that spark scorched-earth campaigns. Clarify that your underlying goal is to strengthen the relationship, not to win at all cost. Winning at the expense of your partner means losing at the expense of the relationship. Avoiding that perilous outcome requires that now and then you meet your partner a little more than halfway. Instead of fretting over what you feel you lost, focus on what you gained. Consider taking a breath, maybe smiling, and gently saying, "I get the feeling that this is really important to you, so it's important to me."

+ *Avoid personal archeology.* Ancient history has its place in museums and the yarns you spin at your own expense—not in relationships. Rather than dredging up old problems that can't be changed, ask yourself what can be changed right at that moment: "What can we do to minimize future disagreements?"

+ *First move through your fury.* If you're really angry, just steaming, breathe, exercise, pray, meditate—whatever, apart from your partner—before hashing over the issue. Once words are said, they can be smoothed but never taken back. When negative emotions guide our logic, we *react* out of defensiveness rather than *act* out of love.

It is critical to do everything we can to make relationships work. The greatest pangs of regret issue from the "woulda, coulda, shoulda's" that course through our minds long after the last mending opportunity passes. No one has all the answers. Sometimes there is no answer. What counts is a commitment to do our best, a sound foundation for a strong relationship. Take advantage of any and all tools—courses, workshops, books, couples counseling, individual psychological work, spiritual growth. United by an intention to learn, love, and stay together, odds improve substantially that your relationship will flourish.

Closing the Circle

Not every relationship, alas, is built to last. Just as they begin and evolve, some relationships inevitably end. Completing a relationship, as I prefer to call it (whether it's a romantic, personal, or a close business relationship), can be some of the greatest chaos we ever face. We'd like to think that it's possible to do this gracefully; the reality is that it sometimes takes the distance of time to show us the positives we've gained. Even when it's clearly time to separate, we still must unravel the myriad strings that intertwine two lives. The longer the relationship, the more string.

Ending a marriage is the most complicated. Having experienced the dissolution of a twenty-five-year marriage, I suggest divorce only as a last resort. I had heard how devastating its impact is on children, friends, and career (not to mention oneself and one's spouse). But nothing could prepare me for the actual event. It trumped my worst nightmare.

Let no one tell you that divorce is the easy way out. And don't underestimate the seemingly endless consequences and emotional dynamics that erupt from divorce, even if it is your only course of action. That said, ask yourself if you've genuinely done everything you can to grow personally and gain a perspective that supports your relationship as a couple. If you can honestly answer yes, and you still don't feel able to accomplish your mission if you stay in the relationship, then make a decision based on your convictions, values, and beliefs.

Children: Parenting the Next Generation

Without a doubt, life yields daily lessons, some heartwarming, some gut-wrenching. Limited to our own lives, this acquired wisdom is valuable. Passed on to our children, that wisdom gains the priceless potential of forging a positive link with those who will inherit our world.

Ours is a society that's wired into the Internet, TV, and an infinite array of gadgetry. But that's no guarantee we're in touch with our children. Parenting is among the most rewarding and the most challenging of relationships. The stakes are high. As children of our own parents, we want to preserve the best of what they gave us. As parents, we want to pass on to our children the best baton possible, improving where we can. Parenting is a unique relationship that evolves with the cycle of life. We begin being parented, become parents ourselves, then often become parented again in our old age.

Growing Up Together

I once overheard a man at a New York City bistro tell a friend, "My kids are growing up. I just hope I become an adult before they do." Children add a dimension of responsibility that immediately shifts parents' perspective on their own behavior, spirituality, relationship, money, career, and future. Actions and decisions that used to affect just you and your mate now affect an innocent child who has no say in whether you spend more time at work or save less money for college. Some parents see their own psychological or spiritual growth mushroom as the competing demands of children, career, and marriage draw to the foreground every conceivable issue. The consequences of unhealthy behavior become severe when you have the ability to pass on patterns to children who don't know any better. While some people gripe, "Kids these days...," it's our legacy that creates the next generation.

I believe it's a healthy sign that young couples are having children later in life. They're giving themselves a chance to grow up and learn to relate, first as a couple, second as a family. While we learn at each stage of life, the ideal progression in my mind is growing oneself first, then growing as a couple, and, finally, growing as a parent. Each stage holds its attendant challenges and can be melded with the others. Each, however, can greatly benefit from focused attention absent the others.

Passing the Baton

I'm blessed with two sons who teach and inspire me every day. Trent, in his early thirties, is a reporter for *Newsweek* magazine, and Chris, in his late twenties, produces still pictures, videos, and films under his company name—Signal Pictures. They're more than capable of running with the family baton into the next generation, sprinting with their own unique talents and passions. I don't believe parents can take credit for the success of their adult children (or that they should bear the blame for their challenges), yet they can share in their kids' lives from the sidelines, enjoying and empathizing.

Parents do, however, have a responsibility to prepare their kids so that when the baton is passed, the little ones are ready to carry it. Following their child's high school graduation, parents can take on additional roles, such as friend and mentor. As the young adults mature, these new roles become stronger while the role of "parent" recedes.

Balance, Please

Encouraging evidence suggests that fathers are spending more time with their children than they did twenty years ago. I'm happy to see that, in general, today's corporate culture allows for more time with children than it used to. In an earlier era, a child's illness, soccer game, or parent-teacher conference was only in the rarest instance a valid excuse for a manager to miss a meeting. It simply didn't play in Peoria. The passage of the Family and Medical Leave Act of 1993 gave parents "flex time," in-house day-care, and increased understanding from management. Now more mothers and fathers can balance their commitments to children and careers. Even two decades ago it was inconceivable that an employee would turn down a relocation offer, even if it uprooted children in critical years. Today families are more likely to make these decisions together, and allow for vetoes.

This does not minimize the harrowing balancing acts carried off by dual-career, multi-child families. In an effort to stay competitive, or to appease Wall Street, some companies still feel obliged to apply pressure on employees in order to ease the stress of rising costs and greater competition. Nevertheless, the trends I see hold positive signs for the health of families—and businesses that do their best to support the balance of work and home priorities.

A-Level Parenting

Good parenting is founded on a quality relationship between yourself and your partner. Strain on a couple, combined with Inner Team turmoil, hinders our ability to deal with our children fairly, carefully, and appropriately. We're constantly surprised by how much children observe and remember. They're like tiny microphones, picking up everything, especially the actions and words of people they are close to. I know that when I rattle off to my parents things they said a long, long time ago, they're flabbergasted that I heard—and remember.

Because your actions make an indelible impression on your children, it's worth doing everything you can to put yourself on a road that will help lead you and them to a healthy future. Living life fully and passionately sends an undeniable message indeed. As Carl Jung observed, "Nothing has a stronger influence psychologically...on their children than the unlived life of parents." Self Coaching skills that enhance your own wellness and strengthen your primary relationship will fuel your tank for this part of the journey. And you'll find that many of the skills you pick up in parenting—encouraging another's self-esteem, constructive discipline, teaching empathy, for example—also apply to relationships in the workplace.

An indescribable confluence of factors—his unique personality, his genes, the behavior of his parents and peers, his community—shape a child. We can guide our children, even rule them with an iron will, but ultimately they must engage in the same process of learning, understanding, and relearning that we go through as adults. Examining behavior, positive and negative, and making decisions to repeat or drop a behavior are skills children can learn and benefit from, even at an early age. I enjoyed teaching my sons, and wouldn't trade those memories for anything—coaching their athletic teams, showing them how to ride a bike, tie a tie, play Ping-Pong, drive a stick-shift car.

Schoolwork is one of the most important areas in which you can spend time teaching and mentoring your children. Monitor their progress. Help them structure time. Create a dedicated study space that supports learning, without pressuring them into achievement. The study table I used in my college fraternity house singlehandedly saved my grades. The idea works well at home. My former wife and I would review and assist in our kids' schoolwork (I still remember some pretty tough math flash cards).

Encouraging children to achieve some level of excellence is not easy. Everyone has standards, of course, from schools to parents to peers. But the real quest should be to find the level that's right for the child, and challenge him to learn and grow without pushing him too far outside his capabilities. Shoving a child toward a goal set too high can instill a sense of failure, or a fear of trying. Rather than digging in when the learning gets tough, she may be more apt to quit, only to regret later that she didn't stick it out. It's sometimes a challenge to remember that a parent's standard of achievement is not the same as a child's. Negotiating the space between takes care and sensitivity.

Show Unconditional Love

A child's sense of self-worth is built on unconditional love. You can make a lot of errors in parenting. Yet, if you get this one right, there's a pretty good chance your kids will emerge as adults who know how to love themselves and others.

I see badges and bumper stickers proclaiming "Proud Parent of a Burnsville Hockey Player" and "Proud Parent of an Honor Student." In the best of all possible worlds I would also see bumper stickers that gloat over parental pride disconnected from accomplishment: "Proud Parent, Unconditionally." My parents love my brothers and me unconditionally, and I give this same unconditional love to my own children. Love that waxes or wanes based on behavior isn't love for the child; it's love of behavior. Whether you're angry or proud of what your child does, love for her as a human being should be what shines brightest.

Kids need a whole lotta love. Love, however, doesn't mean a whole lotta spoiling and coddling. That only sets up unrealistic expectations and does little to prepare them for the reality of working and living with others. An upbringing with no boundaries eventually makes it difficult for an adult to recognize healthy boundaries in relationships or jobs. Childhood would be an impossible act to follow. No employer or companion would ever be enough. Spoiling creates dependence. The goal of healthy parenting is to foster independence, which leads the way to interdependence.

Caring, Constructive Discipline

There are two distinctly different forms of discipline. The type that's caring and constructive can mean the difference between tearing down someone's self esteem and building it up with learning opportunities. Discipline, like feedback around difficult issues in the workplace, frequently occurs in the heat of the moment. If you yourself didn't receive caring discipline when you were a kid, the moment you begin disciplining your children is when your worst fear—that of repeating your parents' mistakes—can manifest itself. If you're susceptible to this, take a moment to calm down before addressing a hot issue. Be honest with yourself about your own motivations and feelings.

Harmful discipline is the kind that's motivated by an impulse to prove something: "I'll show YOU!" What's instructive is gently yet firmly telling a child why his behavior is not okay, how it could be hurtful. This lets him know he's loved unconditionally, and separates the action from the child. "Your behavior is not okay" is very different from "You are a bad kid!"

Help your children learn from their mistakes. The lesson will cut both ways. When—*not if*—you make a mistake, apologize to them and ask (when it's appropriate) for forgiveness, and move on. Your kids will respect you more if you don't try to hide your mistakes (which they'll see) or make excuses (which they won't buy).

It's in parents' job description to define rules and boundaries and draw out the consequences of violating them—a tricky balance. I remember my son Trent sometimes saying as a teenager, "Don't threaten me." Other times he'd protest, "You didn't tell me what would happen if I did that." If it's communicated in a caring way, children—anyone, for that matter—will interpret a consequence as a natural effect of going outside the established limits, and not as a punishment. Children constantly test boundaries; it's one of the most important ways they learn about the world around them. It's also how they learn about their parents. For their part, parents must be ready and able to let go, when the time is right, so that their children can test their wings. Be prepared to find a middle ground, again and again, to allow children new responsibility while sheltering them from parts of life they may still be ill-equipped to handle.

Years may go by before the benefits of constructive discipline emerge. In fact, the pain in your kids' faces may make you feel as if it's better to give in. But the reward comes down the road, when it's apparent that you've raised children who respect themselves and the rights of others. In some cases they may even thank you for it—later.

Teaching Children to Accept Responsibility

Learning responsibility is an incremental process. Structured opportunities to learn, which give children a sense of responsibility and consequence, form the foundry in which they forge their independence and confidence.

Give kids responsibility around the house, a natural arena for independence. As they become a contributing part of the household, they see that their actions affect, and can add value to, the lives of those around them. It's an obvious parallel universe from which they'll draw lessons on future relationships they'll enter into.

Allowances are a great area of opportunity to teach real-life lessons. Given the pressures of our consumer culture, it's never too early to start allocating an allowance. It's an important, youthful lesson in managing money and spending it wisely. The way I figure it, it's better to go broke at twelve than at forty-two. To mirror real life, we tied a portion of our kids' allowances to specific responsibilities. As Trent and Chris grew into their late teens, we even entered into simple, handwritten contracts with them. They signed on the dotted line for car privileges and college support, the latter of which was prorated based on grade-point averages.

Another important vantage point for teaching lies in giving kids a candid glimpse of work time. A tour of the office is a good start, but nothing is more instructive than giving your kids (when they're old enough) a peek at the nuts and bolts of your workday. Every now and then since their late teens my sons have sat in on critical Tires Plus meetings. During one, a particularly tense negotiation with the Bridgestone Tire Company in the mid-1980s, Trent watched me knock heads in a heated debate. Afterward, he said, "That was really intense." That was real-life responsibility in action. No dinnertime lecture could convey what Trent learned with his own eyes that day in Los Angeles. Nevertheless, things like Take Our Daughters (or Sons) to Work Day are great ways to demystify the office and break down the divisions between our professional and personal lives.

It's a given in the parenting game plan that there's always room for improvement. I take to heart my sons' feedback, particularly their regret that they weren't challenged enough when they were young. When Chris was in junior high school, for instance, he talked us into letting him quit piano lessons. Now he wishes we'd forced him to carry through, but he's redressing that by learning as an adult and proving that it's never too late to give parents a chance to attend their kids' recitals. Both sons say that, in retrospect, they lament that we didn't hold the academic bar high enough during their high-school years. Raising teenagers in the 1980s, one of our guiding lights was "let 'em do their thing" philosophy, born of the free-love sixties notion that if it doesn't hurt, it must help. Well, not exactly, it turns out. If I had it to do over, I'd strive for a middle ground, somewhere between allowing them enough slack to develop decision-making skills and reining them in more often during situations they were too immature to handle.

Are the Lines Open?

Many parents relate to children on a surface level without cracking their hopes, dreams, and fears. And often we don't share our own with them. Just as it's important to understand the needs and wants of a partner in love or business, it's vital to understand the needs and wants of the children for whom we're responsible.

Keep an eye out for moments when they're open, curious, or relaxed, or find themselves in a reflective mood. If they come to you, bingo: Stop what you're doing and make the time, right then and there. Among other things, ask them what they want out of life and how you can help them get it.

While in their college years, my sons each approached me about their careers, seeking advice about the prospects of joining Tires Plus. Rather than answer, I lobbed the question back: "What do *you* think about coming into the business?" In both cases, we openly and objectively discussed the pluses and minuses. I didn't want to lead them one way or the other. In the end, they both chose careers outside my career and industry, and it's worked well for them—and thus for me.

Try asking something risky, like "What do you like about our family? What would be different if you were the parent?" Listen carefully to their answers. Value them, explore them. Help your children set short-term goals and add long-term goals. Follow up on previous conversations. Correspondingly, share with your children what's happening in various parts of your life. Be real (while respecting their age and maturity) about what's going well and not so well.

Sex, alcohol, and drugs are important topics whose handling will benefit from established lines of communication. Given the headlines, and what hits the big screen (and small), there's no shortage of opportunity to hash over these things. They're not the sorts of lessons to abdicate to the schools. Mishandled, these issues can engender lifelong consequences. Abuse of sex, drugs, and alcohol is so closely tied to issues of self-worth and healthy love and intimacy that parents have a particular obligation to help their children negotiate this complex terrain. Create an atmosphere in which they feel free to confide absolutely anything without fear of reprisal.

Availability at work is important. I've always had a rule at my office regarding my sons. Anytime they call, I'm available, and they've never abused it. Whoever answers the phone tracks me down, regardless of the situation. Still, there were days when I was too preoccupied, days before I developed stress-management methods like my four-step prayer and focused breathing. It wasn't always possible to switch gears from workplace concerns into my sons' concerns. I recall anxious days fraught with doubts over meeting the following week's payroll, not exactly a state of mind conducive to fully hearing out my sons. When stressful days arise—for many of us, that means every time the sun rises—and that blinking Line Two is your child, your first priority could be to take a deep breath, relax, calm down, pull it into perspective, and put your mind into the moment for them. It can be a challenge, but it's worth the practice.

Children, it's been said, speak a language all their own. They live under the same roof with you, but their perspectives and experiences can be vastly different from your own. Just as you can't assume that someone in your workplace understands words the same way you do, don't assume children will, either.

Try to bridge generation gaps as they develop. Granted, today they are fewer and further between, given the speed of global communications and the rise of the lingua franca of pop culture. But do what you can to see life through the eyes of your children. Enter their world, but don't expect them to bound into yours. This will broaden your perspective and demonstrate that you value your girl's world. A Motown fan, I once found myself spending an afternoon in the basement with my son Trent listening to the entire double-record album of one of his favorite punk-rock bands (the Clash's *London Calling,* for those of you keeping score at home). The effort it takes to find common ground (in this case, ringing ears for a few hours) is well worth the rewards of easier communication and mutual respect.

Quantity and Quality Time

The debate over quality time versus quantity time still simmers. To me, a mix is necessary. Quality time can happen anytime. The activity doesn't matter so much as your attentiveness. Mundane tasks like washing dishes or raking leaves together can be a rich opportunity to catch up. Vacations create a framework for exploring places, ideas, and each other, things you're less likely to do at other times of the year. Schedule vacations and other regular time together just as you would any other important appointment, lest they fall by the wayside in the face of speeding, competing priorities. A regular Tuesday-night father-daughter pizza outing or a big, family-wide weekend dinner gives everyone something to look forward to and count on.

Regret that they didn't spend more time with their children is a common regret of parents of grown children. Unfortunately, wishing won't bring back those days. I remember taking Trent to college and being hit squarely with that sudden insight. Following my wake-up call and my subsequent growth in awareness, I felt tremendously guilty about all the things I could have done with my sons, and how I could have been more present, had I known better, earlier. It took years to get over this. I had to accept my imperfections and understand that I did the best I could with what I knew at the time. Likewise, I had to recognize what I did right by my boys. Sure, regrets still creep in. Although I can't go back, those regrets now inspire me to make the most of the time I still have with all my loved ones.

The primary responsibility for child-rearing rests on parents. But an extended network of family and friends is also vital. The time my sons spend with their grandparents, aunts, and uncles gives them a strong sense of history and a feeling of belonging, as it did for me. Some of my fondest memories? Rocking back and forth for hours with my grandparents on their front porch, talking about everything from the motorcycle passing by on the street to how Grandma and her sisters banded together after their father died. Rooting childhood dreams in the context of family helps us take wing as adults.

Family Mission Statement

A business has a mission statement to communicate its reason for being. We've talked about the importance of a personal mission statement, and seen how those principles can be applied to create a guiding financial mission statement. Why not a family mission statement? The family unit is another organization that can benefit from a jointly created mission statement. It lays out baseline expectations of behavior, values, and purpose, and provides a benchmark against which every family member can measure their actions, as well as the actions of others.

Pete Selleck, COO of Michelin Americas Small Tires, related to me this story about the value of a family mission statement. He was playing golf with Christopher, his thirteen-year-old son, one summer day. On the fifth hole, Christopher's game fell apart, and with it came a temper tantrum. After an appropriate warning with no reaction over a ten-minute span, Pete ended the round on the spot.

When they got home, Christopher was sent to his room with a copy of the family mission statement that the entire Selleck family, including Christopher, had just developed the month before. Pete told his son to write down which parts he had failed to live up to on the golf course, and what he needed to do to change in the future.

Two hours later, Christopher presented his analysis to his father, along with a sincere apology. Since then, Pete reports that golf rounds with his son (after a four-week period of no golf as a reminder) have become much more meaningful. And the Selleck family is another step closer to achieving its vision as expressed in the family mission statement.

Family Meetings

A company would never consider functioning without meetings. Similarly, meetings can strengthen a family. The hectic schedules of family members can create a great deal of miscommunication in the absence of a clear forum for exchanging information. That message board on the refrigerator may work for a while, but the busier a family gets, the more it makes sense to have regular, face-to-face meetings.

Choose a day of the week, like you would for a business meeting, and a consistent time that works for everyone—say, following the big Sunday night dinner. Get commitments from everyone. Go ahead and set an agenda, focus on unfinished business from the previous meeting and ponder new items for discussion. Updating schedules of events and activities outside the home is usually a top order of business. There are questions of tasks, goals, and priorities in the home. Before moving to new items, check in with how everyone did with last week's ideas. Encourage, don't harass, when a caring nudge is called for. Make an agenda item out of positive feedback. If someone raises a specific issue, respond with a potential solution. If meetings haven't been part of your family's regimen, family meetings might seem a little awkward, perhaps too formal. Minimize the formality as much as possible without compromising the focus. After a few, everyone will ease into the groove.

Handling Life's Curve Balls

Life throws us plenty of curves, some that are easy to hit and others that can smoke right by you. Handling tough pitches can pull a family together or tear it apart, depending on how they're handled. The three swings to handle these pitches? Heart, faith, and courage.

Facing the potential loss of a child is one of the wildest pitches imaginable. Few can imagine handling it. I couldn't. When he was twelve years old, my son, Chris, was hit by a car while riding his bike and sent flying. When I finally got the ambulance service on the phone, I blurted, "Is he alive?" "He is right now," the service answered, "but you better get here quick." I was astonished and deeply anguished. A teammate drove me to the hospital, but to me the car couldn't go fast enough. At stoplights I was so desperate to keep moving that I got out of the car and kept walking, only to be picked up a few hundred feet down the road. As Chris lay in a coma for two days, the family came together with amazing strength. I continuously sang songs to him, hoping he would hear me. Finally, the most joyous moment of my life: Chris opened his eyes. Every day I give thanks for both my sons and do my best not to take their presence for granted.

A divorce rate hovering around 50 percent winds up pitching many families and kids a curve. I'll never forget the night Chris told me, "Dad, we're not a family anymore." Steeped in sadness, I could only stammer, "We're still a family…always will be, even though it will look different now." Divorce temporarily tore the heart out of our family; I experienced intense and debilitating guilt over it for years. Seeing my young sons' trusting faces, I felt only that I'd failed them. It took years, anger, tears, sorrow, and personal growth for each of us to find a way to construct a new sense of family.

Difficulties will arise. Working through tough times with compassion, support, and a spirit-filled attitude is a great mirror for the trials your kids will inevitably face. In fact, consider difficulties gifts and opportunities that help your family prepare for the future.

Parents and Elders: The Generation Ahead

Just as we were all once children, we hope to be elders someday. Turning our focus to the generation ahead, we see a wellspring of seasoned sagacity. In mature cultures, elders are respected more than everyone else in the community. Connection with elders is considered a most revered relationship. Most of Western society, however, prizes nothing more than youth and innovation. The younger generation moves in and pushes out the elder generation. Too many people consider elders passé. In fact, they're a full step ahead in terms of experience and wisdom, and many of their life lessons offer precious perspective on our speed-addicted world.

Appreciating Parents

To cultivate appreciation for elders, I start with my parents. Bar none, my mother, Elizabeth, was the single greatest source of nourishment during my youthful growth. As far as I could tell, my brothers and I were her only concern. She had us blissfully fooled. In short succession, she was jumping from the University of Houston's first graduating class on their current campus, to supporting the war effort on an airplane parts factory floor, to our rural Indiana bungalow in the 1950s, where she remade herself into an entrepreneur operating a weight-reduction salon out of our basement, as well as raising three children. When I went to college, she went to graduate school, taking courses toward a master's degree, so she could hop onto a new career track in social work. In her eighties, retirement hasn't lightened her load. Now, friends, bingo, bridge, and travel pack her schedule.

In the 1950s, when I was growing up, mothers raised kids, fathers made money. Mom did both, a tough model to pull off so beautifully then, as today. She regularly read to me, and used warm praise to encourage good behavior. The pleasure I'd get from one of her compliments still rings in my ears, and on the flip side I learned the importance of giving compliments and common courtesy. She recently sent me a framed thank-you note she helped me write to my grandmother when I was five. It reminded me of the care she heaped on my brothers and me, and the sensitivity she encouraged in us.

Because I knew Mom loved me, no matter what, I learned a lot, including how to love myself. She empowered me, told me I could be anything I wanted to be, and pointed me to solutions rather than handing me ready answers. Because she listened to me, I knew my thoughts mattered.

My father, Bill, is a different sort of hero. That he has any empathy and generosity at all is a triumph of will, given the slings and arrows he's faced during his seventy-eight years. Abandoned by his father, his mother reluctantly sent him off to be raised by his grandmother. At twenty-two he became a lieutenant in the U.S. Army's Fourth Armored Division (part of General George S. Patton's Third Army), and trudged off to the European theater of World War II, where he landed on Utah Beach eighteen days after the D-Day Invasion. There he built bridges, ensured that troops crossed safely, and blew up what he'd built, the better to slow the enemy.

At times, close friends were cut down by his side. It was a horror suffered by hundreds of thousands of men and women of Dad's generation, without whom the world would look very different today.

In the war's aftermath, Dad and many others faced their postwar challenges—alone, for the most part. It was a time when almost nothing was known about post-traumatic stress syndrome, or combat fatigue, as it was called then. Still, he persevered, beginning as a home developer and moving through more trying times as a haberdasher before settling into his niche as an extremely successful mausoleum salesman and, in his sixties and most of his seventies, a car salesman.

My teenage years saw Dad and me grow tight. One winter evening he even drove from one end of Indiana to the other just to watch me play basketball (we lost, but having him in the stands took the sting out of the defeat). His generosity and understanding taught me many a lesson, like this one, about cars: I was sixteen and thinking I just had to spend eight hundred dollars, my entire life's savings, on a 1956 Chevy convertible. When I asked him for his advice, he said, "It's not what I think that's important, Tom. It's what you think about it." Well, I bought the car, and it fell apart in pretty short order. What did I own? On one hand, a disintegrated car. On the other, my first major decision, a doozy. But I had no one to blame but myself. Today, I kick a few more tires before I commit—to a car or any other important decision.

Once I graduated from college, Dad became more of a mentor and friend, doling out his own brand of uncommon sense and kitchen-table wisdom. While their financial lot was a rollercoaster ride, Dad and Mom never lost their sense of giving. When the organ in our church fell into disrepair, they stepped up and bought a new one. They were facing their own financial challenges, but they made a higher priority of music in the service of God and the community.

Age-Old Honor

When we're kids, we presume that everything before us is ours, as our God-given right. This city, it seems as if it has always been here, right? That hill over there, it was always that high. Sometimes we need to be reminded that, in fact, the landscape and shape of our world has been sculpted down the ages by people determined to build and change the face of their own lives. We're only one link in that infinite chain of change. We owe a debt of gratitude to those who bequeathed us our lot. I'm grateful to my parents and the entire postwar generation for their sweat and sacrifice.

It's easy to forget our elders' contributions, as the ravages of age blur their accomplishments. But, as Sir Isaac Newton observed more than three centuries ago, if we see farther than our forebears, it is by standing upon the shoulders of giants. But nature decrees that our parents go from being the shoulders we stand on to the shoulders we support. Harbor a sense of gratitude for their essential place in your life. It will remind you to nurture and encourage them when frustration tempts you to be impatient with their changing capabilities and bodies. My mother and father are both wiser for their years. Don't be fooled by an aging outer shell, failing eyes, and spent legs.

My father's favorite word is *empathy*. Try it on. Empathize with how you'll feel at your parents' age. Empathize with the disappointment of a worn-out body. Imagine every day facing the common assumption that loss of *some* ability is tantamount to the loss of *all* ability. Empathize with the loneliness of a world too busy to spend time with you. Empathize with feeling that your experience and stories are bankrupt.

Losing any degree of physical and mental ability is frightening and frustrating. Instead of the usual expansion of learning and experience, every day carries the specter of new restrictions. Close your eyes. Imagine being eighty years old. See yourself, and imagine the changes in your life. Now hold that awareness the next time you call on an elder, whether stranger or kin.

Each day I have with my parents is a gift. I honor them, seek their counsel, encourage them. While our time may whistle by, elder time moves slowly. The days that they've gone without hearing from us can seem like months. Phone calls and letters are a golden tonic that takes scant effort to brew compared to the years our relatives doted on us. We all treasure my weekly connect-up calls.

In my yearly action plan, I map out trips with my parents. In 1990, Mom and I attended her fifty-year class reunion at the University of Houston. Twice now, Dad, Chris, Trent, and I have retraced his steps through World War II, threading through England, France, and Germany. Extended time together creates opportunity to break the surface, to explore how our parents feel about their own childhood, their adult years, their future, their thoughts about life and about death. I ask Dad and Mom questions now so I don't have to wonder later. If you have the opportunity, root yourself in your elders' past so they can grow into your future.

Easing the Transition

The people who spawned the great American baby boom are in their twilight hours, prime time for boomers to begin facing the death of their parents, and their parents' friends, and take an honest look at how to be of service at this important juncture.

Often, adults never get over living anything short of the best childhood possible. Not enough love. Not enough encouragement. Not enough guidance. Not enough support. In most cases, parents did the best they could with what they knew. Still, that doesn't stop people from being troubled by their upbringing, or from hanging on to lingering resentments that prevent a fully honest embrace of those who brought us here. Those resentments, large or small, sometimes stand in the way of giving parents the respect they deserve for the part they played in our lives.

A person's state of mind at the moment of death is considered in many faiths a bridge to the next plane of existence. By resolving conflict, whether active or dormant, in a gentle and caring way today, we can help our parents toward a more peaceful transition. In the final moments, when it's often difficult to sum up feelings, caregivers say that what a dying person most wants to hear are the simplest expressions of human love and kindness: "Forgive me." "I forgive you." "Thank you." "I love you." "Good-bye."

Simple words, yet a troubled personal history can make saying them seem insurmountable. If you feel such a barrier, I encourage you to explore whether resolution is possible, before it's too late. Straight confrontation with your parents can work, but it's not always the most effective course. Counselors can offer effective methods to resolve these issues, a worthwhile pursuit that's possible even if parents are no longer alive.

Similarly, if you have adult children, try asking them to reflect on their youth. Ask them what they're happy about and what they wish had been different. If regret stirs inside you, share it and apologize for not giving your kids more. Treat them the way you want your children to treat you. Sooner or later, we get what we give.

How About Today?

No matter what has gone before and what is yet to come, all we really have is today. We can't change yesterday, and we can't predict tomorrow, but we can affect today. For some years now I've played a little time-travel trick on myself. There are certain moments when I'll try to think about what's happening as if I were reflecting back a few decades from now. What will I think of this choice then, I'll wonder. Will I smile at the memory, or will I cringe? If it's the latter, it's time to call an audible and readjust my game plan.

Imagine a world where each generation builds upon the best of the one before it. Feel the joy and power of lessons being handed down like an inheritance, preserved and capitalized upon. Instead of relearning the same thing over and over again, the legacy could blossom exponentially. Four, five, ten generations later, imagine how your family might evolve and grow in their own life fulfillment. Start this process now, using the motivating wisdom I heard years ago: "I will be a warrior, so my children can be statesmen, so their children can be poets."

Friends Old and New

Parents and children are given; friends we choose. The funny thing is, the best family members are also friends, and good friends feel like family. At any gathering where toasts are made to friends and health, I realize the circle grows wider with each passing year. Friends and health...to me they're one and the same. As keys to mutual giving and learning, friends become key to our health. Anyone who crosses our path is a potential friend, on some level. Common interests, background, values, and direction make some friends closer than others.

My parents are model friends to others. Dad extends a hand and a grin to everyone he meets. To him, the world holds no strangers, just unmet friends. At Mom's eightieth birthday party, one of her friends told me, "Lib has the ability to make all of her friends feel like her best friend."

I love the notion that a friend is someone who knows you're not perfect, but still treats you as if you were. Friends cut you slack, accept you, yet don't back down from telling you straight—with due care—the messages you need to hear. They simultaneously support you and challenge you to do better. Goethe knew well the meaning of friends. He counseled, "Treat people as if they were what they ought to be, and you help them to become what they are capable of being."

Some Are Silver, Others Are Gold

It's said that friends aren't *made* so much as they're *recognized*. That means close friendships arise in any stage of life. I'm fortunate to have close friends that span my life, and that kind of history preserves a refreshing lack of pretense between us. Memories of childhood adventures keep us on even ground as adults, even though our lives have all gone in different directions.

New friendships are enriching in a different way, especially when they aren't acquired at the expense of old friendships. While we don't share a common history with newer friends, we're more likely to have similar interests and values. Together, we're great spiritual traveling companions.

Driving down new roads, we can teach each other and become guide to places one or the other has yet to explore.

Technology has made meeting and keeping up with people even easier. While surfing the Internet to research a European trip, my son, Chris, met people from Spain and Italy who wound up hosting him and becoming friends. In many ways, phones, faxes, and e-mail have transported people a world away to the same space your next-door neighbor occupies.

Friendships need attention to remain intact, yet some friendships can go months without water and still look like plush May grass. Others need frequent sprinkling. Either way, friendships need tending. I do my best to make special efforts to attend friends' lifecycle celebrations and milestones. Supporting them at celebrations of births, weddings, and funerals acknowledges the range of our human experience and binds us together indescribably. Be it your presence at an event, a quick postcard, a phone call, e-mail, lunch or a long visit, let your friends know you care and that they're important.

Close-Knitting Your Community

Loved ones and friends help us get in touch with the gentler side of our missions, and that often impacts our worldview. Feeling closer to friends and family, you may also find yourself yearning for an evolving relationship with community. It may nudge you to peruse your neighborhood and hometown, then your state and the country, until eventually you find yourself asking what you can do to touch the lives of people anywhere. Near or far, large or small, whatever available time or money you do have is needed by any number of people and organizations. There's sure to be one that is consistent with your mission.

Once we were a people bound by geography, now we're bonded by common causes. Emissary organizations fill voids that used to be filled by close-knit communities. Neighbors in many American communities hardly recognize one another. Charitable organizations and volunteerism create an alternative support net; they have the effect of connecting us with people for reasons beyond economics. It may be quixotic to believe we can recapture the close ties of the towns and villages of yesteryear. But we can forge new connections, the kind that better embrace society's irreversible and simultaneous expansion and specialization. The world of cold shoulders that brush off the needy is only the real one if we allow it to be.

Lending a Helping Heart and Hand

Outside of family and work and alongside monetary contributions, volunteerism is the most powerful way there is to spread our mission. What a different world it would be if every one of us volunteered a single hour each week. Or each month, for that matter. It would transform the world. People like Colin Powell, President Jimmy Carter, and Elizabeth Dole are only the most visible faces of volunteerism. There are millions of people who are adding to the lives of others every day. They may have touched your life.

Feel you can't make a difference? Heed anthropologist Margaret Mead's famous observation: "Never doubt that a small group of thoughtful, committed citizens can change the world. Indeed, it's the only thing that ever has." Greenpeace, Mothers Against Drunk Driving (MADD), the World Foundation for AIDS Research and Prevention—they were all once an idea in someone's head that wound up energizing a handful of people dedicated to a common cause, who in turn parted entire seas of possibilities. Often in the face of intense opposition, they inspired millions. In 1998, when the USDA proposed loosening standards for organic agriculture, 200,000 people told them that it was clearly unacceptable. Today, the standards for healthy food remain high.

Look hard enough and you'll find opportunities to simultaneously give of yourself and receive. Baby boomers are moving into their empty-nest and early retirement years. If this describes you, try reconnecting with the community and reestablishing the balance that might have been lost when children and careers consumed every burst of energy.

If not us, who? If not now, when? Consider committing yourself to a cause consistent with your mission statement and action plans that extends beyond your immediate family. Be creative. A friend of mine celebrated her fortieth birthday by inviting her friends to a "day party" during which they built a home supervised by a Habitat for Humanity volunteer.

The Future Is in Our Hands

As we train our awareness on serving others, it's common to rethink where we spend our time, energy, and money. More and more, financial service groups are investing only in ethical businesses. Cigarette companies are out; corporations like Target and Working Assets Long Distance, who watch their charitable yardstick as closely as they do their bottom line, are in. Other companies get into the game of community support by matching funds with employee contributions to nonprofits, sponsoring walks and rides to raise research dollars and awareness for medical concerns such as breast cancer and muscular dystrophy, as well as a host of other causes.

There are people who get up and walk out in the face of Scrooge-like employers. My friend Stuart, for instance, left a prestigious, high-paying position in a large company because he said its leadership couldn't care less about the community in which it operated. "They were only takers," he said, "not givers." This was inconsistent with Stuart's personal mission, and ultimately the internal conflict was too much. He left the firm and found a position at a company whose values matched his own. While he took a hit in the paycheck, Stuart's self-respect and happiness soared. Today, free of regret, he has never felt more successful.

Earth: A Friend in Need

Relationships with people are a two-way street—giving and getting, caring and being cared for. It may not be as obvious, but our relationship with Earth can be in some ways the same. The Earth's dynamic, life-giving structure provides all our sustenance—food, shelter, water, air—and we, in return, do our best to respect and care for it. In our relationship to Earth, however, history has shown our planet to be a more faithful friend to us than we have been to it.

The statistics read like a dystopian science fiction novel: half of the world's temperate rain forests have vanished. Global warming is increasing the spread of infectious diseases and spiking the number of heat-related deaths. Skin cancer is on the rise as the Earth's ozone layer thins. The U.S. industrial-agricultural complex uses pesticides at a rate of some ninety-five pounds per *second*. That same second chews up two acres of U.S. forests. Okay, perhaps it's no surprise that Americans consume more energy per capita than anyone else. But the underbelly of all those glimmering office towers and speeding sports sedans is the world-leading, airborne burst of carbon dioxide they help produce—5.8 tons per person, per year.

We're not a lost cause, however. We've come a long way since the 1970s. Pittsburgh is no longer the pits, Cleveland's Cuyahoga River isn't about to catch fire again, and our emissions-control standards have our cities far ahead of air quality in Calcutta, Mexico City, and Tokyo. We've come a long way, and we still have a long way we can go.

Look around at the web of life and out on the horizon, toward your children, to your children's children, to your children's children's children. Do you care what kind of world they live in? Of course you do. But can you answer just as easily whether your extended offspring will breathe fresh air and drink clean water? Do you see in their lives natural-growth forest filled with wild, native animals? Do their rivers, lakes, and oceans churn with life? The answers rest in our hands. Tomorrow's state of the Earth is made of today's decisions.

It's easy to lose sight of the big picture when it's clouded by the haze of our daily duties. But all our well-intentioned activity becomes moot when people begin living on an ill Earth. What does a thriving business matter if the air slowly kills you and the land can't support growth? What does it matter that we've reached our profit goals this year, if in the process we've hindered the environment's ability to sustain us in the years after?

Some people find it strange to find a tire and automotive retailer, a business typically faced with numerous environmental challenges, speaking out for sustainability. Where there's a will, however, there is a way. For example, Tires Plus recycles old tires into fuel for facilities equipped with specially designed, EPA-approved filtering systems. We recycle waste oil, antifreeze, and old batteries in states that require it as well as in states that don't. Tires Plus installs "earth-friendly" automotive hoists. For years, service center hoists were installed below ground to preserve working space, but when hydraulic fluid leaked or spilled, the space saving set-up caused a major environmental hazard. Using research provided by the EPA, Tires Plus installs hoists that use biodegradable vegetable oil, which cause no contamination in the event of a leak.

On the consumer side, Tires Plus offers informational handouts that contain tips on conserving resources related to automobile use. Among staff and in the wider community, Tires Plus supports organic agriculture and earth-friendly organizations. Doing what we can where we can, we hope these small ripples will help build the growing tide of awareness and care for our environment.

The Earth and its atmosphere give us *everything*. Ponder that for a moment. We tend to think that, physically, anyway, our work and its rewards put food on the table and a roof over our heads. In one way they do, but look beyond the grocery store receipt and the mortgage. Go outside and look under your feet. Gaze up at the sky. Ultimately, that's what sustains us. Take away the bounty of air and water, and time is up. That's why the relationship each and every one of us has with Earth determines the kind of life future generations will enjoy. Or suffer.

That's hard for us to fathom, because many of the changes that are happening won't be evident in our lifetimes. The insidiously slow shifts will only show up after generations, who will look back at us and wonder what we were thinking—or *if* we were thinking. It brings to mind an uncomfortable story I've heard: tossed into hot water, a frog will spring right back out. Put into lukewarm water that's brought slowly to a boil, a frog will stay in the water and simply die. Death, whether slow or quick, still lands us and future generations in the same place.

Where to Begin

Most people aren't out to harm the Earth; they just don't realize the ways, large and small, that they may be unknowingly contributing to the problem. The decision to walk to the store instead of drive, recycle paper instead of dumping it, eat more plant-based foods instead of meat,use natural fertilizers on a lawn instead of chemicals, all have the possibility of impacting your effect on the Earth. It may not seem like much, but don't underestimate the accumulated power of positive action. Sustainability is a lifestyle choice that's not difficult to adopt, and in fact it's now hip to be green. Is caring for Earth on your mission assignment? Check the Resources section for more info, then go forth a little more aware and a little more prepared.

The Universe and Beyond

Science probes the galaxies and the innards of electrons. Philosophers tinker under the hood of the mind. Theologians seek the nature and the truth of the Divine Source. They all pursue the same questions: Where do we come from? Where are we going? What guides us? Is our life span seven decades long, or just a blink of the universal eye?

It took some determination to seek my mission. Yet the question lingers: Did my own higher wisdom determine it? Or did my mission come from elsewhere, "somewhere beyond"? Maybe, just maybe, I really was rediscovering, traveling back in time to the memory of the divine being who approached me back even before I was born: "Are you ready? Are you willing?" When I accepted, the mission became forever mine, and my real journey began. Through this rediscovery and journey, I began seeing my mission in context of a larger purpose, a purpose that did not begin with birth and will not end with physical death. My life, my energy, my purpose—all reside on a larger circle of being that brought me here and stretches far beyond my Earthly life.

A good deal of fear is drained from the future when I understand that the death of my physical body merely enacts a transition between one state of being and another. I imagine the moment of death will be like the purchase of a ticket home. As *A Course in Miracles* says, "Death is the central theme from which all illusions stem. Is it not madness to think of life as being born, aging, losing vitality, and dying in the end?...What is born of God and can still die? God is, and in Him all created things must be eternal...be not deceived by the 'reality' of any changing form.... Heaven is here. There is nowhere else. Heaven is now. There is no other time."

Coming Full Circle

Is it as Dorothy discovered in *The Wizard of Oz,* that the ticket home is right where our heart is? Is it in the recognition that "home" is where we came from and where we'll return, and there's no other place like it? Envisioning my return home to my Source reminds me of how precious these days really are. No matter what our beliefs about what will come next, envisioning the end of our life as we know it vests us with a renewed appreciation of today's potential.

If you're willing, join me on a short, awakened peek at the end of this phase's mission. Take a deep breath and imagine you're on the cusp of saying your last good-bye. Friends, memories, legacies...all are there in your mind's eye. In some ways, it's very scary. In others, it's exciting to project forward, secure in the belief that for every door that closes, another opens. It's the end of many, many miles. Look back for a moment and see how far you've come.

Discovering your mission was the first play in the game—no small beginning. Motivation came in the form of understanding and acceptance of our higher, mission-driven purpose. With game plan in hand and feet firmly planted, we did our best to stay on course through the Seven Take-Action Steps and COPPS traits, challenging ourselves to successfully negotiate life's twists and turns. Lifetime learning and communication skills supported and enhanced our efforts. We learned to take the tough calls in stride, rested, regrouped, then enjoyed the game.

We took care of our Inner Team and used key plans to tune up our bodies, juice our intellect, work through psychological roadblocks, and fuel our spiritual connection to others, the world, and God. We learned to teach, mentor, and be a friend, offering to those who needed us what we could, when we could. We learned the lessons that came to us, even when they arrived in the most unlikely forms. From our closest love to the most distant person, we learned to recognize that every living being is part of the great circle of relationships that bind us all together with our mission purposes. Respecting the foundation that supports our life, we learned to tread a little lighter on the Earth. We evolved and grew, felt lighter and less burdened, uplifted by Spirit, who helped us with our duties.

Going into Overtime

Here, now, as the game comes to a close, are you ready to consider it over? Your focus, even in the final moments of life, remains on moving forward. What will the future bring? What's beyond? What happens after the lights go out? Do we crumble to dust? Are our electrons flung off into space at the speed of light? Is our body resurrected? Do we return to learn more? Do we fly up to a heaven of a thousand pleasures? Do we synthesize into a state of pure being? Without the limits of time and space, does here become there? Does now become then? Is there a past and a future or only an eternal present?

Answers matter less than your trust and satisfaction in that moment. You know you've played out your own life game plan the best way you knew how and discovered that winning means something different than racking up the most points or raising yourself higher than others. Instead, you've centered winning and success on learning and achieving your mission, playing your role in a vast cosmic puzzle unified in its chaos. You feel good about having done your best, albeit imperfectly. You played with dedication, strength, humor, caring, and wisdom.

Fully in the game, awakened and energetic, ordinary moments become extraordinary. Fears disappear. Satisfaction turns to bliss. You come face to face with your true potential. Is that heaven out there, or is it right here?

Additional Acknowledgments

Many people have touched my life to help me become the person who could write this book. My deep gratitude goes to all of them:

My family mentors—brothers Tim and Gary Gegax and sister-in-law, Pam, whose love and support have taught me what family is all about.

My personal mentors—Dr. Deepak Chopra, Leni Erickson, Earnie Larsen, John Robbins, Brenda Schaeffer, and Carole Morning Smiley.

My business mentors—John Berg, the late Curt Carlson, John Leach, and Dick Schulze.

My business mentors early in my career—Dean Bachelor, Greg Higham, and Joe Steger.

My mentors in love—those women who spent valuable years in relationships with me, helping me to grow and become a better man.

My mentors-at-a-distance, people who have inspired me through their books and work—Edwin Bliss, James Fadiman, Robert Frager, Christopher Hegarty, Napoleon Hill, Dr. Dean Ornish, James Redfield, Helen Schucman, William Thetford, Neale Donald Walsch, Dr. Andrew Weil, and Mary Ann Williamson.

My Tires Plus teammates—all two thousand of you. Our success is a team effort. The Tires Plus Head Coaching team—George Argodale, Jim Bemis, John Hyduke, Kyle Kennedy, Sherri Lee, Pat Madigan, Scott McPhee, Eric Randa, Wayne Shimer, and Dave Wilhelmi.

My Tires Plus partner from the start—Don Gullett. Your undying loyalty and incredible patience with me over our twenty-three years together, your hard work and good heart have helped build a company of which we can both be proud. And to partner Larry Brandt, who has assumed more and more leadership as the company has grown.

In addition to the friends and associates mentioned in the front of this book, many others read the manuscript-in-process and added their energy, ideas, and enthusiasm to help it become more than the sum of its parts. My thanks to Kevin Cashman; Larry Dennison; Scott Edelstein; Leni Erickson; Janet Feldman; Jose Ferreira; Colleen Childers-Fogarty; Porter Gale; Tad Hargrave; Charlie Hoag; Bill Jorgensen; Elizabeth Kautz; Dr. Lawrence H. Kushi; Tom MacIntosh; Charles Maxwell Jr.; Dr. Tu Nguyen; Prakash Puram; Ocean Robbins; Dr. M. Viktoria Sears; Carole Morning Smiley; Dr. Russell Smiley; Julie Swenson; and Doug Toft.

Resources

See Bibliography for additional resources.

Aging and Longevity

Carter, Jimmy. *The Virtues of Aging*. Ballantine Books, 1998.

Chopra, Deepak. *Ageless Body, Timeless Mind: The Quantum Alternative to Growing Old*. Three Rivers Press, 1998 (re-issue).

Salls, Donald J. *Live and Love to Be 100: 161 Natural Ways to Reverse the Aging Process and Live a Longer, More Vital Life*. Crane Hill, 1995.

Bodywork Practices (see also Whole-Person Wellness)

Berry, Carmen Renée. *Is Your Body Trying to Tell You Something? Why It Is Wise to Listen to Your Body and How Massage and Body Work Can Help*. Pagemill Press, 1997.

Brennan, Richard. *The Alexander Technique Manual: A Step-by-Step Guide to Improve Breathing, Posture and Well-being*. Charles Tuttle Co., 1996.

Gach, Michael Reed. *Acupressure's Potent Points: A Guide to Self-Care for Common Ailments*. Bantam Doubleday Dell, 1990.

Rondberg, Terry. *Chiropractic First: The Fastest Growing Healthcare Choice Before Drugs or Surgery*. Chiropractic Journal, 1996.

The, Robert. *5-Minute Massage: Quick & Simple Exercises to Reduce Tension & Stress*. Sterling Publications, 1995.

Communication

Carnegie, Dale. *The Quick and Easy Way to Effective Speaking*. Pocket Books, 1990.

Krannich, Caryl Rae. *101 Secrets of Highly Effective Speakers: Controlling Fear, Commanding Attention*. Impact Publications, 1998.

Sandra, Jaida n'ha. *The Joy of Conversation: A Complete Guide to Salons*. Utne Reader Books, 1997.

Tannen, Deborah. *Talking from 9 to 5*. Morrow, 1994.

Toastmasters International, P.O. Box 9052, Mission Viejo, CA 92690. Phone: 949-858-8255. Website: www.toastmasters.org

Community Building

America's Promise: The Alliance for Youth. 909 North Washington St., Suite 400, Alexandria, VA 22314. Phone: 703-684-4500. Website: www.americaspromise.org (National not-for-profit organization led by General Colin Powell.)

Bobo, Kim, et al. *Organizing for Social Change: A Manual for Activists in the 1990s*. Seven Looks Press, 1996.

Utne Reader Neighborhood Salon Association. 1624 Harmon Place, Suite 330, Minneapolis, MN 55403. 612-338-5040. Website: salons@utne.com

Volunteer America! P.O. Box 1788, Blairsden-Graeagle, CA 96103. 800-508-8497. Website: www.volunteeramerica.com (Clearinghouse for volunteer opportunities and volunteer vacations nationwide.)

Death and Dying

Kübler-Ross, Elisabeth. *On Death and Dying*. Collier Books, 1997.

Kübler-Ross, Elisabeth. *The Wheel of Life: A Memoir of Living and Dying*. Touchstone Books, 1998.

Nuland, Sherwin B. *How We Die: Reflections on Life's Final Chapter*. Vintage Books, 1995.

Earth and Its Creatures

Daly, Herman E. *For the Common Good: Redirecting the Economy Toward Community, the Environment, and a Sustainable Future*. Beacon Press, 1994.

MacDonald, Mary. *Agendas for Sustainability: Environment and Development into the Twenty-First Century*. Routledge, 1998.

Meadows, Donnella. *Beyond the Limits: Confronting Global Collapse, Envisioning a Sustainable Future*. Chelsea Green, 1993.

Perkins, John. *The World Is as You Dream It*. Destiny Books, 1994.

Recycling Hotline. 800-CLEANUP. Website: www.1800cleanup.org

Williams, Rees E. *Our Ecological Footprint: Reducing Human Impact on the Earth*. New Society, 1995.

Wright, Machaelle Small. *Behaving as if the God in All Life Mattered*. Perelandra, 1987.

Family and Love Relationships

Covey, Stephen. *The 7 Habits of Highly Effective Families*. Golden Books, 1998.

Gray, John. *Men Are from Mars, Women Are from Venus*. HarperCollins, 1992.

Hendrix, Harville. *Getting the Love You Want: A Guide for Couples*. Henry Holt and Co., 1988.

Moore, Thomas. *Soul Mates: Honoring the Mysteries of Love and Relationship*. Harper-Perennial, 1994.

Ornish, Dean, M.D. *Love and Survival: The Scientific Basis for the Healing Power of Intimacy*. HarperCollins, 1998.

Walch, Mimi Doe. *10 Principles for Spiritual Parenting: Nurturing Your Child's Soul*. Harper-Perennial, 1998.

Food and Nutrition

The American Dietetic Association. 216 W. Jackson Boulevard, Chicago, IL 60606-6995. 312-899-0040. Website: www.eatright.org

EarthSave. 800-362-3648. Website: www.earthsave.org

Ingram, Colin. *The Drinking Water Book*. Ten Speed Press, 1996.

Levin, James, M.D., and Natalie Cederquist. *A Celebration of Wellness*. Glo, Inc., 1992.

Lieberman, Shari, and Nancy Bruning. *The Real Vitamin and Mineral Book: Going Beyond the RDA for Optimum Health*. Avery Publishing Group, Inc., 1990.

Ornish, Dean. *Eat More, Weigh Less*. HarperCollins, 1993.

Robbins, John. *Diet for a New America: How Your Food Choices Affect Your Health, Happiness, and the Future of Life on Earth.* H. J. Kramer, 1998.

Sinatra, Stephen, M.D. *Optimum Health: A Natural Lifesaving Prescription for Your Body and Mind.* Bantam, 1998.

Intellectual Wellness and Creativity

Cameron, Julia. *The Artists Way: The Spiritual Path to Higher Creativity.* Penguin/Putnam, 1992.

Dyson, Esther. *Release 2.1: A Design for Living in the Digital Age.* Broadway Books, 1998.

Hart, Archibald. *Habits of the Mind: Ten Exercises to Renew Your Thinking.* Word Books, 1996.

Masters, Robert, and Jean Houston. *Mind Games: The Guide to Inner Space.* Quest Books, 1998.

Lifestyle Management

Carlson, Richard. *Slowing Down to the Speed of Life: How to Create a More Peaceful, Simpler Life from the Inside Out.* Harper, 1997.

Covey, Stephen. *First Things First: to Live, to Love, to Learn, to Leave a Legacy.* Simon & Schuster, 1994.

St. James, Elaine. *Inner Simplicity: 100 Ways to Regain Peace and Nourish Your Soul.* Hyperion, 1995.

Sheehy, Gail. *New Passages: Mapping Your Life Across Time.* Random House, 1995.

Physical Improvement

American Heart Association. *American Heart Association Fitting in Fitness: Hundreds of Simple Ways to Put More Physical Activity into Your Life.* Times Books, 1997.

Anderson, Bob. *Stretching.* Shelter Publications, 1987.

Cook, Brian B. *Strength Basics: Your Guide to Resistance Training for Health and Optimal Performance.* Human Kinetics Publishing, 1996.

Meditation, Movement and Related Practices

Campbell, Don G. *The Roar of Silence: Healing Powers of Breath, Tone & Music.* Theosophical Publishing House, 1989.

Easwaran, Eknath. *Meditation: A Simple Eight-Point Program for Translating Spiritual Ideals into Daily Life.* Nilgiri Press, 1991.

Goldstein, Joseph. *Insight Meditation: The Practice of Freedom.* Shambhala Publications, 1994.

Huang, Alfred. *Complete Tai-Chi: the Definitive Guide to Physical & Emotional Self-Improvement.* Charles E. Tuttle Co., 1993.

Johari, Harishi. *Chakras: Energy Centers of Transformation.* Inner Traditions International Ltd., 1988.

Mehta, Mia. *How to Use Yoga.* Rodmell Press, 1988.

Mentoring

Albom, Mitch. *Tuesdays with Morrie.* Doubleday, 1997.

Girzone, Joseph F. *Joshua.* Collier Books, 1983.

Huang, Al Chungliang. *Mentoring: The Tao of Giving and Receiving Wisdom.* Harper-SanFrancisco, 1995.

Otto, Donna. *The Gentle Art of Mentoring.* Harvest House, 1997.

Money Management

Blix, Jacquelyn. *Getting a Life: Real Lives Transformed by Your Money or Your Life.* Viking Penguin, 1997.

Needleman, Jacob. *Money and the Meaning of Life.* Jacob Needleman Audio, 1997.

Orman, Suze. *The 9 Steps to Financial Freedom.* Crown Publications, 1997.

"Am I Putting Enough Away for Retirement?" Website: www.allstate.com/news_issue1/money/money_2.html (An interactive, online calculator from Allstate Insurance.)

Personal and Career Achievement

Boldt, Laurence G. *Zen and the Art of Making a Living: A Practical Guide to Creative Career Design.* Viking Penguin, 1993.

Carter-Scott, Chérie, Ph.D. *If Life Is a Game, These Are the Rules.* Broadway Books, 1998.

Hegarty, Christopher. *7 Secrets of Exceptional Leadership.* Executive Books, 1970.

Jenner, Bruce. *Finding the Champion Within: A Step-by-Step Guide for Reaching Your Full Potential.* Simon and Schuster, 1996.

Jones, Laurie Beth. *The Path: Creating Your Mission Statement for Work and Life.* Hyperion, 1996.

Mackay, Harvey. *Beware the Naked Man Who Offers You His Shirt: Do What You Love, Love What You Do and Deliver More Than You Promise.* Ballantine Books, 1996.

Meehan, Mary, Larry Samuels, and Vickie Abrahamson. *The Future Ain't What It Used to Be.* Riverhead Books, 1998.

Stephan, Naomi. *Fulfill Your Soul's Purpose: Ten Creative Paths to Your Life Mission.* Stillpoint Publishing, 1994.

Ziglar, Zig. *See You at the Top.* Pelican, 1985.

Psychological and Emotional Wellness

Baron, Renée. *The Enneagram Made Easy: Discover the Nine Types of People.* Harper-SanFrancisco, 1994.

Beatty, Melanie. *Co-Dependent No More: How to Stop Controlling Others and Start Caring For Yourself.* Hazelden, 1996.

Borysenko, Joan. *Guilt Is the Teacher, Love Is the Lesson.* Warner Books, 1991.

Hazelden Foundation, P.O. Box 11, Center City, MN 55012. 800-257-7810. Email: info@hazelden.org

Earnie Larsen Enterprises. 612-560-4197, 800-635-4780. Website: www.earnie.com

Lee, John, and Bill Stott. *Facing the Fire: Experiencing and Expressing Anger Appropriately.* Bantam Doubleday Dell, 1995.

Marshall, Jeanie. *Affirmations: A Pathway to Transformation—Empowered Development by the Day, by the Month, by the Year.* Jemel Publishing House, 1996.

Myers, Isabel Briggs. *Gifts Differing: Understanding Personality Type.* Consulting Psychologists Press, 1995.

Schaeffer, Brenda. Website: www.loveandaddiction.com

Retreats

Burt, Bernard. *Fodor's Healthy Escapes: 244 Resorts and Retreats Where You Can Get Fit, Feel Good, Find Yourself and Get Away from It All.* Fodor's Travel Publications, 1997.

Lederman, Ellen. *Vacations That Can Change Your Life: Adventures, Retreats and Workshops for the Mind, Body and Spirit.* Sourcebooks Trade, 1996.

Miller, Jenifer. *Healing Centers & Retreats: Healthy Getaways for Every Body and Budget.* John Muir Publications, 1998.

Sleep

Buchman, Dian Dincin. *The Complete Guide to Natural Sleep.* Keats Publications, 1997.

Lavery, Sheila. *The Healing Power of Sleep: How to Achieve Restorative Sleep Naturally.* Simon and Schuster, 1997.

Maas, James B. *Power Sleep: The Revolutionary Program That Prepares Your Mind for Peak Performance.* Villard Books, 1998.

Spirituality and Spiritual Practice

Elkins, David N. *Beyond Religion: A Personal Program for Building a Spiritual Life Outside the Walls of Traditional Religion.* Quest Books, 1998.

Feng, Gia-Fu, and Jane English. *Tao Te Ching—A New Translation.* Vintage Books, 1972.

Kabat-Zinn, Jon. *Wherever You Go, There You Are: Mindfulness Meditation in Everyday Life.* Hyperion, 1995.

Jackson, Phil, and Hugh Delehanty. *Sacred Hoops: Spiritual Lessons of a Hardwood Warrior.* Hyperion, 1995.

Miller, William A. *Make Friends With Your Shadow: How to Accept and Use Positively the Negative Side of Your Personality.* Augsburg Fortress, 1981.

Time Management

Hedrick, Lucy. *Five Days to an Organized Life.* Nightingale-Conant Audio, 1990.

Koch, Richard. *The 80/20 Principle: The Secret of Achieving More with Less.* Currency/Doubleday, 1998.

Winston, Stephanie. *The Organized Executive: New Ways to Manage Time, Paper, People, and the Electronic Office.* Norton, 1994.

Whole-Person Wellness

American Cancer Society. 1599 Clifton Rd., Atlanta, GA 30329. 800-227-2345. Website: www.cancer.org

American Heart Association. 7272 Greenville Ave., Dallas, TX 75231. 800-AHA-USA1. Website: www.amhrt.org

American Lung Association. 1726 M Street N.W., Suite 902, Washington, D.C. 20036. 800-586-4872. Website: www.lungusa.org

Childre, Doc and Bruce Cryer. *From Chaos to Coherence: Advancing Emotional and Organizational Intelligence Through Inner Quality Management.* Butterworth-Heinemann, 1998.

Chopra, Deepak, *Deepak Chopra's The Wisdom Within: Your Personal Program for Total Well-Being.* (CD-ROM edition). Random House, 1997.

Chopra Center for Wellness. 7630 Fay Avenue, La Jolla, CA 92037. 888-424-6772.

Hay, Louise. *101 Ways to Health and Healing.* Hay House, 1998.

"MedWeb: Alternative Medicine." Website: www.gen.emory.edu/medweb/medweb.altmed.html (Online directory maintained by Emory University Health Sciences Center Library of links to alternative health topics.)

Myss, Caroline, and C. Norman Shealy. *Anatomy of the Spirit: The Seven Stages of Power and Healing.* Random House, 1997.

Ornish, Dean. *Dr. Dean Ornish's Program for Reversing Heart Disease Without Drugs or Surgery.* Ballantine Books, 1992.

Robbins, John, and Riane Eisler. *Reclaiming Our Health: Exploding the Medical Myth and Embracing the Sources of True Healing.* H. J. Kramer, 1998.

Weil, Andrew, M.D. *Eight Weeks to Optimum Health.* Fawcett, 1998 (reissue).

Workplace Wellness

Anderson, Bob. *Stretching at Your Computer Desk.* Shelter Publications, 1997.

Cashman, Kevin. *Leadership from the Inside Out: Seven Pathways to Mastery.* Executive Excellence Publishing. 1998.

Fahlman, Clyde H. *Laughing Nine to Five: The Quest for Humor in the Workplace.* Steelhead Press, 1997.

Fox, Matthew. *Reinvention of Work: A New Vision of Livelihood for Our Time.* HarperSanFrancisco. 1994.

Larrañaga, Robert. *Calling It a Day.* HarperSanFrancisco, 1990. (Twelve Step self-help book for workaholics.)

Weisinger, Hendrie. *Emotional Intelligence at Work: The Untapped Edge for Success.* Jossey-Bass, 1998.

Bibliography

I'm particularly indebted to the following people, who helped me clarify my thoughts in their particular areas of expertise:

Chapter 1. Brenda M. Schaeffer, M.A., C.A.S., for mission-discovery exercise.

Chapter 4. Ron L. Fronk, Ph.D., water and breath; Prof. Carl V. Phillips, Ph.D., and John Robbins for nutrition; Dr. Viktoria Sears for supportive bodywork.

Chapter 5. Earnie Larsen; Brenda M. Schaeffer, M.A., C.A.S., and Dr. Robert Simmermon for psychological wellness.

Chapter 6. Rev. Mark Holman, Rev. Kurt Kalland, Rev. Duke Tufty.

Chapter 8. Michael D. Norman for public speaking.

Chapter 9. Brenda M. Schaeffer, M.A., C.A.S., for love relationships; Charles Maxwell Jr. for financial planning; John Robbins for environmental awareness.

American Cancer Society. "Cancer: What Is It?" 1998. Website: www.3.cancer.org/cancer info/gen_main_cont.asp?st=wi

American Heart Association. "Cardiovascular Diseases." 1998. Website: www.amhrt.org/ Scientific/Hsstats98/03cardio.html

American Lung Association. "Trends in Cigarette Smoking." 1997. Website: www.lungusa. org/data/smk2.htm

American Medical Association. "Nutritional Basics." 1998. Website: www.ama-assn.org/ insight/gen_hlth/nutrinfo/part3.htm#p01

Anthony, William A. *The Art of Napping.* Lompoc, CA: Larson Publishing Company, 1997.

Balch, Phyllis A., and James F. Balch, M.D. *Prescription for Dietary Wellness: Using Foods to Heal.* Garden City, NY: Avery Publishing Group, 1998.

Batmanghelidj, F., M.D. *Your Body's Many Cries for Water.* Falls Church, VA: Global Health Solutions, Inc., 1997.

Begley, Sharon. "Do Parents Really Matter?" *Newsweek,* 7 September 1998, 52–59.

Besdin, Abraham. *Reflections of the Rav, Volume One.* Hoboken, NJ: KTAV Publishing House, 1993.

Bliss, Edwin C. *Getting Things Done: The ABCs of Time Management.* New York: Charles Scribner's Sons, 1991.

Brody, Jane. *Jane Brody's Nutrition Book.* New York: W.W. Norton, 1981.

———. "Drunk on Liquid Candy, U.S. Overdoses on Sugar." *The New York Times,* 24 November 1998.

Buchholz, Steve, and Thomas Roth; Karen Hess, ed. *Creating the High Performance Team.* New York: John Wiley and Sons, 1987.

Burfoot, Amy. "Like Father, Like Son." *Runner's World,* August 1994, 45.

Centers for Disease Control and Prevention. "Trends in years of potential life lost before age 65 among whites and blacks—1979–1989," *JAMA* 268(24):3423, 1992.

Chopra, Deepak. *Perfect Health: The Complete Mind-Body Guide.* New York: Crown Publishers, 1991.

————. *The Seven Spiritual Laws of Success: A Practical Guide to the Fulfillment of Your Dreams.* San Rafael, CA: Amber-Allen Publishing New World Library, 1993.

————. "Seduction of the Spirit." Workshop. San Diego, CA, 1995.

Cousins, Norman. *Anatomy of an Illness as Perceived by the Patient: Reflections on Healing and Regeneration.* New York: Bantam Doubleday Dell, 1991.

Covey, Stephen R. *7 Habits of Highly Effective People: Powerful Habits in Personal Change.* New York: Simon and Schuster, 1989.

Cowley, Geoffrey. "Cancer and Diet." *Newsweek,* 30 November 1998, 60.

Dalai Lama. *The Way to Freedom,* San Francisco: HarperSanFrancisco, 1994.

Easwaran, Eknath. *Take Your Time: Finding Balance in a Hurried World.* New York: Hyperion, 1997.

Fadiman, James. *Unlimit Your Life: Setting and Getting Goals.* Berkeley, CA: Celestial Arts, 1989.

Glasser, William, M.D. *Positive Addiction.* New York: HarperCollins, 1985.

Goleman, Daniel. *Working With Emotional Intelligence.* New York: Bantam, 1998.

Gould, Meredith. "Power Napping." *Nation's Business.* February 1995, 65.

Grady, Denise. "Articles Question Safety of Dietary Supplements." *The New York Times,* 17 September 1998.

Gurdjieff, G. I. *All and Everything: Beelzebub's Tales to His Grandson.* Aurora, OR: Two Rivers Press, 1993.

Hendler, Sheldon Saul, M.D. *The Oxygen Breakthrough: Thirty Days to an Illness-Free Life.* Old Tappan, NJ: Pocket Books, 1989.

Hill, Napoleon. *Napoleon Hill's Keys to Success: The 17 Principles of Personal Achievement.* New York: Dutton, 1994.

Jung, Carl, ed. *Man and His Symbols.* New York: Dell Publishing, 1964.

Kushi, Michio, Aveline Kushi, and Alex Jack. *Macrobiotic Diet.* New York: Japan Publications (USA), Inc., 1992.

Larsen, Earnie, and Jeanette Goodstein. *Who's Driving Your Bus?: Codependent Business Behaviors of Workaholics, Perfectionists, Martyrs, Tap Dancers, Caretakers and People Pleasers.* San Francisco: Jossey-Bass, 1993.

McGaulley, Michael T. *Selling 101: Essential Selling Skills for Business Owners and Non-Sales People.* Holbrook, MA: Adams Media Corp., 1995.

Maggio, Rosalie. *The New Beacon Book of Quotations by Women.* Boston: Beacon Press, 1996.

Martin, Rick, and T. Trent Gegax. "'Sell In,' Bliss Out." *Newsweek,* 8 December 1997, 72.

Mehrabian, Albert. *Silent Messages: Implicit Communication of Emotions and Attitudes.* Belmont, CA: Wadsworth, 1981.

Merriam-Webster, Incorporated. *Merriam-Webster's Collegiate Dictionary, Tenth Edition.* Springfield, MA: Merriam-Webster, 1997.

Moody, Raymond A. Jr., M.D. *Life After Life: The Investigation of a Phenomenon—Survival of Bodily Death.* New York: Bantam Books, 1988.

Nørretranders, Tor. *The User Illusion: Cutting Consciousness Down to Size.* New York: Viking, 1998.

Omnigraphics. *Diet and Nutrition Source Book: Basic Information About Nutrition, Including Dietary Guidelines for Americans.* Detroit, MI: Omnigraphics, Inc., 1996.

Ouspensky, P. D. *The Psychology of Man's Possible Evolution.* New York: Random House, 1973.

Peck, M. Scott. *The Road Less Traveled: A New Psychology of Love, Traditional Values and Spiritual Growth.* New York: Simon and Schuster, 1978.

Pitchford, Paul. *Healing With Whole Foods: Oriental Traditions and Modern Nutrition.* Berkeley, CA: North Atlantic Books, 1996.

Rechtschaffer, Stephan, M.D. *Timeshifting: Creating More Time to Enjoy Your Life.* New York: Doubleday, 1996.

Redfield, James. *The Celestine Prophecy: An Adventure.* New York: Warner Books, 1993.

Reichheld, Frederick F., ed. *The Quest for Loyalty.* New York: McGraw-Hill, 1996.

Robbins, Ocean. "Choices for a Healthier World." Brochure. Soquel, CA: Youth for Environmental Sanity, 1998.

Schaeffer, Brenda. *Loving Me Loving You: Balancing Love and Power in a Codependent World.* New York: HarperCollins, 1991.

———. *Is It Love or Is It Addiction?* Revised edition. Center City, MN: Hazelden Foundation, 1997.

Schoen, Elin. *Growing With Your Child.* New York: Doubleday, 1995.

Schucman, Helen, and William Thetford. *A Course in Miracles.* Mill City, CA: The Foundation for Inner Peace, 1975.

Schuré, Édourd. *The Great Initiates: A Study of the Secret History of Religions.* San Francisco: Harper and Row, 1961.

Shenk, David. *Data Smog: Surviving the Information Glut.* New York: HarperCollins, 1997.

Solomon, Robert C., and Kathleen Marie Higgins. *A Short History of Philosophy.* New York: Oxford University Press, 1995.

Spragins, Ellyn. "So What's the Score?" *Newsweek,* 19 October 1998, 90.

Stewart, Thomas, and Jane Furth. "The Information Age in charts." *Fortune,* 4 April 1994, 75.

Sullivan, Scott. "In Memory of 'Uncle.'" *Newsweek,* 22 January 1996, 43.

Tagore, Rabindranath. *Gitanjali: Offerings from the Heart.* New York: Simon and Schuster, 1997.

U.S. Department of Commerce, Bureau of Census. *Statistical Abstract of the United States.* 1997, 117th Edition, Table 130.

U.S. Department of Health and Human Services. *The U.S. Surgeon General's Report on Nutrition and Health.* Public Health Service DHHS (PHS) Publication No. 88-50211, 1988.

———. *Vital Statistics of the United States, 1992,* v.II, part B, Hyattsville, Maryland, 1996.

Vecsey, George. "Sports of the Times; Many Joys of a Home Run Lovefest." *The New York Times,* 8 September 1998.

The Staff of the Wall Street Journal, Ronald J. Allsop, ed. *Wall Street Journal Almanac,* New York: Dow Jones and Company, 1998.

Walsch, Neale Donald. *Conversations with God: An Uncommon Dialogue, Book 1.* New York: G. P. Putnam's Sons, 1995.

Washington, James Melvin, ed. *The Essential Writings and Speeches of Martin Luther King, Jr.* New York: HarperCollins, 1986.

Weil, Andrew. *Spontaneous Healing: How to Discover and Enhance Your Body's Natural Ability to Maintain and Heal Itself.* New York: Alfred A. Knopf, 1995.

———. *Natural Health, Natural Medicine.* Wilmington, MA: Houghton Mifflin Company, 1998.

Williamson, Marianne. *Return to Love: Reflections on the Principles of a Course in Miracles.* New York: Harper, 1994.

Wolff, Michael. *Where We Stand: Can America Make It in the Global Race for Wealth, Health, and Happiness?* New York: Bantam Books, 1992.

World Wide Fund for Nature. "State of the Climate: A Time for Action." 1998. Website: www.panda.org/climate_event/climate.doc

For more information on Tom Gegax or Tires Plus, including Tom's speaking schedule and availability, please write to:

Tom Gegax
Tires Plus
600 West Traveler's Trail
Burnsville, MN 55337

Or visit www.tiresplus.com

Index